WARRIOR'S
RAGE

WARRIOR'S
RAGE

The Great Tank Battle of 73 Easting

Douglas Macgregor

NAVAL INSTITUTE PRESS
Annapolis, Maryland

Naval Institute Press
291 Wood Road
Annapolis, MD 21402

Library of Congress Cataloging-in-Publication Data
Macgregor, Douglas A.
  Warrior's rage : the great tank battle of 73 Easting / Douglas Macgregor.
    p. cm.
  Includes bibliographical references and index.
  ISBN 978-1-59114-505-9 (alk. paper)
  1. 73 Easting, Battle of, Iraq, 1991—Personal narratives, American. 2. 73 Easting, Battle
of, Iraq, 1991—Influence. 3. Persian Gulf War, 1991—Tank warfare. 4. Macgregor,
Douglas A. 5. Command of troops. I. Title.
  DS79.735.I73.M33 2009
  956.7044'242—dc22

                                                                      2009027749

Printed in the United States of America on acid-free paper

14 13 12 11 10 09   9 8 7 6 5 4 3 2
First printing

To the memory of
Sgt. Nels Andrew Moller
1st Platoon Scouts, Ghost Troop, 2nd Squadron,
2nd Armored Cavalry Regiment, U.S. Army
Killed in action on 26 February 1991

And to all
American, British, and allied
Soldiers, Sailors, Airmen, and Marines
killed or wounded in Southwest Asia
since the beginning of America's war with Iraq
in January 1991

This book is humbly dedicated

Contents

Illustrations

Introduction

We have good corporals and sergeants and
some good lieutenants and captains, and those
are far more important than good generals.

GEN. WILLIAM T. SHERMAN (1820–91)

Late in the afternoon of 26 February 1991, barely twenty-four hours after more than fifty thousand soldiers of Iraq's Republican Guard Corps began their withdrawal from Kuwait and southern Iraq, the two lead cavalry troops of "Cougar Squadron," the 2nd Squadron of the 2nd Armored Cavalry Regiment, finally caught up with Iraq's Republican Guard Corps. Taken by surprise, a defending Iraqi armor brigade arrayed along the north–south grid line of a military map referred to as the "73 Easting" was swept away by salvos of American tank and missile fire that devastated the Iraqi fighting positions.[1]

Metal smashed against metal as killing round after killing round slammed into the Iraqi army's Soviet-made tanks. A few hours later, the few surviving Republican Guards, exhausted men in dirty green uniforms, huddled together as prisoners of war in the nighttime cold. Most of the captured Iraqi troops just stared into the darkness through eyes empty of feeling or expression while their wounded comrades lying nearby on the desert floor received medical attention from the American soldiers who had just defeated them.

Splendid battle that it was, however, the battle of the 73 Easting bore no abiding fruit. Instead of continuing a successful attack, an attack with almost no U.S. losses that had destroyed the Iraqi rear guard, Cougar Squadron was halted, ordered to break contact with the enemy, and even to withdraw behind a meaningless limit of advance. Contact thus broken, the Republican Guard Corps' main body escaped.

The speed and power of Cougar Squadron's attack demonstrated the Iraqi enemy's inability to survive a determined U.S. ground assault. It utterly destroyed the Iraqi enemy's last defense, but it made no difference. The generals and colonels commanding the lead divisions and brigades in the VII Corps attack were much more concerned with what the enemy *might* do to *them* than with what they could do to the enemy. Though their fears were never justified by the facts, their fears were real enough in their own minds to slow the VII Corps' movement to a snail's pace.

The fruits of victory, the total destruction of the Republican Guard, rotted on the vine while the commanding generals of the U.S. Army's VII Corps wasted precious hours herding their divisions into a "tight fist" for a fight that was already passed. By the time the corps' divisions arrived and "attacked," little of the Republican Guard remained, with the exception of the Iraqi armored brigades that mounted a last-ditch defense for the rest of the retreating corps, and much of its equipment had already been abandoned.

What the soldiers of Cougar Squadron won on the battlefield—the opportunity to pursue and complete the destruction of Saddam Hussein's base of power, the Republican Guard Corps—was lost by an U.S. Army chain of command that never saw the Iraqi opponent in a true light and never grasped the strategic implications of their own actions. The result was the escape of the Republican Guard and its subsequent use by Saddam Hussein to destroy the Kurdish and Shiite Arab insurrections that had been encouraged by the George H. W. Bush administration.

When it became clear the Republican Guard had escaped, the generals resisted the idea of extending the war by moving ground troops toward Baghdad until American security demands were met. As a result, President Bush and his top generals sacrificed the opportunity to leverage American military power for significant political gain. Meanwhile, Saddam Hussein regrouped his Republican Guard forces, two to three divisions of which had been spared by VII Corps' inaction and the premature cease-fire.[2]

Now is a good time for Americans to reassess the conduct of Operation Desert Storm, against the backdrop of Operation Iraqi Freedom. "The

Agreement on Complete Withdrawal" (in plainer English, a status of forces agreement) has just been agreed upon by the governments of the United States and Iraq. Washington is now obligated to remove its forces from Iraq's cities and towns in the summer of 2009 and to withdraw its forces completely before the end of 2011.[3]

A new phase is beginning. Understanding how we got here is vital.

Just as World War II began where World War I left off, Operation Iraqi Freedom began where Desert Storm ended in 1991. Despite its initial showy successes on television, reminiscent of the first Gulf War, Americans eventually discovered that Operation Iraqi Freedom (OIF) was fundamentally flawed. Other than removing Saddam Hussein from power, Operation Iraqi Freedom lacked a coherent strategic design, with catastrophic results in human and monetary terms for the United States and Iraq.[4]

This negative assessment is an insight not easy to develop. Desert Storm, as the 1991 war is generally known, was publicized to the world as a total victory and a triumph of American military might. Subsequent press coverage, books, memoirs, and TV documentaries—despite considerable evidence to the contrary—served to reinforce massively that conventional wisdom rather than to question it. Medals and high-media profiles are wonderful things, and wars are wonderfully photogenic if appropriately sanitized—and Desert Storm was nothing if not sanitized.

After Desert Storm, the generals owned the store, and no civilian— and Congress contained an ever-dwindling band of members with military experience—would dare to question the men and women who wore splendid uniforms laden with rows of medals and other honors (mostly awarded by each other for nothing more than bureaucratic deeds, but which looked dazzling from afar).

Within the American system, a polarized celebrity culture conditioned to respond to emotional buttons, clichés, slogans, uniforms, and badges has quite astonishing power. Besides, senators and members were up to their eye-balls in dubious practices themselves, so they were scarcely in a position to accuse general officers of careerism, conflicts of interest, or of feathering their own nests at the taxpayers' expense. In fact, all that the politicians who were nominally in charge of overseeing the military seemed to care about was getting their shares of defense dollars, which was easy enough, given that the U.S. was spending more on defense than the rest of the world combined, a truly mind-boggling statistic and one that did not seem to register with the average American taxpayer—who otherwise might have asked, "Why?"

Readiness and preparing for the next war were neglected as too disruptive. Instead, the generals argued, "Why change? After all, we won Desert Storm, didn't we?"

The Desert Storm campaign had gone exactly as planned, went the lie, and it had yielded a brilliant victory. Mission accomplished. Back to the main business of the Army, which certainly was not war, as far as the generals were concerned.

True, it was unfortunate that the Shiite Arabs and the Kurds, who had risen against Saddam Hussein on President Bush's instigation, had not been helped by U.S. troops and had been massacred, but what was that when compared to the sound bite of a "Hundred-Hour War"?

After Desert Storm, no one asked about any of that. The club of generals became unstoppable. General officers were no longer just generals—they were iconic figures, in the eyes of the American people, and they would show up as commentators on television, basking in book deals, consultancy sinecures, and directorships, and lobbying for contracts for decades.

The lie, as is so often the case where war is concerned, became institutionalized; therein lies the real tragedy. If the critical weaknesses in U.S. Army generalship displayed in 1991 had been identified and remedied, not deliberately concealed, things in Iraq might have been very different a decade later. Whether one agreed with the decision to invade Iraq in 2003 or not, the truth is that the blame for the cruelty, carelessness, and incompetence of the intervention and occupation of Iraq lies more with the Army generals in charge of the execution of policy than with the policy makers. Policies determine focus, but execution—effective implementation—is what makes life work.

It is customary to blame the politicians—and they are rarely blameless— but the record shows that whereas bad policies can often be saved in wartime through effective implementation by competent commanders on the battlefield, the reverse is rarely true. In short, political rhetoric is a fine thing, but it is what the senior military leaders on the spot do, or, fail to do, that counts. And here the willingness of the generals to act decisively, to study their professions seriously, and to stand up to their political masters if a wrong course of action is ordered, was noticeably lacking.

The good news is that the lower ranks of the U.S. Army are replete with excellent soldiers. The problems are at the top, not at the bottom. And these problems are very serious, because as a Vietnamese proverb would have it, "A fish rots from its head."

If the Army were a corporation with a track record like Iraq, its shareholders would be up in arms, its generals would have been fired en masse long ago, and federal agents would be investigating its probity—and the investigators would have no difficulty in finding matters of serious legal concern.[5]

The activities of the generals attracted scant attention in the 1990s, but some were exposed, in all their greed and pettiness, by the exigencies of war. Our soldiers and Marines lacked body armor and appropriate armored vehicles because we weren't prepared for war; we weren't prepared for war because too many of the generals in charge did not do their jobs. These conditions did not emerge under "Dubya's" administration. They emerged in the 1990s after Desert Storm.

One might think that a watchful media would be alerted by so much blood and so many hundreds of billions of dollars wasted, but the generals found wrapping themselves in the flag made them effectively media proof. No editor or reporter wants to be accused of stabbing the soldiers in the back in time of war—and they confuse soldiers with generals, which is like confusing ordinary citizens with senators and presidents. Most of the U.S. Army does not consist of generals, who today are rarer than hen's teeth when it comes to being near direct enemy fire. So this book focuses on the true heroes who went in harm's way; the soldiers who fought, died, and won in 1991.

In war, the quality of leadership does not just matter, it's fundamental. Like the United States itself, the U.S. Army is a living thing, built of flesh and blood, not just iron and steel. Courage and competence are its driving force. And here I speak from hard-won experience: I was involved with both Operation Desert Storm and Operation Iraqi Freedom. I had the honor and the privilege of leading American soldiers into battle, to witness firsthand the gallantry and intelligence of the American soldier under direct enemy fire.

All of us in Cougar Squadron—the 2nd Squadron, 2nd Armored Cavalry Regiment—were deeply affected by our experiences in Iraq, both personally and professionally. It would have been strange had we not been. We saw and did terrible things, because such is the nature of war, but we also experienced combat soldiering at its peak and knew with certainty what was possible.

Direct-fire combat is the crucible that separates the warriors from the corporate careerists, and it seasons soldiers fast. The hard truth is that where the profession of arms is concerned, there is no substitute for exposure to the business of killing, or being killed, as a way to focus one's attention on the difference between what is important and what is mere process, pomp, and careerism.

The battle of the 73 Easting was a brutal affair. It occurred when 2nd (Cougar) Squadron, an 1,100-man battle group of the 2nd Armored Cavalry Regiment, was assigned to act as a spearhead for the U.S. Army's VII Corps, the massive force of 110,000 troops tasked with the destruction of Iraq's eighty-thousand-man Republican Guard Corps.

Cavalry are scouts, albeit heavily armored scouts in our case, so our job was to find and fix the enemy long enough for the main force, VII Corps, to rumble up and finish the job. Fixing an enemy—essentially, keeping him in place so he can be destroyed—means fighting, but it was clear that on the day of the battle, 26 February 1991, the colonels and generals were thinking in terms of air strikes and artillery, tools that would not get the job done.

But the plans of generals rarely survive contact with the enemy, and all that much-hyped electronic surveillance seldom works as advertised, so in this case we suddenly found ourselves in a sandstorm up against a much larger force that had the added advantage of being dug in. The sandstorm meant no timely air support; so much for fixing the enemy with air strikes and artillery from a distance.

We were on our own, with a very good chance of being permanently "fixed" ourselves unless we could come up with something fast.

What transpired had less to do with the kind of long-distance video game, much characterized by the media as the face of modern war, than with the proverbial knife fight in a telephone booth. The Republican Guard and we were very much in range of each other. Each side had the means and the opportunity to wreak havoc on the other.

In reality, such combat bears no resemblance to a game at all. Real people die—they don't come back—and you can see, taste, hear, and smell the manner of their dying. Later, you can think about their mothers and wives, and their other loved ones and friends. No one, even if unharmed physically, is unscathed in such a battle, and the memories linger.

This was a close fight of extraordinary violence and intensity, and the lead troops of Cougar Squadron, Eagle and Ghost troops, facing a superior, dug-in armored force supported by mines, artillery, and infantry equipped with antitank weapons, could have been in a great deal of trouble. Military wisdom has it that the attacker should outnumber the defender by at least three to one. In our case, the reverse was more akin to the reality.

But we were confident combat soldiers at the peak of our professional readiness. As a unit, Cougar Squadron was exceptional, and when you are that good, as history has shown throughout the ages, being outnumbered is no longer an issue. The battle of the 73 Easting is an important reminder that victory in battle is a question not simply of slinging masses of troops at the enemy but of positioning, tactics, and thoughtful adaptation of men and machines to new forms of conflict to achieve decisive victory over the enemy.

We also had faith in ourselves and in our weapons. And we knew that being second in a tank gunfight is not a place you want to be, because the penalty is death. Victory in close combat goes to the sure and the swift.

The destruction of a tank and its crew is called a "catastrophic kill" for good reason. Armored warfare is hair-trigger fast, frighteningly lethal, and unforgiving. Men are vaporized, eviscerated, blown apart, asphyxiated, or burned to death when an incoming tank projectile or missile strikes, and the margin between victor and vanquished can be a fraction of a second.

As those of us who fought along the 73 Easting reflect on the many thousands of Americans killed and wounded since American forces entered Iraq in March 2003, we are more convinced than ever that this battle should have profoundly shaped the thinking of the Army's generals about expeditionary warfare. The value of armor-protected mobility, combined with accurate, devastating direct fire in any environment, urban or desert, should have been self-evident after Desert Storm, but it was not. Our soldiers and Marines paid a high price in blood for the lack of mobility, firepower, and protection during Iraq's occupation.

In terms of raw fighting power, in 1991 the 2nd Armored Cavalry Regiment (which hereafter I'll refer to as the "2nd Cavalry") was composed of more than four thousand soldiers and 350 tracked armored fighting vehicles, including scouts, tanks, and self-propelled guns. With the reinforcement of supporting artillery and, for the first twenty-four hours of the ground war, an AH-64 Apache battalion, the 2nd Cavalry grew in strength to eight thousand.

Devised primarily for fighting the Soviet enemy in Central Europe, the 2nd Cavalry was organized into three reinforced ground squadrons of nearly

Figure 1. Cougar Squadron in 1991

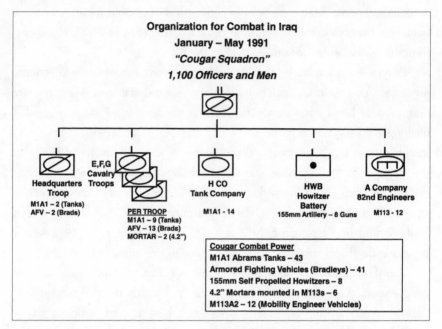

Organization for Combat in Iraq
January – May 1991
"Cougar Squadron"
1,100 Officers and Men

Headquarters Troop
M1A1 – 2 (Tanks)
AFV – 2 (Brads)

E,F,G Cavalry Troops
PER TROOP
M1A1 – 9 (Tanks)
AFV – 13 (Brads)
MORTAR – 2 (4.2")

H CO
Tank Company
M1A1 - 14

HWB
Howitzer Battery
155mm Artillery – 8 Guns

A Company
82nd Engineers
M113 - 12

Cougar Combat Power
M1A1 Abrams Tanks – 43
Armored Fighting Vehicles (Bradleys) – 41
155mm Self Propelled Howitzers – 8
4.2" Mortars mounted in M113s – 6
M113A2 – 12 (Mobility Engineer Vehicles)

1,100 troops each, with tanks, armored fighting vehicles, engineers, and artillery; one aviation squadron of scout aircraft and helicopter gun ships; and one support squadron for logistics. To simplify radio communication, the squadrons used nicknames. The 1st Squadron was called "War Eagle," the 2nd Squadron was "Cougar Squadron," the 3rd Squadron was "Wolf Pack," the 4th Aviation Squadron "Red Catcher," and the Regimental Support Squadron "Muleskinner."

But who were these fine young Americans, and how did they come to be that good? Why did we kill so many of the enemy if, in retrospect, there was no point to it? And why did Sergeant Moller, a young gunner in Ghost Troop, die in action?

With life still streaming toward him, Sgt. "Andy" Moller gave up everything. Like thousands of soldiers, sailors, airmen, and Marines since the beginning of America's war with Iraq, he did so without complaint or fear. He believed we were right and that we would win.

Was Moller's faith misplaced? Had his life been the down payment on the victory we fought to achieve? Would we complete the assigned mission and smash the Republican Guard, thus ending this destructive war and the regime in Baghdad that had started it? I was reluctant to ask these questions in 1991, but I worried that the generals would declare victory before the job was done. The signs were already there.

The offensive to destroy the Republican Guard called for bold, decisive leadership from the front, but we saw none of this from the senior officers commanding us during our advance across southern Iraq. Running the Republican Guard out of Kuwait was not enough. We knew the regime in Baghdad had to go.

To me and to the soldiers, sergeants, lieutenants, and captains I led into battle in February 1991, that meant destroy the Republican Guard, or Iraq would come back to haunt us.

ONE

Unfinished War

To our front, black smoke streamed from burning T72 tanks. Secondary explosions from fuel and ammunition ripped apart what remained of the burning hulks and the defensive positions to our front.

"Why are you stopping?" asked the Republican Guard commander who had survived our assault and was now a prisoner of war in the hands of the 2nd Armored Cavalry Regiment.

"Why do you not go to Baghdad? You have the power. Your army rules the heavens and the earth. Do you think we love Saddam? Saddam killed our best generals. He kills everyone." In a voice filled with more anguish and frustration than fear, my new Iraqi prisoner of war looked me straight in the eye and said in heavily accented English, "Major, you must go to Baghdad and end this. You must save Iraq. . . ."

But I knew there was no appetite at regiment or corps to do any such thing. From the time we crossed into Iraq, the generals saw only danger, never opportunity. I said the only thing to the Republican Guard officer that I could think of: "We are ordered to halt. I have orders. I cannot advance. That's the way it is."

. . . Along the 73 Easting in the Iraqi desert 2200 hours, 26 February 1991

A jolt of clear-air turbulence shook my seat in the jet aircraft and refocused my eyes on the 2nd Cavalry regimental coin I held in my hand. The coin had taken me back to the fighting in February 1991 almost from the moment the jet left the gate at Reagan National Airport.

Every major unit in the Army has its own distinctive coin, an item its members are supposed to keep on them for good luck. If they are "challenged" by another soldier from the unit and don't have it with them, they end up buying drinks for everybody. But for me, the 2nd Cavalry coin is about more than drinks and better times. The green and gold regimental crest, emblazoned with the fleur-de-lis, symbolizes much more than a readiness to fight. It represents courage and character under fire, the essence of professional soldiering.

However, on 17 January 2002, I was carrying much more than just the 2nd Cavalry coin. I knew I was about to be challenged for stakes much higher than drinks. Now, on the final approach to Tampa–St. Petersburg Airport, the mild turbulence prompted me to put the coin away and focus on the meeting at U.S. Central Command (CENTCOM), a meeting I had traveled from Washington, D.C., to attend.

Captain Melissa Wilson, a smart, attractive woman from CENTCOM's public affairs office, met me at the gate. She was assigned to escort me to CENTCOM headquarters. If Florida's intoxicating warm air and sunshine tempted me to forget this trip was official business, her presence was enough to gently remind me this trip was no vacation.

Actually, the trip to CENTCOM had begun much earlier, on a chilly Saturday morning in December 2001 when I met with Newt Gingrich, at a place not far from my home in McLean, Virginia. Gingrich, who was acting as a behind-the-scenes advisor to Secretary of Defense Donald Rumsfeld, had read my 1997 book, *Breaking the Phalanx*, a book that set forth the vision for a new, reorganized, and reformed twenty-first-century Army. After a few minor pleasantries and some exceptionally good coffee, Gingrich had come straight to the point.

"In the last thirty to forty days, Secretary Rumsfeld asked GEN Eric Shinseki—the Army chief of staff—and the Joint Staff for their assessment of what force levels would be needed to invade Iraq and defeat the Iraqi army."

Gingrich then paused to sip his coffee before ending his statement with, "You should know the Army chief of staff told the secretary that such an operation would require more than 550,000 troops."

I smiled a little. There weren't that many troops in the entire active-duty Army! So much for the decade-long fiction of the near-simultaneous, two-major-regional-contingencies strategy maintained by every Army chief of staff since 1991, I thought.

Newt Gingrich sipped his coffee and continued.

"Based on your combat experience during the first Gulf War, what do you think? How many troops do we need to reach Baghdad and eliminate the regime? And how long do you think such an operation would take?"

So the decision was made. We would go back to Iraq, ostensibly to finish what we had begun in 1991. I was amazed. Only 120 days had elapsed since the terrorist attacks on New York City and Washington.

Knowing the widespread opposition among the senior Army generals, both active and retired, to any plan for military intervention in Iraq, I saw that the Army's numbers were obviously inflated with the hope of raising the cost of the operation so high that the Bush administration would drop the idea immediately. This approach had been tried in 1991, but President George H. W. Bush had complied with all of General Schwarzkopf's troop requests, making it impossible for the Army generals to duck the fight.

Conditions were different now. In the air and at sea, our capacity to strike quickly and effectively against concentrations of enemy ground forces in open terrain had dramatically improved, but in the intervening years since 1991 the Army had become a smaller replica of the one that fought in 1991. Thanks to cuts implemented by the Army's four-star generals in 1998, our combat battalions contained 25 percent fewer combat troops and armored fighting vehicles in 2001 than they had in 1991.

But I knew the quality of American combat troops, Army and Marine. They were excellent, and I knew from personal experience how incapable the Iraqi army had been in 1991. There was no reason to believe that the sanctions imposed on Iraq since 1991 had made Iraq's already weak army any better.

I was, therefore, confident in responding to the question with a very different answer and a radically different plan of attack.

"Sir, given the impact of sanctions on an already incompetent Iraqi force, I suspect that with the right organization and mix of equipment, a surprise assault from a cold start by fifty thousand armored combat troops, with the potential for rapid reinforcement with additional soldiers and Marines to restore order, could do the job of eliminating Saddam Hussein's regime in a week to ten days."

Gingrich did not balk at my response. He explained that Rumsfeld was not unaware that the Army four-star generals inevitably choose men with the same attitudes as themselves—men with whom they were personally comfortable—to fill important command and staff posts, as well as to succeed them in authority when they retired. This condition, Gingrich noted, was particularly true of the officers that populated the Army chief of staff's inner circle advising him.

The upshot of the discussion was that three weeks later I provided the secretary of defense with a briefing that emphasized the importance of a ground force organized for velocity. The force I outlined was composed primarily of mobile, armored troops tightly integrated with airpower, designed to go fast as hell, brush aside opposition, defeat any counterattack, and remove Saddam from power in Baghdad. On reaching Baghdad, the plan called for 15,000 light infantry to fly into Baghdad's international airport to reinforce and restore civil order in the aftermath of Baghdad's fall until Iraqi troops replaced them.

Occupation was never mentioned. I was never asked to plan or even contemplate the long-term occupation of Iraq. My task was to develop a concept for the rapid takedown of Iraq's government by removing Saddam Hussein in his capital through an in-and-out expeditionary approach. Reorganizing the entire Middle East by imposing American democracy through the use of force, as the neocons eventually wanted, was not my task.

Rumsfeld liked the presentation. He sent the presentation and me to U.S. Central Command, where the members of the inner staff of the commander, Gen. "Tommy" Franks, viewed the briefing with considerable apprehension— and me with suspicion. CENTCOM was settled into a comfortable routine of managing operations in Afghanistan. War in Iraq, whatever the threat of weapons of mass destruction (WMD) may have been, was the last thing anyone at CENTCOM wanted to think about.

Within an hour of my arrival in Tampa, I was hurried out of the airport and taken to MacDill Air Force Base and CENTCOM headquarters. A few minutes later, Captain Wilson presented me to Col. Mike Hayes, Chief of Strategic Planning and close confidante of General Franks.

Mike was very helpful. He explained that Secretary Rumsfeld had directed General Franks to bring me to Tampa for general discussions concerning future operations in Iraq. Mike finished up with a mild warning not to be surprised by the CENTCOM commander's liberal use of profanity.

The next day, I met with General Franks. His office was what you would expect a four-star general's headquarters to be—plush and beautifully decorated, but comfortable nonetheless.

The tall, lanky General Franks was cordial. Despite his years of service in an Army with an institutional culture that equates general-officer rank with intelligence and wisdom, Franks managed to conceal skillfully any contempt he felt about Rumsfeld's sending an out-of-favor Army colonel, long ago identified as an "outcast" by the active and retired Army three and four stars, to propose a new concept of operation. Franks conducted himself as a gentleman throughout the meeting, which, although originally scheduled for forty-five minutes, lasted an hour and a half.[1]

Joining Franks for the meeting were the CENTCOM deputy commander, the J-2 (that is, the deputy chief of staff for Intelligence), two or three other senior officers, Colonel Hayes, and Franks' executive officer, a Navy commander.

After brief introductions, the meeting opened with a twelve-minute monologue by General Franks during which he assessed the state of affairs in Iraq. His comments were laced with quite a bit of profanity and were difficult to follow. When General Franks finished his remarks, he asked for my opinion.

In roughly seven minutes, I outlined the following points. First, whatever we undertook, it would have to involve actions the Iraqi opponent did not expect or anticipate. Second, a robust, tracked, armored, and highly trained force should strike directly at Baghdad, avoiding contact with the Iraqi army as much as possible, to induce an early and complete collapse of the regime. By avoiding contact with the Iraqi army in the south, I argued, we would preserve as much of the army as possible for use in the postconflict stability phase.

Third, surprise depended on a skillful manipulation of both American and Southwest Asian (SWA) perceptions. Although I argued against a bombing campaign, I made the point that U.S. ground forces would have to be tightly integrated with air forces. This arrangement would allow us to attack from a "cold start."

General Franks listened patiently and said the following in his colorful, heavy southern drawl: "Attack from a cold or standing start, I agree. Small and fast, I agree. Straight at Baghdad, I agree. Simultaneity or sequentially, simultaneous is probably better, I am not sure yet."

Franks then mused for another ten to fifteen minutes about what he called a "generated start" along with a series of political-military considerations and comments about carrier battle groups and air forces. He then returned to the subject and said: "What size force are you suggesting?"

"Initially," I answered, "no larger than 35,000 to 40,000 ground troops, primarily armored combat troops, with rapid reinforcement during the advance and subsequent immediate occupation of Baghdad by 15,000 light infantrymen."

"You mean about two divisions," asked Franks. "No, sir," I replied, "I meant four or five five-to-six-thousand-man armored battle groups on at least two axes." Armored forces could ignore most of the minor skirmishes that would consume light infantry units dependent on airpower and artillery for survival. The collateral damage would then also be minimized.

The 15,000 infantrymen would be prepositioned in Oman, with a cover story that they were training for employment in the horn of Africa. When Baghdad fell and the airport was ours, they would fly into Baghdad. Backed by armored firepower, they would secure the peace by restoring calm and public order in the capital city until Iraqi soldiers could replace them.

This plan was consistent with the idea of thoroughly controlling Baghdad while leaving the rest of the country under the control of Iraqi army units that cooperated with us until we could turn over Baghdad too. No one at CENTCOM suggested that American soldiers and Marines should occupy and control Iraq.

Based on my experience in 1991, I was sure that if left out of the fight, the Iraqi army and its officers would be useful in restoring order to the country under the direction of a new government. In the concept plan prepared for Rumsfeld I argued that, if possible, Iraqi military units should be integrated into our advance on Baghdad, ensuring that we arrived with Iraqi army troops capable of policing the capital with us. Sympathetic Iraqi army units also offered us the best chance for discovering and securing WMD sites, along with Baathist police and intelligence centers.

Flooding Iraq's villages, towns, and cities with American soldiers and Marines was a prescription for serious anti-American violence, and I strongly opposed the idea. The Arabs would regard such an intrusive presence as public humiliation, not as liberation.

On the whole, General Franks reacted more positively to my proposal than I expected, although I was unsure at the time whether this was just a performance designed to mollify Secretary Rumsfeld. Since I was nobody's "boy," in the sense that I had no four-star sponsor pushing me, I fully expected to be curtly dismissed and guided out of Franks' office. Instead, Franks talked for some time. Then, once he had made it clear that he was finished expressing his views, he invited the other attendees to give their opinions.

Franks' deputy commander, Gen. Michael "Rifle" Delong, was the first to speak. He started by raising questions based on the threat from chemical, nuclear, or biological weapons, referred to simply as "WMD."

DeLong seemed to favor a long air bombardment campaign and a larger buildup on the ground over time, which, in my view, would make the use of WMD much more likely.

I listened politely to his views and then told him that the alternative to a long buildup, a lengthy air campaign, and a ponderous, linear assault on the Desert Storm model was a swift strike at the jugular to collapse organized resistance—a strike that moved faster than the enemy could react. The importance of minimizing strikes from the air against a country that was already exhausted from years of sanctions and whose civil populations needed the water, power, and sanitation infrastructure intact was beyond the generals' comprehension. The very notion that we should focus our attack away from the Iraqi army, which I was convinced would not fight much—if at all—was ignored.

But the discussion continued. The deputy commander was not satisfied with my responses.

It was now the J-2's turn to question me.

The deputy chief of staff for Intelligence began by criticizing my concept of operation on the ground that the time frame equated to the period when Iraq's ground forces achieved their highest state of training readiness. To me this comment was ludicrous; frankly, I did not think that the Republican Guard could stop a toilet from overflowing. But I kept my cool.

Franks interrupted and asked me about the quality of the Iraqi enemy.

I told him that surely, as former assistant division commander of the 1st Cavalry Division, he too recognized that our soldiers and their armor were vastly superior to anything the Iraqis could put into the field against us.

General Franks was trapped. He found it impossible to disagree with this assertion.

When the meeting finally ended, I was led out of Franks' office into another room, where the discussion continued with the J-2, an Army brigadier general, who—like, unfortunately, most of the officers I talked to—had little or no personal experience of direct-fire combat in Iraq or anywhere else.

When I was asked what we would do in the event that the Iraqi armored formations inside Basra decided to come out of the city and attack near An Nasiryah, I replied, "Great! This will give our air forces something to do. They will annihilate them in minutes."

My confident reply did not impress the J-2. He strongly objected to my faith in the effectiveness of American airpower as a tool to deal decisively with threats to our flanks or rear, claiming that I overestimated airpower's effect and the willingness of the U.S. Air Force to cooperate with the Army.

Interservice squabbling seemed to be as alive and well as ever. All too many of those in high command seemed to be permanently afflicted with a high-school mentality.

Though I tried to listen attentively to the general, his lecture grew tiresome and my mind wandered. I had heard these views before—how my ideas and concepts of operation were too risky, why if we did what I proposed our open flanks would crack under Iraqi counterattack, why weeks of bombing and hundreds of thousands of American soldiers would be required to defeat the pathetic Iraqi army. I remembered how the Army generals of 1991 had initiated potentially brilliant maneuvers only to abort them and squander victory because they lacked the will to see them through to completion.

The general sitting in front of me could just as easily have been a general from 1991—nothing had changed in the Army generals' thinking about war. And why should it? The generals select their friends to succeed them. Thus, it was no surprise that the views of this man were the same as those I heard ten years earlier. We obviously had learned nothing about Arabs or Iraq during the twelve years since the first Gulf War. Still, I was truly shocked when I learned later that General Franks expected that a ground offensive to take Baghdad might last as long as three months—I could not imagine any Iraqi force resisting a determined ground attack by American armored forces for more than a few minutes.[2]

The Army generals who had seen disaster waiting for them on the other side of every sand dune in 1991 had cloned themselves, producing a new generation of risk-averse, uninspired, uniformed bureaucrats who pretended to be bold leaders but actually were troubled with doubt and fear.

The one glaring difference was that most of the Army generals sitting at CENTCOM and Third Army headquarters had no personal experience of direct-fire combat against the Iraqi military or, in most cases, against anyone who knew what "right looks like." The names and faces of the generals who would eventually lead Army forces into Iraq for a second time were well known to me. Like their four-star mentors, they were only as good as the canned tactical methods they knew from the training centers and simulations. None of them were inclined to ask what else might work.

Fearing that President Bush and Secretary Rumsfeld would do what Lyndon Johnson and Robert McNamara had done and go to war with the generals they had found on taking office I was overcome by the premonition that whatever plan the generals followed, the outcome would be disastrous. The generals I knew did not know enough about Iraq or its people, and like their mentors in 1991, they were filled with fear of fighting a robust Iraqi army that simply did not exist. They were not the generals we needed. We did not need generals sitting in front of a TV screen watching icons and video feeds while our soldiers fought it out on the ground with an enemy who did not conform to the generals' plans. Iraq, I feared, would prove to be a nightmare.

I grew weary of the discussion.

Time was suspended while a kind of monumental inner silence filled me. I no longer wanted to listen to the generals' endless list of fears and concerns. I wanted to go back in time to a different place. I wanted to be with soldiers who did not take counsel of their fears—soldiers I admired and loved—soldiers who advanced under fire without hesitation, following officers who understood combat leadership from the front, the meaning of mobility and firepower, who were always ready to issue concise, relevant "orders from the saddle."

In the deep recesses of memory, I could still see these men behind me in long columns of armor, submerged in a swirling sea of sand, wind, and black rain. Drifting away from the confines of CENTCOM headquarters, my mind echoed with the noise of tanks grinding against the desert floor of southern Iraq.

After all, I had fought in Iraq once before.

TWO

Getting Ready for the Fight

Hard on the training ground, easy on the battlefield.

MARSHAL ALEKSANDR VASILYEVICH SUVOROV (1729–1800)

ORDERS BRIEF, EASTERN SAUDI ARABIA, 18 DECEMBER 1990

To American soldiers deploying to Saudi Arabia in 1990 with romantic visions of the colorful desert and exotic Bedouin Arabs based on David Lean's Oscar-winning movie *Lawrence of Arabia*, Saudi Arabia's desert landscape was a huge disappointment. There were no shifting hills of golden sand bleaching in the sun, no spectacular red mesas or glowing mountains in the distance, just flat sand and gravel, stretching for endless miles.

In the Arabian Desert, the full moon was so bright that both soldiers and vehicles would cast distinct shadows. But this clarity was missing on a moonless night a week before Christmas when the 2nd Cavalry's squadron commanders and their operations officers were told to assemble at the regimental Tactical Operations Center (TOC) for a future-operations briefing, we made damn sure to get there before dark.

Army TOCs are quite large concentrations of wheeled and tracked command-and-control (C2) vehicles with packed tons of communications gear and computers manned by dozens, sometimes hundreds, of soldiers, sergeants, and officers. At the regimental, division, and corps levels, the mass of interconnected vehicles looks from a distance like a series of large olive-drab circus tents.

In theory, TOCs (rhymes with "clocks") are information-processing centers for colonels and generals, people who in wartime are otherwise often overwhelmed with more information than they can absorb and exploit. The canvas walls that surround the areas between the C2 vehicles are covered with paper or electronic maps that are constantly being updated by legions of staff officers to provide senior officers with visual representations of past, current, and potential future events on the ground.

In practice, these field headquarters are the modern equivalents of World War I headquarters inside French chateaus where senior officers waited for news from the front and watched staff officers move little flags and blocks of wood around maps, the difference being that the mass of interconnected tracked and wheeled vehicles is somewhat, but not much, more mobile. When major briefings or operations orders are issued to subordinate commanders and their staffs, an ample supply of folding steel chairs are arranged in rows, with specific seats marked for squadron commanders and their operations officers.

Such was the setting for the 2nd Cavalry's first major operations briefing in Iraq. Training in Germany where the 2nd Cavalry was stationed was always good, but it was very predictable, almost staged. Obviously, Cougar Squadron would need a different approach, one that would give the soldier the means and the leadership to work through chaos.

I was Cougar Squadron's operations officer, and developing that new approach was my job. The squadron operations officer is in charge of staff section three (S-3). He plans and supervises the conduct of all war-fighting and training operations. In a 1,100-man cavalry squadron battle group, the S-3's role is vitally important, and for a major in the tank corps, it is arguably the best job in the U.S. Army.

There was nothing calculated about my assignment to the 2nd Cavalry. From the time I was five years old, I had wanted to go to West Point, and from the time I entered the U.S. Military Academy, I had wanted to join the U.S. Cavalry. It was that simple.

We had some idea in December 1990 of what we would be told. Gen. Norman Schwarzkopf, the U.S. CENTCOM commander in chief, had already given Lt. Gen. Frederick M. Franks, VII Corps commander, his marching orders.

"I think it's pretty obvious what your mission is going to be, Fred," Schwarzkopf said, moving his hand along the desert corridor to the west of Kuwait. "Attack through here and destroy the Republican Guard. Once they're gone, be prepared to continue the attack to Baghdad. Because there isn't going to be anything else out there."[1]

Schwarzkopf's order to Franks that he was to destroy the Republican Guard could not have been any clearer. There was no ambivalence. Its destruction was his mission.

For the officers of Cougar Squadron, the news that the 2nd Cavalry would lead VII Corps in the attack was electrifying.

Unlike the regular Iraqi army, which consisted of conscripts led by cautious, fearful officers, the Republican Guard units were presented to us as well paid, well equipped, and often extremely violent. Having brutalized their own people to enforce Saddam Hussein's rule inside an Iraq otherwise subdivided into Kurdish, Sunni, and Shiite populations, many of the Iraqi Republican Guard troops were reportedly repeating the same behavior in Kuwait.

For the Republican Guards, being in control meant imposing terror, turning Kuwait's occupation by Iraq into a nightmare of frightening dimensions. Thus, destroying the Republican Guards was seen by us not only as a strategic imperative but as morally justified.[2]

But we were unaware that our corps commander, General Franks, was not so enthusiastic. Franks' response to Schwarzkopf was underwhelming: "We can do this. We'll make it happen."[3]

Schwarzkopf seemed to sense the discomfort in General Franks' statement and quickly followed up with a comment on the importance of "killer instinct" in his commanders.

Staring directly at General Franks, Schwarzkopf said, "I cannot afford to have commanders who do not understand that it is attack, attack, attack, attack, and destroy every step of the way. If you have somebody who doesn't understand it, I would strongly recommend that you consider removing him from command and putting in somebody that can do the job."[4]

Clearly, Schwarzkopf should have followed his own advice. Not only was he aware of Franks' overcautious nature and therefore, as we would discover, that he was the wrong man for the job, but Schwarzkopf clearly understood the strategic consequences if Franks failed to destroy the Republican Guard—Saddam Hussein would survive in power.

But this is where the corporate mentality of the club of generals came into play, rather than the pragmatic professionalism required of a true soldier. Franks was one of the "good guys." Schwarzkopf, Franks, and Gen. Carl Vuono, then chief of staff of the Army, had been friends at West Point.

And so Schwarzkopf did not act.[5] He did not do what he must have known to be his sworn duty. Despite the bluff and bluster and his commanding presence on television, he lacked the character required of a true wartime leader who had the lives of hundreds of thousands of his own men to consider, as well as the responsibility of delivering a decisive strategic result to the nation. It is hard to find a better example of the difference between the character required of a military leader and the mentality of corporate careerism that in fact prevails.

Though we were unaware of the uneasy relationship between Franks and Schwarzkopf, when Maj. Doug Lute (later a lieutenant general), the regimental S-3 (or operations) officer, began the briefing, we were ready for the mission to attack the Republican Guard.

Lute was tall and thin, with a keen eye for whatever it took to please his boss. Ambitious and high-strung, Lute was no wild-eyed risk taker. His mission was simple: give the boss whatever the boss wants, period.

As in Germany, the briefing opened with a series of presentations by the primary staff officers—operations, intelligence, personnel, logistics, and civil affairs—explaining that the regiment's task would be to find and fix the Republican Guard Corps so that it could be attacked and destroyed by the main body of VII Corps' divisions. Lute's initial presentation was consistent with what an armored cavalry regiment would do in Central Europe, deploying forward of, or to the flanks of, an armored corps. In fact, everything related to future operations that the regimental staff presented was predictable. Only the geographical setting was different.

Sitting next to me was 1st Lt. John Hillen (later assistant secretary of state for political military affairs under the administration of President George W. Bush). Hillen was my assistant operations officer. He was also one of the most capable officers I have known. He was to play a key role in everything the squadron did before and during combat in Iraq.

What endeared Hillen most to me was his willingness to argue with me, to challenge my views on a range of issues. I needed Hillen around to ensure that my rank, my size (height six feet two inches, weight 210 pounds), and the force of my personality did not inadvertently shut down dissent.

When Lute outlined the mission, Hillen was quick to wink in acknowledgment of a mission that we expected all along. Lute's explanation went something like this: "The regiment will set the terms of battle for the corps and serve as its base of fire and observation. If the enemy is moving, the regiment destroys the advance guard battalions and develops the situation.

If the enemy is stationary, the regiment fixes the enemy, finds his flanks, and assists in getting the divisions into the fight."

As presented, the mission could have been written for a movement to contact with the Third Guards Tank Army of the Group of Soviet Forces in Magdeburg, Germany. Adding a new flavor to the standard mission profile from Central Europe, however, Lute mentioned in passing that armored formations in the desert would operate like ships at sea. This was not an unreasonable analogy, given the obvious parallels between oceans and deserts, but there was little in any of the presentations to suggest that we would actually operate differently from the way we had trained in Europe.

The planned advance across southern Iraq struck me as slow, deliberate, and overly cautious, given the paucity of enemy forces reported in the area. Even the absence of any obstacles to movement—rivers, embankments, rail lines, or bridges—made no difference to anticipated rates of advance. Psychologically, we were still in Central Europe.

Stranger yet were the numbers of "phase lines" on the map of the flat and open Iraqi desert. Phase lines have been with us since World War I, and they were originally designed as control measures to limit or constrain movement so as to keep advancing infantry formations on line. The use of so many phase lines was very much out of place in a featureless desert, for what we anticipated would be a war of rapid movement. Since there was nothing to canalize or divert our movement on the ground, why, I wondered, were we using the multitude of phase lines?

This is nonsense, I thought. The infantry still thinks at two or three miles an hour. Infantrymen take cover and call for air strikes or artillery at the first sign of resistance and see the enemy-occupied foxhole fifty meters ahead of them as the Clausewitzian "center of gravity in war." It's just dumb.

Major Campbell, the regimental intelligence officer, was next in line. Like Lute, he presented a "doctrinally correct" brief creating the impression that we faced a Soviet-like enemy with an order of battle of which Stalin would have been proud.

In broad terms, the regimental intelligence officer explained that the Iraqis, roughly twenty-six conscript infantry divisions totaling nearly 310,000 men, were deployed forward in a prepared defensive belt along Kuwait's border with Saudi Arabia. Behind them were another eighty to ninety thousand troops in nine Iraqi army mechanized divisions of higher quality, including the eight

Republican Guard divisions. These were located well to the rear of the main Iraqi defense.[6]

From the first intelligence briefing, however, every day, every week, every month, the U.S. Army's estimates of Iraqi forces suggested an ever-growing Iraqi ground force filled with veterans of the Iran-Iraq War equipped with top-quality Soviet equipment. Though I was hardly an Arabist or Middle East expert, my instincts told me these assumptions were over the top.

Key questions—like, "How many tank rounds do the Iraqis fire in training, and how often do they train?" Or, "How far do they move on maneuvers, in what formations, and how often?"—were not asked or addressed.

Intelligence officers habitually assess what they can count, which means they normally fail to consider such factors as troop quality, morale, cultural context, terrain, or weather, and so on. They often ignore the factors that count most when it comes to the fight. Intelligence officers, particularly those with no personal experience of direct-fire combat, have a natural inclination to project worst-case scenarios. Given that most of our generals are not sufficiently widely read or informed by combat experience to have the confidence to put their own stamps upon the available intelligence, this is often a serious problem. But in December 1990, I judged it too early to reach any conclusions. Perhaps, I thought, the approach and thinking at regiment, corps, and army levels would change.

When the staff finished its presentation, Col. Don Holder, the regimental commander, rose to speak.

Lieutenant Colonel Steve Robinette, the deputy regimental commander, always liked in briefings to call Don Holder "E.F.," or "E. F. Hutton," referring to a television commercial, popular at the time, in which it was insisted that when stock broker E. F. Hutton talked, everyone listened. Robinette's comment was not without merit, and Robinette was in a position to know. He made it his business to know the officers in the regiment personally and to serve as a mentor to them as well as to assist the commander in personnel matters. In a generally cutthroat, competitive Army culture, selfless mentorship is a rare trait, but Robinette had character in spades.

In Nuremberg, Germany, before the war, during one of the 2nd Cavalry's quarterly training briefings for General Franks, Robinette had listened as Franks criticized scout training across the corps, insisting that we simply did not know how to develop good reconnaissance skills.

When General Franks finished making his comments, Robinette spoke up, saying, to Colonel Holder's horror, "Sir, you're wrong. In the 2nd Cavalry we know what we are doing."

Holder then said, "Sir, that's not really what Steve meant."

"Oh, yes, he did," insisted Franks.

Though Franks personified orthodoxy in all matters pertaining to the Army, he also knew Robinette well from service in Vietnam. So Robinette probably had latitude to speak more bluntly than other officers in VII Corps. In this way, Robinette's influence magnified Holder's credibility, ensuring that Holder always had the captive audience he needed when he spoke.

Holder's subsequent comments were consistent with the doctrinal thinking to which he had contributed so much when he co-wrote the 1986 version of Army's field manual *Operations,* known as FM 100-5. Holder reiterated the mission, noting that the details concerning the exact deployment of the divisions behind the 2nd Cavalry had yet to be worked out. Most of the division deployments, he added several times, were still incomplete.

Colonel Holder also argued in favor of an attack on a narrow front, with the 2nd Cavalry in the lead and the divisions in column behind us, a comment that made perfect sense to us. When the main body of the Republican Guard Corps was detected, Holder said, we would hand off the battle to the divisions, moving to the flank or striking northeast to Basra, depending on circumstances at the time.

No surprises here, though I doubted that movement across the flat, open desert would or should mirror movement in Central Europe. Still, Hillen and I were happy to get the basic guidance that would allow us to plan and train at the squadron level, but we found the atmosphere in the regimental staff to be puzzling. Everyone at the meeting was working hard to seem unassuming and self-effacing, but their mood was actually tense and uneasy. Levity was forced, not natural, and the officers were merely workmanlike in their tone. Combat tasks were dutifully explained, but without any detectable enthusiasm for the fight ahead.

As usual, Hillen did not miss a thing, whispering to me, "Don't expect any sweeping cavalry attacks around the flanks of the enemy or anything daring from this bunch."

I nodded slightly but kept silent.

But Hillen was on to something serious. There was a very strong sense of skepticism about whether this offensive would work—and, yes, the officers were obviously scared.

No harm in that, I figured, as long as fear does not overrule common sense. Hell, though no one ever says it, no rational man who thinks about it would ever willingly cross the line of departure in war to fight.

Mercifully, the briefings in the regimental TOC did not take very long, and when the evening ended, we left quickly. Lieutenant Colonel Paul Larson (not his real name), the Cougar Squadron commander, met with me briefly after the meeting to compare notes, then drove straight back to squadron.

Larson, who bore a modest resemblance to the actor Luke Perry on the television show *Beverly Hills 90210*, was a diminutive figure with a high-pitched voice and an occasionally brusque manner that his detractors in the 2nd Cavalry said bordered on arrogance. I did not share this view of Larson, but I was constantly aware that Larson was uncomfortable in his dealings with the tall, remote, and contemplative Holder. Larson had also been thrust into command of Cougar Squadron after a popular and widely respected lieutenant colonel had been removed from the command list, moving Larson from the alternate to the primary list.

His prior experience was limited to the command of a headquarters unit as a captain and a year as an executive officer of a tank battalion as a major. This narrow professional background put him at some disadvantage vis-à-vis Colonel Holder, and he was acutely sensitive to it.

Larson knew that Holder and I had known one another since Holder taught me as a West Point cadet. Though at first suspicious of this relationship, Larson eventually came to regard it as an advantage in his dealings with Holder. I say "eventually," because my assignment to the squadron had come unexpectedly to Larson.

While I was regimental adjutant, Holder had decided to assign me to Cougar Squadron before my year as adjutant was up. Holder had summoned me to his office, where he was characteristically brief and to the point: "Toby Martinez, the Cougar Squadron S-3, is going to be the corps commander's new aide de camp. You will replace him as soon as possible. You have a lot of work to do. You have to turn Cougar Squadron into a hard-riding outfit that can fight. I see no evidence that the soldiers, noncommissioned officers, or company-grade officers are the problem, but beneath the 'spit and polish' surface, the squadron is not what it should be. You will have to go down there, turn things around, and get along with the squadron commander." At first, Colonel Holder's words puzzled me, but a few days later, when I was in the job, the meaning of his words became clear: it would be my job to prepare Cougar Squadron for war and to lead it into battle.

It was now pitch black. Though nights in the desert can be like perpetual visits to the local planetarium, on a night without any moonlight and nothing more than a compass and odometer to guide us, we could have been in trouble. Fortunately, we decided to drive toward the "Tapline" road, which stretches east–west across Saudi Arabia, refuel our vehicle, establish our position, and chart a course home from there. It was a good thing we did. The Tapline road was the artery carrying supplies, people, and equipment from the Persian Gulf to the Army's assembly areas in the flat, open desert of northeastern Saudi Arabia. In American terms, it was the military equivalent of I-95, the road with traffic that never stops. Anyone in the Army coming into or leaving Saudi Arabia ended up on the Tapline road. Of course, it was also a lucrative target for air or missile attack, but given American air supremacy, that possibility seemed remote to us. It was here that I reconnected with Cpt. Tony Ierardi, a former troop commander and assistant S-3 in Cougar Squadron.

Captain Ierardi, Hillen's able predecessor in the assistant S-3 job, had promised me when orders assigned him in the early fall to the Army's combined-arms staff officers course at Fort Leavenworth, Kansas, that he would find a way to return and join us in the desert. Ierardi had been an integral member of my team in Germany, and I wanted him with me in the desert. Though I never doubted Ierardi's sincerity, I was skeptical that he could do it, given the bureaucratic constraints the Army personnel system imposes on its officers; Ierardi had no orders reassigning him to the 2nd Cavalry. But, then again, I figured that since he was from Philadelphia like me, he would find a way to get back. (There were more than a few of us from Philadelphia in the squadron, and that too became a factor in Cougar Squadron's success.)

Then, while my driver refueled my Humvee at one of the many refueling points along the Tapline road, a solitary figure, tall and mysterious, weighed down with a duffle bag and backpack, walked toward me out of the darkness. At first, I put my hand on my .45-caliber automatic, not knowing who or what this person might be. There was no need. Having literally hitched one ride after the other on Air Force transports from central Kansas to Saudi Arabia, here was Captain Ierardi, a young, Bruce Willis look-alike, with all the gear he could carry. I was jubilant.

I walked over and threw my arms around him and said excitedly, "Tony, I don't know how the hell you found us, but I am damn glad you did."

We climbed into the Humvee, and I listened with great glee to Ierardi's story of how he had managed his miraculous feat of finding us in the desert. When we reached Cougar Squadron's Tactical Operations Center, Ierardi stowed his gear in my "General Purpose, Small" tent, as it is called in the Army.

My mind was at ease. Tony Ierardi would become my unseen "right arm," acting decisively and intelligently in the TOC to quickly solve a host of internal housekeeping problems and leave me to focus like a laser on what counted most—the fight. The division of labor allowed me to maneuver the troops while Ierardi dealt with the machinery of Cougar Squadron's command-and-control support requirements and, when necessary, Dragoon Base (regimental headquarters). The operations team of Ierardi, Hillen, and Cpt. Rhett Scott (a brilliant intelligence officer about whom more will be said later) was now in place.

CHRISTMAS IN TAA SEMINOLE

Tall, handsome, and always moderate in his language and conduct, Operations Sgt. Maj. Sherman Catchings made the squadron's tactical operations run efficiently and effectively. The only two things that offended Catchings' sensibilities were wet toilet paper and dumb second lieutenants. Otherwise, I never saw any senior noncommissioned officer assert his authority with soldiers and officers with greater ease. Catchings was one of the few soldiers who had combat experience in Vietnam. His advice and counsel to me were invaluable. His leadership consisted of a mix of firmness and compassion creating instant confidence in the soldiers he led. He simply embodied every virtue an officer seeks in a senior noncommissioned officer. I came to revere him, to trust him completely.

When engineer bulldozers were sent to Cougar Squadron for the purpose of digging in our tanks and armored fighting vehicles, I declined to immobilize the Cougar's armored fighting power. The idea of digging in tanks and armored fighting vehicles designed to fire on the move and smash through enemy defenses at 35 or 40 mph made no sense to me. Instead, I asked Sergeant Major Catchings if he would plan and supervise the digging-in of Cougar Squadron's Tactical Operations Center. Given its size and composition, the TOC vehicles had little armament and moved far too slowly to cope with sudden air attacks. If we did have to deploy suddenly in response to the threat of a renewed Iraqi offensive, it made more sense to keep the combat vehicles in a state of readiness to move on short notice.

Sergeant Major Catchings understood completely and created a work of art. All of the armored vehicles in the tactical operations center now sat in a large man-made depression, perhaps fifty feet by fifty feet across and ten or twelve feet in depth below the surface of the desert floor. Above the armored vehicles hung camouflage nets, creating a convincing picture of nothingness to overhead surveillance. One side of the square depression gently sloped downward, allowing vehicles to drive in and out from under the nets. From the desert floor or from the air, the command center was scarcely visible.

It turned out that the unorthodox setting was so remarkable, since everyone else in the 2nd Cavalry buried their tanks and "Brads" in the sand, that when Colonel Holder was informed he would receive a visit from the Army Chief of Staff, General Vuono, and the Deputy Chief of Staff of Operations, Lt. Gen. Dennis Reimer (later chief of staff), he decided to brief the VIP generals in Cougar Squadron's TOC.

Though I was not terribly excited about the brass dropping in for a regimental dog-and-pony show, I was in no position to object. In fact, at the time, I was really ill.

The day before Christmas, I had been offered a fresh banana from the Philippines. Stupidly, thinking that the outer skin made it safe to eat the banana flesh inside, I took it.

Dumb. Dumb. Dumb. By midnight I thought I would expire. I spent Christmas Eve with severe intestinal pain.

Christmas morning, the day of the VIP visit, began with soldiers setting cans of excrement on fire. Soldiers found the experience distasteful, commenting later that they remembered seeing shit-burning details on a television show about Vietnam called *Tour of Duty*. Abercrombie in Hawk Company actually volunteered to accompany one of the details on Christmas morning so he could say, "This is what I did on Christmas Day, 1990." Thankfully, by the time the Army's top four-star generals arrived on the scene the shit burning was over.

Though my intestinal condition made sitting through Colonel Holder's presentation to the generals impossible, I did want to check on the event, so I walked the short distance from my dug-in tent to the TOC. Just outside I was surprised to find Maj. Dave Petraeus, the chief of staff's aide de camp. Dave Petraeus (later a four-star general) and I had taught in the Department of Social Sciences at West Point, so I felt comfortable raising the issue of the plan of attack with him.

As always, Dave was cordial. However, when I told him I was concerned that General Franks planned to attack at a painfully slow speed, that this could be disastrous, and that General Vuono might want to look into the matter, Dave made some soothing remark suggesting that things would work out but declined to involve himself. He, like Major Lute, who was always near when generals were about, were both far more concerned with keeping the two VIP generals on schedule for their next celebrity visit in the desert than with a corps attack that seemed a distant possibility. As the care and feeding of four-stars was not my concern, I thanked Dave for his time and moved on.

Inside the TOC, General Vuono expressed his admiration for the regiment, adding grimly, "If we do have to fight and, God, I hope we do not, because we all know what that means, I know you guys will do a great job."

ADJUSTING TO THE DESERT

We now had two or three weeks to put into practice the focused training we had developed in Bamberg, Germany. We needed the training badly, because the routine of life in our assembly areas was tiresome.

A part of the garrison-like routine soldiers particularly disliked was "Stand To." "Stand To" meant everyone dressed, awake, and manning his respective weapon, ready to fight. In the desert, the 2nd Cavalry executed Stand To daily at 0500 hours.

Normally, I would walk into the squadron TOC just before 0500 hours to receive the report from the Cougar Squadron's cavalry troops, tank company, and howitzer battery. When Lieutenant Colonel Larson was satisfied with the report from the troops, I would signal Dragoon Base that we had executed Stand-To and were resuming normal duties. It was on one of these cold, windy desert mornings that I earned a nickname that I personally found strange but that the soldiers seemed to like a lot.

Walking into the TOC one morning at Stand To, I must have looked particularly rough, and Specialist Kyle, one of our most gifted and competent vehicle mechanics, said, "Hey, look at that, the major looks just like Sid Vicious!"

Everybody broke into hysterics. Perplexed by the whole thing, I revealed my ignorance of popular culture with the question, "Who the hell is Sid Vicious?"

Of course, the question elicited even more laughter. Too tired and too cold to understand, I smiled and asked if I was now stuck with this name.

Staff Sergeant William Burns, the squadron's Bradley master gunner, who was now standing behind me, said, "Sir, in the morning you look pretty rough, just like Sid Vicious. Haven't you seen the movie *Sid and Nancy*? Sid Vicious was a bad motherf——er."

Burns was the most original human being I had ever known. His origins were British, Egyptian, and African via Manchester (England), New York City, and Lincoln, Nebraska. Against this guy, the Iraqis never had a prayer.

"No, I never heard of the guy. Who was he?" I asked.

"Sid Vicious? Who was Sid Vicious?" asked Burns.[1]

The tall, energetic Burns was incredulous, amazed at my lack of knowledge about popular culture, but when I shrugged my shoulders in response, Burns quietly whispered to me, "He was a rock star who killed his girlfriend with a knife—a real burnout with a bad attitude."

"Hmmm," I grunted. "Well, as long as he killed somebody, I guess it's all right."

Not realizing that everyone in the TOC was listening, I was surprised when my statement elicited laughter. The next morning, anarchy signs appeared on the side of my tank turret, and somebody had painted "Sid Vicious" on the tank's gun tube. The nickname stuck.

While the TOC crew was having some fun at my expense, Cpt. H. R. McMaster, the Eagle Troop commander, was involved in a much more serious discussion with Lieutenant Colonel Larson. Apparently, Larson had decided to drive over to Eagle Troop early to see how Eagle Troop executed Stand To.

Unfortunately, on this occasion, not everyone in Eagle Troop was quite up for the Stand To, and a confrontation ensued.

When I had first encountered H.R. McMaster, he looked like a short, stocky, and intense version of the country and western singer Garth Brooks. Like me, H.R. was from Philadelphia, and I think this created an instant rapport between us. In addition to being a 1984 graduate of the Military Academy, McMaster was also a graduate of the Valley Forge Military Academy in Wayne, Pennsylvania—a military school I knew well from my days at the William Penn Charter School in Philadelphia.

Werner Binder, the father of a German family with whom I had lived as an exchange student for twelve months from 1969 to 1970, had once told me, in reminiscing about his wartime experience as an officer on the Eastern Front during World War II: "Your best commander is always your most difficult subordinate. He always asks hard questions and offers new ways to do things, because he thinks. He may be quick-tempered and occasionally insubordinate, but if you have one like this, give him the freedom to do what he thinks is right whenever possible."

In 1991, these words fit the young, exuberant Eagle Troop commander like a glove. For me, the key was keeping up McMaster's morale, because beneath the energetic exterior, McMaster was a man of great sensitivity and emotion, full of affection for his men but quick to anger if he sensed injustice.

Unfortunately, these attributes were of little help when Eagle Troop's Stand To was not quite up to standard. Unfortunately, the diminutive Lieutenant Colonel Larson now addressed McMaster in his best high-pitched nasal voice, saying, "Captain McMaster, to whom must I speak in Eagle Troop to ensure that my orders are carried out?"

Larson was being sarcastic in the worst way possible, in the hope of provoking McMaster—and McMaster was responding.

"Sir, that person would be me."

"Apparently not, captain," Lieutenant Colonel Larson shot back, "since my guidance was ignored."

Larson then systematically listed the deficiencies that he noted during Eagle Troop's Stand To, everything from soldiers not shaved to gun-tube orientation, meaning guns pointed in the wrong direction.

More embarrassed than anything else, McMaster glared back at the squadron commander, forcefully responding with, "Sir, if I am not performing to your expectation, it is your privilege to relieve me at any time."

And so it went. Hearing the verbal exchange, however, and knowing full well that the discussion was escalating pointlessly in the wrong direction for both officers, Lt. John Gifford, Eagle Troop's executive officer, moved in cautiously with a phony message that one of the scout platoon leaders was on the radio for McMaster.

John Gifford was a very gifted and intelligent officer who spent a great deal of time managing McMaster's frustrations and temper. I seriously doubt that Eagle Troop would have performed as brilliantly as it did without Gifford's steady hand.

Mildly amused at the confrontation he had provoked, Lieutenant Colonel Larson apparently decided to take advantage of Gifford's intervention, his point made. Larson told McMaster to tend to his troop and left him to stew in his embarrassment.

Although McMaster was extremely competent, he was also the sort of commander whose supply room and administration were usually in disarray. If the activity in question had no immediate value to Eagle Troop's readiness to deploy and fight, McMaster generally ignored it. In one of our first meetings in Bamberg McMaster had decried the lack of focus on readiness to deploy and fight.

"What we need," McMaster had told me, "Is a war to straighten out the damn Army. Too many people have forgotten what we're really all about."

Obviously, I sympathized with McMaster, but I warned him, "Be careful what you wish for; you may get it." However, I could not prevent the friction between McMaster and Larson that was to ensue. Refereeing the ongoing match between them turned out to be one of my supporting missions as the Cougar Squadron operations officer.

BUILDING THE SHARK

Cavalry units, or armored reconnaissance outfits, are like deep-sea sharks, which have to swim to eat and live; without sea bladders, they sink when they do not move. As long as an armored cavalry unit is in motion, it finds and devours its enemy. Like the shark, an armored force that stops for more than a short time to refuel and rearm is at great risk. But the shark I wanted for the war was not yet ready for deep water. The shark from Bamberg would have to learn new ways in the Arabian Desert.

If the training was tough enough, I thought, it would engender far more unit cohesion, by promoting confidence, an automatic response to anticipated orders, and aggressiveness. Thanks to the 2nd Cavalry's fine training programs in Germany, gunnery skills were already superb. We would keep these skills in good shape, but for Cougar Squadron, adaptation to the new desert environment entailed tough, new maneuver training at the crew, section, platoon, troop, and squadron levels.

In the fast-paced action of armored combat, discipline had to become habitual. To the extent that I could make it so, the quality and content of our training would have to approximate real combat and inculcate routine actions. With any luck, our relentless preparation for offensive operations would also suppress the soldiers' natural inclinations to fear and homesickness and enable soldiers to fight in a relatively autonomous state under conditions of extreme stress.

Fortunately, Cougar Squadron was blessed with the time in Saudi Arabia to "get our house in order" before our first combat actions began. Borrowing from Field Marshal Erwin Rommel's playbook, I resolved to put my tactical command post (TAC) in an armored Bradley fighting vehicle that would follow me in my tank. This would allow me to intervene personally in combat to tip the scales in a fight if it became necessary on a fluid, nonlinear battlefield. Of course, I did not yet have a tank, but I kept pressing for one until I got one.

Before turning to the troop commanders for their views on training, however, I turned first to Hillen and Staff Sergeant Burns. Both Hillen and Burns had more recent experience at the platoon level than I did, and they were both more familiar with the heavy requirements my proposed training program would impose on the soldiers and their equipment. As the master gunner for the Bradley M2/3 weapon system, Burns was responsible for everything from crew personnel stability to weapon system readiness. His technical and tactical competence was unsurpassed.

Some readers may question the wisdom of expecting a young first lieutenant or even a senior noncommissioned officer to take on these tasks and execute them successfully. But competence, character, and intelligence are generally independent of rank, experience, and age. Experience helps, but not enough to compensate for the absence of competence, character, or intelligence. This explains why just a few years before James Gavin distinguished himself in command of the 82nd Airborne Division in the fall of 1944 he was still a captain of infantry![7]

Turning first to Hillen, I made it clear that his whole world would now revolve around boundaries: he would be issuing control points, maintaining contact with Ierardi at Cougar Base and Dragoon Base, reporting significant actions taken, developing battle drills and formations.

Next, I asked Staff Sergeant Burns to work closely with Staff Sergeant Pierce, the tank master gunner, to set up ranges and renew the weapons training we had begun in Germany during October 1990. I asked Burns and Pierce to assume responsibility for setting up the ranges and developing the gunnery training. I left artillery training, as always, in the able hands of Cpt. Sam White and his first sergeant.

Sam's eight-gun battery could deploy and shoot faster than any other battery I have ever seen, but a small element of tension did exist with the 4.2-inch mortars. First Lieutenant Danny Davis, the Eagle Troop fire-support-team leader, was not only Eagle Troop's critical link to the artillery but also controlled the troop mortars. Davis was always anxious to try anything that had not been done before. A very bright and enthusiastic artilleryman, Davis was devoted to just two things: Jesus Christ and Eagle Troop. He never failed either one, but his unbridled enthusiasm sometimes got him into trouble.

Since we had never maneuvered in the open desert, integrating mortars into Eagle Troop's battle drills was a truly new event. In discussions with McMaster, Davis devised an ingenious tactic that made perfect sense but was entirely unorthodox by conventional U.S. Army standards and would take a lot of practice to perfect: As soon as the enemy was sighted, the troop's tanks would move to the front, scouts would move to the flanks, and the mortar section of two M113 tracked armored vehicles, each carrying a 4.2-inch mortar, would immediately move one hundred meters to the left or right of the advancing troop and begin dropping rounds on top of the enemy. The initial shots would be, of necessity, white phosphorous rounds, designed to mark the enemy's location for friendly forces in the air and on the ground. If the enemy is moving, direct hits are unlikely, though possible, but the real point of suppression fire is to disorient and confuse the enemy and keep his head down.

As Eagle Troop repeatedly practiced this drill, the time for displacement the mortars needed to hip-shoot at the enemy was compressed. Mortars, however, are high-angle-fire weapons and need a minimum range of approximately 560 meters. Thus, hip-shooting always presents the danger that range may be misjudged or simply set incorrectly. It was probably inevitable that the crew would eventually get the elevation and charge wrong in one of its practice hip-shoots, with the result that four rounds went over the horizon into parts unknown.

Unfortunately, these particular "parts unknown" belonged to the XVIII Airborne Corps deception TOC. Deception TOCs are established to transmit false electronic signals and offer the appearance of a real operational headquarters to overhead surveillance. Though the event was probably the closest any of the military intelligence soldiers ever came to real action, the unhappy residents of the corps deception TOC were not amused, and they complained bitterly.

For the next two months I coped with queries that came down from VII Corps headquarters, doing everything I could to stonewall inquiries that I feared might be used as a justification to relieve or punish McMaster. In those weeks before real action began, the Army's garrison culture, which exalts unquestioning compliance with dumb ideas above tactical war-fighting prowess, continued without much interruption. The desire to punish the slightest infraction persisted. As I learned repeatedly, this culture creates a real incentive for officers in leadership positions to conform, but not necessarily to perform.

After the conflict, two days after the cease-fire was called, while sitting in an assembly area just inside Kuwait, I received a directive from corps headquarters to provide a formal report on the incident. I could no longer stonewall. Fortunately for me, corps headquarters was flush with victory. They were in a forgiving mood, and the matter was closed.

The other event worth noting involved a lost tank from Ghost Troop. One of Ghost's tanks became disoriented and nearly drove into Kuwait. Fortunately, Saudi National Guard troops stopped the tank before that happened and with the help of an interpreter managed to inform us of what had happened. It was the unhappy and embarrassing task of Cpt. Joe Sartiano, the Ghost Troop commander, to find and bring back the missing tank. Like McMaster, Sartiano was a graduate of the West Point class of 1984.

When Sartiano met me for the first time, he was not bashful about what he wanted but came right to the point. "Sir, I don't know what H.R. told you, but I really want to get out of Seventh Army Training Center and command a cavalry troop in the 2nd Cavalry. McMaster tells me great things about Cougar Squadron and you, so I thought. . . ."

I interrupted him: "Please spare me the bullshit. If you want to command a cavalry troop, that's fine. You don't need to kiss my ass to get in the door."

Though clearly a little surprised at my remark, Sartiano instantly dropped the obsequious nonsense that is all too common in our Army. I asked him how his family felt about moving from Grafenwoehr to Bamberg. Joe said he was divorced and that moving across Germany was not an issue. We talked for approximately ten minutes. I liked what I saw and heard.

Sartiano looked like a combination of Dean Martin and Andy Garcia, with a deceptively relaxed manner. His demeanor was a virtue in an Army of far too many soldiers serving under vitamin D–deficient, anal-retentive, obsessive-compulsive careerists without a shred of compassion for their troops. There was, however, more to Sartiano than his looks. After graduation from George C. Marshall High School in Falls Church, Virginia, Joe had been recruited to play football for West Point, where he started as a punter all four years. He also had a healthy sense of humor.

When he returned from recovering the lost tank, I asked him about his visit with the Saudi National Guard and how he had been treated. He said, "Not bad, Sir, until they offered me the usual combination of goat's eyes and monkey balls. At that point, I had to decline their hospitality and get the hell out of there."

Sartiano, McMaster, and their lieutenants understood that training, if it is to be effective, must inspire soldiers with the desire to fight. When the quality of the training and leadership is high, soldiers can do things in moments of extreme danger on the battlefield that they had previously thought impossible. In the final analysis, what the American soldier does in prewar training, he also does in wartime. The notion that exposure to hostile fire suddenly awakens new attributes in the soldier that were not already there is some Hollywood moviemaker's wet dream.

In addition to the demanding training regimen, two further events occurred with profound consequences for our development into the shark. The first involved the arrival of brand-new M2A2 infantry versions of the Bradley fighting vehicle and Global Positioning System (GPS) sets for the Cougar Squadron's scout platoons. These armored fighting vehicles offered not only more room to store gear and ammo, an improved machine-gun mount, a better transmission, and more speed but also more armored protection.

The new GPS equipment, though primitive by today's standards, was marvelous. With the exception of the hours between 0500 and 0700, when the required number of satellites were not in position over the Middle East the GPS equipment gave our scouts, artillerymen, and Air Force liaison section the confidence to plan and direct operations and attacks with speed and precision.

The other major development in training was "Quickstrike." Colonel Holder instituted a series of alerts, under the name of "Quickstrike," designed to posture the combat elements of the squadron for deployment to Saudi Arabia's border with Iraq. With no warning at all, the squadron would be required to get its combat elements moving within fifteen minutes and the rest of its supporting elements within thirty minutes. Our opportunity to test this readiness for real was to come much earlier than expected.

In mid-January we received word that a force of Iraqi tanks in battalion strength had broken through the berm along the Saudi–Iraq border and were presumably executing an end run through the Wadi al Batin toward King Khalid Military City.

Soldiers literally tumbled out of their cots and into their vehicles. The tanks' turbine engines roared and mini-sandstorms kicked up behind their armored fighting vehicles pulled out of their assembly areas, moved into formation, and raced toward the border.

As I moved out in the Bradley fighting vehicle, Hillen jumped into one of the tactical command-and-control vehicles—a tall, tracked armored vehicle called an M577—and tried to keep up. (The M577 was an M113 light tracked armored fighting vehicle with a raised roof to give room to stand up and look at map boards, and with multiple radios and an electrical generator.) Before long, however, the underpowered behemoth vanished, and I lost sight of him. Over the radio, as we moved, the battle stations reported their combat power in succession. I responded with, "Battle stations, battle stations, this is Cougar 3, battle carry sabot, over." This directed the tanks to load tank-killing rounds into their guns.

As the executive officers or troop, company, and battery commanders answered, I could hear the excitement in the soldiers' and officers' voices. This was the first time we had ever loaded service sabot ammunition in anticipation of a real tank battle.

The effect was electrifying. As they say in the U.S. Navy, this was no drill. Even though it turned out that the moving-target indicators spotted by the Joint Surveillance and Targeting Radar System (JSTARS—a Boeing 707 jet with ground surveillance radar) were camels, not tanks, the drill was also a good introduction to maneuver warfare in the desert. After dark, the troop commanders ran into one another in Cougar Squadron's TOC and gave each other great handshakes, with huge smiles on their faces. All agreed that the Quickstrike reaction drill demonstrated that our soldiers could indeed "walk the walk"!

BATTLE DRILLS IN THE ARABIAN DESERT

Combat units are always created before battles, not during them. Combat either solidifies or destroys them. The best small units become imprinted with the character and personality of their commanders. This imprinting process is a result of how small units prepare to fight.

Mobile desert warfare requires great skill and high-speed performance of combat formations that fight. Centralized control of events is impossible, and success depends heavily on informed initiative, as well as the inculcation of an offensive spirit into every soldier, noncommissioned officer, and officer. The opportunity for success when it does come is fleeting; immediate advantage must be taken by soldiers at all levels, based on an understanding of the unit commander's intent. Armored fighting vehicles and attack helicopters are of little use if the men inside them do not think and are afraid to act.

To take offensive action, the American soldier must be trained relentlessly to attack—and this is exactly what we did. In the desert, warfare is a gunfight. The side that shoots first wins. To win, the soldier must have complete confidence in himself, his weapon, his fellow soldiers, and his leaders.

I resisted any suggestion that Cougar Squadron practice defensive tactics. The troop commanders agreed, and we all struggled to erase the very word "defense" from our soldiers' thinking.

Nothing like this is easy to achieve. In every organization there are always "acolytes," who will follow the leader anywhere. There are also "swing voters," who "go along," provided things go well. Unfortunately, there are "passive resisters." Knowing this to be the case, I tried every way possible to integrate, co-opt, and incorporate everyone's ideas. The reason is very important.

Leadership and tactics in a wartime environment, characterized by uncertainty and ambiguity, are inseparable. Leaders at every level must have complete confidence in the validity of their thinking about war. When they do, they perform a hell of a lot better. Solutions imposed from above by commanders, one-man shows, do not work. This is why the subtle differences in the way the Cougar Squadron troop commanders organized their formations to fight are instructive.

In Eagle Troop, for instance, the respective integrity of tank and scout platoons was always preserved; while the scout and tank platoons cooperated well, there was no permanent teaming of scouts and tanks. In Ghost Troop, Sartiano decided that the best use of the scouts' superior gunsights required the integration of the Abrams tanks with the Bradleys into teams. Sartiano called this practice "scrambling the troop."

In Fox and Eagle troops, the mortars moved in formation between the scouts and the tanks. In Ghost Troop, the mortars and fire-support team traveled in a wedge behind Captain Sartiano's tank, the *Godfather*, or Ghost 66, as the troop commander's tank is normally called. Eagle and Fox troop commanders normally led with their scouts but positioned the mortars farther forward between the scout and tank platoons.[8]

In drills, once contact was made with the enemy it was the Ghost Troop fire-support team leader's responsibility to watch over and conduct mortar fire in support of the scouts in contact. It was another version of the tactic of holding the enemy's nose with scouts and mortars as the tanks moved to punch him, but with a slightly different twist from the approach of Eagle and Fox troops. As the initial round was fired, the fire-support team leader would move to the scout platoon into contact to observe the engagement area. This gave the fire-support team leader the ability to observe and to report to the attacking tank platoon leaders "Rounds complete," so they wouldn't get caught by any shots still in the air.

Eagle Troop did things differently. Eagle Troop pushed the mortars as far forward as possible. Frankly, I saw the merits of both arguments and did not

Figure 2. Key Leaders and Equipment in Ghost Troop

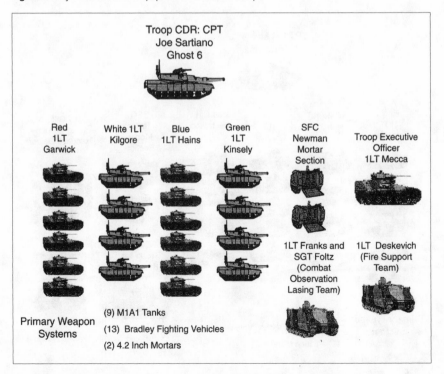

interfere. The troop commanders were always free to develop their own tactics, provided their tactics worked within the framework of Cougar Squadron's battle drills and formations.

In Eagle and Ghost troops, the commanders adapted their tactics and their leadership to suit not only their own preferences but the personalities of the soldiers, sergeants, and lieutenants they led. McMaster organized and led his troop as though it were a rugby team on its way to the World Cup Finals. As a commander, he was a player-coach, leading on the field through every scrum but willing to defer to his officers, whose judgment he valued and respected. McMaster's approach worked primarily because he was blessed with a collection of lieutenants and senior noncommissioned officers who liked this kind of down-and-dirty, personal leadership, especially his emphasis on the use of the tank platoons as assault forces, attacking on the move.

McMaster's employment of the scouts forward or on the flanks to develop and shape the battle (that is, find the whole enemy force and determine what it was doing) was equally appealing to the scout platoon leaders, who were

Figure 3. Key Leaders and Equipment in Eagle Troop

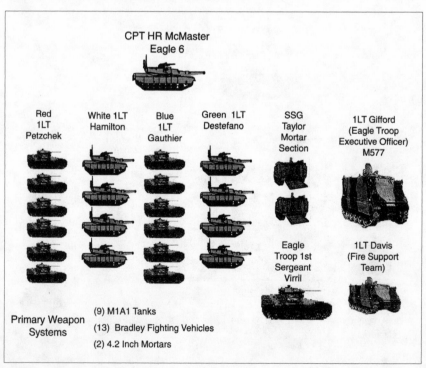

eager to cooperate closely with the tank platoons but still wanted to retain control over their respective formations as much as possible. A fine scout in his own right, with lots of National Training Center experience, McMaster also pushed hard to develop a flair for reconnaissance in his scouts, the true eyes and ears of the cavalry. In the execution of battle drills and formation movement, Eagle Troop was unexcelled.

Ghost Troop diverged in character from Eagle Troop in several important ways. Before leaving Bamberg, Sartiano knew that he had taken command of officers and noncommissioned officers who had great enthusiasm but less experience and much less self-confidence. One of Ghost Troop's best noncommissioned officers, Staff Sergeant Patterson (another Pennsylvanian), was now in Eagle Troop. Patterson was a man of action, easily bored in garrison; fortunately, I had been able to persuade Colonel Larson to transfer Patterson, not permanently hurt him with the extremely harsh disciplinary action that Larson would normally have imposed. In addition, one of Sartiano's tank platoon leaders was a newcomer from another unit in Germany, and this presented Joe with a set of challenges that McMaster did not face.

Sartiano's top priority was to forge a close-knit, tightly integrated unit as quickly as possible. Sartiano's emphasis was on teamwork that capitalized on the depth of gunnery experience in his scout sections through the integration of Abrams tanks and Bradley fighting vehicles. In contrast to the formation smashing practiced in Eagle Troop, Sartiano strove both to refine Ghost Troop's maneuver skills and build up the troop's confidence in its leaders.

None of this is to say that I was an easygoing or completely hands-off leader when it came to matters of training or tactics. I was not. Though I made it a point to always show humor and kindness to soldiers and noncommissioned officers, I could be very brusque with officers who did not perform to expectation.

Soldiers become soldiers for reasons that have nothing to do with the ambitions and delusions of grandeur that frequently influence officers. In contrast to officers, American soldiers ask for and get very little, but they give a hell of a lot.

Being tough on officers was essential to the development of the self-confidence they needed if they were to make quick decisions in combat. Junior officers win or lose battles. If they lack the character, competence, or intelligence to make decisions under fire without consulting higher authority, they will fail and put the lives of the soldiers they lead at risk.

Thoroughly practiced battle drills and formations were critical confidence-building measures. But at the same time, too much uniformity imposed at the lowest level would destroy, not encourage, initiative. Striking a balance between the two was vital. The good news was that we had a wealth of talent at every level that was capable of initiative and risk taking. Training just developed it.

Of course, maneuvering a cavalry troop, tank company, or artillery battery is relatively straightforward. Doing it well takes practice, but there are relatively few moving parts. In the open desert, a captain can generally see most of the elements he commands.

On the other hand, maneuvering a cavalry battle group with nearly two hundred vehicles of various types is much more complex and difficult than anyone who hasn't done it imagines. You cannot clump together, or you make too easy a target; when you are spread out, in anything other than perfect conditions and flat terrain, the elements can easily lose visual contact with each other. So now imagine turning a formation in which each vehicle occupies a space a hundred yards from the vehicle closest to it, and you have some idea of the challenge. That makes the choice of a formation a critical decision.

MANEUVERING IN THE ARABIAN DESERT

Having watched the cavalry troops train, I ruled out the closely packed maneuver formations that we had used in Germany's narrow valleys and dense woods.

I wanted to exploit the full combat power of Cougar Squadron inside formations that provided all-around security as we moved but still facilitated the concentration of fire at the decisive point in battle. To achieve this, every soldier would need to know where he was in relation to the rest of his unit, and if his unit was adjacent to another friendly force, he had to know roughly where his unit ended and where the adjacent unit began. Within formations, routine battle drills assist units in adapting to changing battlefield conditions on a case-by-case basis and give combat leaders at the lowest level the ability to influence the action.

I also wanted the smallest element to make contact with the enemy first. The lead element would then provide the intelligence we needed to maneuver against a moving or stationary force. Ierardi and Hillen favored moving with all three cavalry troops abreast. I was undecided, so I drove over to consult with McMaster. I wanted another solution.

"What I really need," I asked McMaster as I paused to sip some hot coffee, "is your opinion on the fighting formation we should adopt for our offensive maneuver. I know we talked a lot about this in Bamberg. You know I want to lead with at least one cavalry troop, but I am uncomfortable making contact with anything larger. What do you think?"

"The diamond," replied McMaster.

"What?"

"The diamond," answered McMaster.

Smiling from ear to ear, McMaster fell excitedly to his knees and drew a picture in the sand of the squadron battle group with one troop in the lead, two troops on the flanks, a little behind, and the tank company in the middle, just ahead of the squadron's TOC. I did not need a magnifying glass to know that this was obviously the solution to my objection to deploying three troops on line.

"Yes. H.R., the diamond is exactly what we need. Let's see what the frontage will be."

I stopped to pull out my map, placed it on the hood of the Humvee and looked carefully at the distance across our projected zone of attack. Three troops abreast would cover fifteen kilometers. That was too much to present to the enemy at one time. The diamond, with a smaller frontage, would transform the squadron battle group into a more precise maneuver instrument.

"We have twenty kilometers," I remarked. "That will work. If we position ourselves generally in the center, we can spread out over ten kilometers with observation of the five kilometers on either side. That solves the problem. Now, H.R., listen, I've already arranged things with Colonel Larson. I've also spoken to Rudd. He is going to set up a series of scenarios, with enemy forces constituted from our combat trains."

The "combat trains" consisted of thirty to forty wheeled vehicles that hauled and distributed everything from fuel and bullets to medical supplies and repair parts.

"You mean the combat trains in the attack?" asked Gifford.

"Precisely." By now, McMaster and Gifford were laughing pretty hard. They could not imagine the combat trains pulling this off.

"Guys," I said, "I'm serious."

"Sir, I know, I know," answered H.R. through the laughter. "I just can't wait to see those guys in action,"

"Well, Rudd and Master Sergeant Vera [Cougar Squadron's truck master] are ready. We will deploy in the diamond just as we've discussed," I said, motioning to the diamond McMaster had drawn in the sand. "I just have to talk to Sam White about where our artillery battery [Caisson] will be in the formation and where our direct-support artillery battalion, 6-41 Artillery, will fit in." Recently 6-41 Artillery had joined us, and I needed time to integrate them into the maneuver training. "Hillen will work up the GPS waypoints. We'll move out against a stationary enemy in the morning and a moving enemy in the afternoon [though it turned out that we took three days to get that far along]. Then, we'll repeat the exercise at night. What do you think?"

"Sir, this is fantastic," said Gifford. McMaster chimed in, "It's the first time in our lives we will see an entire cavalry battle group dispersed in formation across the desert. We couldn't do this anywhere else in the world, you know that."

"Hell, it's the first time any of us have seen this. But rest assured, we will fuck it up a few times before we get it right."

"Sure, but whatever happens, it will be worth it," responded McMaster.

Indeed, it was worth it.

Three days later, after a series of rehearsals at the troop and platoon levels, Cougar Squadron was heavily engaged in maneuvers. The results were mixed, but we learned a hell of a lot.

The tanks' turbines sucked in so much dust and sand that we had to stop repeatedly and clean the filters to prevent the engines from seizing up. We also determined that whenever we stopped, we would shut down the tank engines, saving enormous quantities of fuel. That way we could get all the way to Basra in six hours on one tank of fuel, even if we drove at forty miles per hour!

After several tries, we eventually managed to refuel all forty-two of the squadron's tanks in less than sixteen minutes. The support platoon became so expert in this task that we could routinely refuel all the wheeled and tracked armored fighting vehicles in the Cougar Squadron battle group in less than forty-five minutes. Refueling hundreds of vehicles would normally take much longer, but the flat, open desert offered us the space to spread out the battle group and execute a refuel on the move (ROM) much faster than we could have done it in the valleys and forests of Germany. We also learned how important additional air filters would be to keep the sand and dust out of our tanks' turbine engines. (When we crossed into Iraq, we would carry three times the normal load of air filters.)

After several days of practice, the cavalry troop commanders also deter-mined that putting engineer platoons forward with the cavalry troops made no sense. Mounted in light armored vehicles and Humvees, the engineers simply added soft-skinned targets to the battlefield when there was no reason to expose them to enemy fire. Instead, we placed soldiers from the engineer company with the scouts to act as liaison elements and sent the rest back, bringing engineer assets forward as required by the situation. By the third day we were maneuvering very comfortably inside the diamond. It was time for the most difficult and yet most important exercise—maneuver against a moving enemy.

Knowing that McMaster understood what it was we were trying to accomplish, I put Eagle Troop in the lead, with instructions to make contact, compel the enemy force to halt, and recommend a course of action—telling us to punch right, around Eagle Troop's right flank, or left, around the troop's left flank. Eagle Troop's scouts moved out smartly, compelling the rest of the squadron to keep up, a condition I had very much wanted to achieve.

Within ten minutes, McMaster saw the column of trucks from the combat trains moving from right to left across his front. He reported the enemy formation and immediately began attacking the lead elements with both direct and indirect fire, only to see Captain Rudd calmly deploy his force into the attack from a column. I had told Rudd not to be an accommodating enemy, and he was taking my guidance very seriously.

Within seconds of making contact, McMaster recommended a punch right to meet and fix the enemy, with the result that Ghost Troop automatically began swinging to the right rear, wide around him, while Fox Troop moved up on line with Eagle Troop, on the latter's left.

The formation moved like an onrushing stream, without any detailed orders, exactly as I had hoped. It was now time for Hawk, the tank company, to move forward around the right of Ghost Troop and deliver the killing blow, but Hawk was nowhere in sight.

Frustrated, I called the Hawk Company commander and told him, "Hawk 6, Cougar 3, punch right, acknowledge, over?"

Eventually, Hawk 6 responded that due to the dust and sand he could not see Eagle Troop. McMaster instantly emitted smoke from his tank and dispatched scouts to lead Hawk forward, but the smoke added the sand-filled air simply made matters worse. To top it off, Sartiano now called with more bad news.

"Cougar 3, Ghost 6, over."

"Cougar 3, send it."

"Cougar 3, Ghost 6, we have a situation here, over."

"What do you mean by situation, over?"

"We have large numbers of local wildlife in front of us, over."

Sitting in his tank turret, Sartiano could see, for about two hundred meters to his front and left, nothing but sheep.

Standing in front of his Abrams tank, "the Godfather," Sartiano's driver was trying to ask a Bedouin politely to move his sheep so that Ghost Troop could continue its attack. The effort, though well intentioned, went nowhere.

"Explain wildlife, over?" I asked.

"This is Ghost 6, we are surrounded by sheep. Break [indicating a pause]. I mean, we can blast through them, but the local nationals may not like that, over."

"This is Cougar 3, roger," I said glumly. "Don't kill the sheep. Catch up when you can, Cougar 3, out."

By this time, Rudd's expertly organized, drilled and trained combat trains were overrunning the squadron, driving past Caisson's guns, which had "dropped trails" and were simulating fire missions called in by Eagle Troop.

Morale among our soldiers who normally supplied bullets, food, water, and repair parts but were now simulating an armored enemy was sky-high. They had outmaneuvered our combat elements, and they knew it.

I must admit that I was truly depressed. Moving a squadron decisively in any given direction was something like turning a battleship at sea; it would take more time than we had left to reset the squadron battle group. All we could do on this last day of our three-day maneuver marathon was hold an after-action review.

After-action reviews (AARs) can be helpful if the officers executing the mission actually do the talking. It was customary in Cougar Squadron for the S-3 to conduct the AARs. The colonel would normally wrap up the AAR with a summation of key points.

So after the dust clouds finally settled and everyone had plenty of water to drink, I opened the after-action review by restating the mission and the general purpose of the exercise, then turning first to Captain Rudd, the commander of the opposing force, for his assessment of our performance. Rudd was exacting in how he described his meeting engagement with us, pointing out our weaknesses with great precision. When he finished, I turned to McMaster for his assessment.

McMaster came forward, pointing out on the large whiteboard depicting the squadron diamond where the enemy had been sighted and what actions he had taken. McMaster finished his assessment with a number of comments on how the scouts would liaise with Hawk Company in the future.

I began by mentioning that the artillerymen had done a splendid job of deploying and firing in response to Eagle Troop's initial calls for fire. This elicited outbursts of animal sounds and "Hooahs!" from Caisson.

I turned next to Sartiano, Ghost Troop's commander.

Sartiano explained how he had managed to hold on precariously to Eagle Troop's flank for the punch right until his encounter with the Bedouin and his herd of sheep. This statement elicited an outburst of laughter and remarks suggesting that Ghost Troop had had designs on the sheep that had caused it to halt and linger with the sheep, and so on, and so on, and so on. Finally, once we regained our composure, I turned to the Hawk Company commander, a young captain in his late twenties.

"Hawk 6, tell us what your mission was and what happened." He came forward and related his version. "Sir, my mission was to follow and support Eagle Troop. When the order came to punch right, I tried to move the company forward but could not identify Eagle Troop."

"Why not?" I snapped.

"Sir, there was too much obscuration."

"All right," I answered. "Then, what did you do?"

"Sir?"

"What did you do?"

"Sir, unable to see what was happening, I decided to halt the company and wait for further instruction."

This comment left me steaming. The thing I disliked most about the U.S. Army's officer corps was its predisposition for inaction and indecision. We would be the first unit into Iraq, the first to fight. We needed officers who would act without orders on the basis of what they knew and thought to be right.

"Captain, you command more combat power than anyone else in this squadron. You have the ability to make or break us in close combat. Doing nothing and waiting for orders is not an acceptable response."

Things now grew very silent as I continued.

"You must be prepared to go forward even in the face of uncertainty. Uncertainty is not an excuse for inaction."

My voice was rising in intensity when Lieutenant Colonel Larson interrupted. Larson could see that for the first time since I had come to Cougar Squadron I was close to losing my temper.

"Major Macgregor's point is valid." Lieutenant Colonel Larson paused before continuing to clear his throat. "But I think that wraps up the maneuver. I have a list of deficiencies that I noted. Some of your load plans are not uniform, and your rear bumpers are not properly marked at night. I will cover those and other matters at the next staff meeting."

I stood back. I was exhausted. I had not slept in three days. Lieutenant Colonel Larson came over and said in his high-pitched voice, "Doug. You were right, but you were too hard on the Hawk Company commander."

Though I did not completely agree with him, I was tired, too tired to argue and too tired to debate. There would be more training, time to fix things, I thought.

"Sir, I'm sure you're correct. I need to think about this stuff for a while and put together some proposals for your consideration on what we may want to do differently next time."

"Yes. We must change some things," answered Larson. "We need to do that before the next command and staff meeting."

Lieutenant Colonel Larson walked away. I slowly walked over to "Cougar Forward," an M577, crawled inside, and sat down. Soon, Ierardi and Hillen showed up. We held our own internal after-action review.

We decided that when my Abrams tank arrived, Hillen and Specialist Wightman would turn my regulation mount, a Bradley fighting vehicle, into Cougar Forward, a mobile command post that would move whenever and wherever I went in my tank and become John Hillen's mobile home for the duration of the operation.

T. K. Wightman would turn out to be the real genius behind this transformation. T.K. eventually also ensured that no matter how many miles away from the regiment we might move, Cougar Forward, mounted in an armored fighting vehicle with a stabilized turreted weapon, could also fight. Whereas a large and ponderous M577 command-and-control vehicle without stabilized armament was easy for an enemy to pick out and target, Cougar Forward in a fast-moving armored battle would appear pretty much like any other Bradley fighting vehicle and could add its own machine guns and 25-mm automatic cannon to the fight.

Our first big maneuver was over. Though our first major undertaking had ended with less fanfare and success than I would have liked and had been hard on the soldiers and their machines, we recognized that the training was paying off. For me, the most important lesson was still to make contact with the smallest possible element long before I arrived with the main body of the Cougar battle group. However, making contact with the smallest element meant making contact with something smaller than a 135-man cavalry troop. The diamond would work, but it was evident that if I was going to issue "orders from the saddle" and direct Cougar battle group effectively, I would need earlier warning of the enemy's presence and posture. I needed a platoon-sized forward-reconnaissance element at least twenty to forty kilometers out in front.

General Heinz Guderian had reached this same conclusion fifty years earlier: "The purpose of reconnaissance is to provide the commander with an accurate assessment of what the enemy is doing; in effect information of this kind furnishes the basis for command decisions."[9]

There was something else. Men in leadership positions from the squad to the squadron level who could not lead could no longer hide. Incompetent or ineffective leaders were exposed. The weak could either step aside or be pushed aside by soldiers who *could* lead. My shark was beginning to swim in deep water.

THREE

This Is Going to Be Bad

Fear unhinges the will, and by unhinging the will it paralyzes reason;
thoughts are dispersed in all directions in place of being
concentrated on one definite aim.

MAJ. GEN. J. F. C. FULLER, *THE FOUNDATIONS OF THE ART OF WAR,* 1926

After General Schwarzkopf's message on 17 January 1991 that Desert Shield
was over and that Desert Storm had begun, there followed more than a month
of effectively uncontested, round-the-clock bombing aimed at destroying the
Iraqi air-defense system, key elements of the Iraqi command-and-control
network, and Iraqi ground forces.

As we prepared to move into our attack positions just short of Saudi
Arabia's border with Iraq, Ierardi and Hillen burned all of the "eye wash" gear
used for briefings, as it is called. Anything without immediate value to the
fight went into the fire, along with papers, cardboard, and canvas.

When Tony and John told me about it, I was delighted. "Wish I had
thought of that," I responded. "I hate all of that crap. Thank God. Good job."

The burnt offering symbolized that we had turned a major corner in the
development of "the Shark." Officers with an exaggerated respect for the
chain of command who were competent but uninspired were now relegated to
positions of secondary responsibility. The key players, the troop commanders
and the staff officers who would develop and supervise the execution of
orders, were men unafraid to act on their own if the situation required it. The
changeover from the garrison lineup to the wartime roster had taken effect.

Figure 4. VII Corps War Plan in January 1991

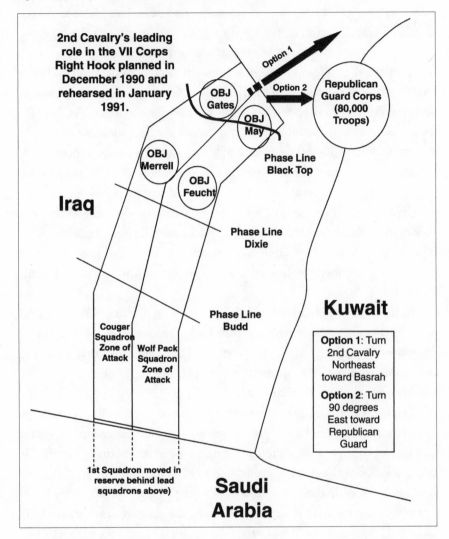

2nd Cavalry's leading role in the VII Corps Right Hook planned in December 1990 and rehearsed in January 1991.

Option 1

Option 2

OBJ Gates

OBJ May

Republican Guard Corps (80,000 Troops)

Phase Line Black Top

OBJ Merrell

OBJ Feucht

Iraq

Phase Line Dixie

Phase Line Budd

Kuwait

Cougar Squadron Zone of Attack

Wolf Pack Squadron Zone of Attack

Option 1: Turn 2nd Cavalry Northeast toward Basrah

Option 2: Turn 90 degrees East toward Republican Guard

1st Squadron moved in reserve behind lead squadrons above)

Saudi Arabia

The Shark was not yet fully assembled, it was not perfect, but it was 80 percent there.

Before moving up to the border with Iraq, however, the 2nd Cavalry conducted one more tactical exercise without troops (TOCEX) designed as a command-and-control rehearsal for the 2nd Cavalry's planned advance across Southern Iraq. Of the command-and-control exercises we conducted, this one was by far the most helpful, if only because we were able to thoroughly test communications along with our ability to coordinate artillery and air strikes.

Acting as General Franks' spearhead force, the 2nd Cavalry began the exercise, moving in front of the divisions toward objectives Gates and May. General Franks determined that depending on the situation at the time, the 2nd Cavalry would either continue the attack northeast to Basra, cutting off the retreat of the Republican Guard, or turn ninety degrees to the right, colliding directly with the main body of the Republican Guard. In this exercise, and in every exercise that I can remember, we always turned right, moving straight for the concentration of Republican Guard divisions. The notion of positioning the 2nd Cavalry behind the Republican Guard was never taken seriously.

Consistent with normal routine, the after-action review for the exercise began with the usual recapitulation of the broad, general mission and commander's intent. Then the two lead squadron commanders, the Wolf Pack Squadron commander (3rd Squadron) and Larson, Cougar Squadron (2nd Squadron) were asked to brief their movements to Phase Line Blacktop, an asphalt road ninety miles inside Iraq running northeast out of Kuwait into Iraq.

Reading from his notes, the 3rd Squadron commander, "Wolf Pack 6," repeated the mission statement for Wolf Pack Squadron and began detailing the movement through the zone of attack. He pointed out that given the ambiguous nature of the situation in the open desert, he planned to refuel roughly every thirty to fifty kilometers.

I thought this was crazy. If we moved at no more than fifteen miles per hour, which seemed to be the preference of the senior leadership, we would take forever to cover a large stretch of flat, open desert containing very few, if any, enemies. But this was mild compared to what happened next.

"Sir," said Wolf Pack 6 to Holder, "I expect," he paused to reshuffle his three-by-five cards, "five percent casualties by the time we reach Phase Line Dixie and 10 percent casualties by the time we reach Phase Line Miller. [These were intermediate phase lines between Saudi Arabia's border with Iraq and Phase Line Blacktop.] These figures are the result of force ratio calculations based on the Iraqi enemy templated by our intelligence officers."

Where in the hell did this come from, I wondered? Force ratios? There was no firm evidence that any serious enemy was actually located in the vast, open desert of southern Iraq. One day, intelligence sources reported nine thousand moving-target indicators on surveillance radar. The next day, only a handful were reported. Anyway, why would you anticipate casualties on the scale suggested on the way up to objectives Gates and May? Ten percent casualties meant the loss of 110 soldiers, killed or wounded.

Larson was surprised too, but for a very different reason. He feared that I had let him down by not providing equally erroneous information and analysis to him.

"Doug, you didn't put together anything about casualties for me," he whispered to me.

"Sir, that's right."

The very idea of predicting American casualties and briefing the predictions in a prewar exercise offended me.

In hushed tones I continued, "Sir, don't worry about it. We aren't going to have any casualties, at least none until we attack the Republican Guard. This is preposterous."

Larson seemed a little distracted by my statement, but when it was his turn he stuck to the script and ignored the casualty issue entirely.

Holder made no comment.

As the discussion about the command-post exercise continued, the operation looked more and more like a World War I offensive, linear and slow behind a storm of moving artillery and air strikes. There was no discussion of striking deep toward Basra or of any real maneuver against the Republican Guard, just crashing head on into it at a painfully slow speed. The idea of *pulling* the corps into battle by striking boldly into Iraq was absent.

When the meeting ended, I was relieved to walk out. The mood, however, did not improve. The consensus among the 2nd Cavalry majors and lieutenant colonels that hung around after the meeting was that a force as huge as the Iraqi army could not be defeated without significant casualties.

According to some of the majors with whom I spoke, Gen. Barry McCaffrey, the 24th Infantry Division (Mechanized) commander, estimated that as many as two thousand soldiers would be killed or wounded. General Luck, the XVIII Airborne Corps commander, had reached a similar conclusion, saying the Marines would suffer 10–20 percent losses.[1] Rumors were also afoot that as many as 16,000 body bags were being shipped into Saudi Arabia in anticipation of heavy casualties.

The most frequently heard comment in the discussions with the lieutenant colonels and majors who gathered to talk after the meeting was: "This is going to be bad. We're going to have lots of casualties."

It was obvious that the tendency among the colonels and generals to see a more powerful and dangerous enemy than actually existed would be very hard to defeat. The burden of proof always fell on the advocate for action. It was far easier for officers to inflate the enemy and argue for inaction than to argue the opposite case.

Clearly, the grossly inflated reports of Iraqi military potential in the media did not help matters.[2]

When I left the TOCEX after-action review I was not quite inconsolable, but close to it. The emphasis on top-down control, on scheduled halts, the very opposite of what Holder had preached in Germany, meant that we would sacrifice momentum as soon as we crossed into Iraq and stopped. We were deliberately robbing ourselves of initiative before the battle was joined. I began to worry that the slow, ponderous advance might make it possible for even the Iraqi Republican Guard to hastily establish more formidable defenses, using chemical weapons and mines.

Hillen did not hesitate to remind me that the men in command above us were extremely uncomfortable with uncertainty and thought it safer to move slowly and deliberately, regardless of the circumstances or potential opportunities.

"Come on, what did you expect? Battlefield opportunism is too dangerous," said Hillen sarcastically.

"Well, John," I said, "We will have to work our way through it. Just work through it."

Of course, I had no idea how I was going to work through it. Despite these frustrating exchanges, the offensive was still a few weeks away, and I was not yet ready to abandon hope that we would come to our senses and exploit the opportunities before us. I would try again before we entered Iraq.

Hillen did note that Larson had stuck with the original script and had not succumbed to the temptation to talk about casualties as the Wolf Pack commander had. Hillen observed, "Larson's has gone through one hell of a transformation, hasn't he?"

I didn't answer. What Hillen did not know was the transformation had begun much earlier, back in Bamberg, when we had been preparing to rotate to the Army's Combat Maneuver Training Center (CMTC) in Hohenfels, Germany.

At Bamberg, predeployment seminars on operations and tactics were held in the squadron conference room, a large elaborate room with paneled walls, a long oak table, upholstered chairs, and red wall-to-wall carpeting. Most of the time, the troop commanders gathered behind Larson in front of the map overlay while I briefed the various missions and potential schemes of maneuver for the squadron. The missions were straightforward, but the first session got off to a difficult start.

The first mission we discussed was a "movement to contact," which was inevitably the first task assigned to armored and mechanized units headed to CMTC.

As I explained the disposition of Cougar Squadron during the movement-to-contact mission, Lieutenant Colonel Larson interrupted to ask me about my plan for "actions on the objective."

This question took me by surprise. In maneuver operations focused on the seizure of a known particular terrain feature, crossroads, or town, a great deal of attention is devoted to the detailed occupation of the objective. For instance, attacks to secure airfields involve lengthy descriptions of where and when elements of the attacking force should be before, during, and after the attack, because these are known quantities. Movement-to-contact operations, however, are conducted when the enemy's exact location and disposition in the zone of attack are unknown. In other words, finding and ultimately destroying the enemy are the true purposes of the maneuver. An objective in the form of a large circle is usually placed on the map for such operations, to generally orient the movement of the attacking force only.

At first, I hesitated to answer Lieutenant Colonel Larson's question, because I was a little embarrassed by it. I had no desire to make the squadron commander feel foolish in front of the troop commanders. He persisted, however, in criticizing me for not planning the seizure and occupation of the nonexistent objective in great detail. Lieutenant Colonel Larson's oft-stated desire to have everything distilled into a checklist ran counter to the uncertainties inherent in a fluid, movement-to-contact operation.

Under the circumstances, I felt compelled to explain that the objective was just a map control point meant to orient our movement through the zone of attack. Because we did not know precisely where the enemy was or what he would defend, I could not provide a detailed plan of attack and occupation of the objective.

Lieutenant Colonel Larson blew up. He told me I was completely wrong and insisted that my response to him bordered on disrespect. Furious, he announced a break in the discussion until after lunch and stormed out of the room.

I was dumbfounded. The troop commanders were just as confused as I was, and I had seen them wince when the squadron commander raised his voice. When the squadron commander left, the troop commanders asked me what I was going to do.

"Well," I said, "I guess I will start planning to seize the objective." In any case, I told them not to worry about it and urged them to go to lunch. Eventually, I was left alone with Rhett Scott to ponder the map.

Not long after the troop commanders departed, Larson returned to the conference room, where I was sitting alone, working on a plan to secure the objective and making it show on the map overlay. I stood up, not knowing what would happen next. The only thing I could think was to wonder what "sin" I had committed had produced this bizarre situation.

To my amazement, Larson stood in the door of the conference room and said meekly, "Doug, you were right. I looked it up in the manual. I fucked up."

Without another word, he turned and walked out. As he turned toward the door, I caught a glimpse of the field manual *Cavalry Operations*, FM 17-95, in his hand. Apparently, he had consulted the book and discovered that I was right after all—I can only guess what would have happened if there had been no "book answer" to turn to, as is so often the case in the real world of combat.

To his credit, however, Lieutenant Colonel Larson had the humility to admit he was wrong. I respected him for it then and I still do. This broke the ice, and from then on, while our relationship was never warm, it was based on Larson's complete trust and confidence in my judgment regarding all things operational.

WE'RE FACING GRAZIANI'S ARMY

News of the destruction of Iraq's 5th Mechanized Division in the battle of Khafji broke soon after our arrival in Tactical Assembly Area Richardson, some three hundred miles inland from the Persian Gulf.

Khafji is a small town in Saudi Arabia close to Kuwait, with port facilities on the Persian Gulf coast. However, Khafji's importance to us stemmed from the fact that on 29 January 1991 it was the scene of a strong but poorly executed attack by Iraqi ground forces.

Naturally, we wanted to know as much as we could about the battle. Unfortunately, our only information about the action came from newspaper reports. Rhett Scott pursued the matter with customary zeal, studied the intelligence reports carefully, and a few days later we had important information on what had actually happened at Khafji.

Scott presented me with a quick "down and dirty" analysis that ultimately confirmed the validity of the conclusions that he, Hillen, and I had reached in early January. According to Scott, we now had irrefutable evidence that without the air-defense technology to neutralize or defeat American and allied air strikes, an Iraqi ground offensive in the open terrain of southern Iraq had no chance of succeeding. But Scott was quick to point out that this expected revelation was by no means the whole story.

Smiling broadly from ear to ear, Scott delivered the message I was anxious to hear: "Iraqi ground forces cannot effectively coordinate fire and maneuver. They also can't shoot straight. Frankly, the most the Iraqi army seems able to do is attack in waves after lining up their tanks and BMPs [Soviet-built tracked infantry-carrying vehicles] in column ahead of time. Bottom line: These guys can't fight worth a shit."

We were ecstatic. This news confirmed what we thought was true all along: the Iraqi enemy was far weaker than the generals said they were. Hillen was inside one of the '577s, heard the ruckus outside, and thought the war was over.

Scott interrupted the jubilation and said, "Wait, there's more. When hit hard, the attacking Iraqi troops seemed to lack the stomach for a real fight. Close with them and they fold."

I could hardly contain myself.

"No shit, Rhett. That's exactly what we thought a month ago. We are up against the Italian army of the '90s. What we have now is the greatest opportunity an armored force has had since the Germans seized Tobruk in '42. Good God, I've got to make these points to Holder right away."

"How are you going to do that? Nobody at Regiment is going to listen," asked Hillen.

"You know, hope springs eternal," I told Hillen. "I once worked for a very smart army general from Boston named O'Connor who taught me an enduring lesson about life in the Army. I had screwed up something because I had not documented a conversation in which I confidentially passed instructions to a colonel on behalf of the general."

"What happened?"

"The colonel blew me off, and I had no record of ever telling him what the general wanted done. Fortunately for me, when the general found out, he did not fire me. He was not a jerk. He just shook his head and said, 'Douglas, never forget something. If it's not on paper, it doesn't exist.' O'Connor was right."

Hillen still did not seem to get it and said, "So, what's the point?"

"John, the point is I must write a memorandum and forward through Holder to Franks. Perhaps if I put it on paper, maybe Holder will listen and talk to Franks about a more decisive and rapid advance."

My comment seemed to sink in with Hillen. Rhett Scott seemed a little puzzled, but Scott suspended judgment, I guess, while I sat down and started to type into a laptop computer that John Hillen had brought along for use by the S-3 and S-2 (operations and intelligence, respectively) sections. (Readers may think of an army in a war zone as being like an old French Foreign Legion movie, soldiers without the means to consider complicated tactical problems as they swat flies and perspire under the searing sun. Not so the American army, which in 1991 had computers in its tactical headquarters.)

In composing the memorandum, I knew that I would have to attack several key concerns as I had heard them expressed by General Franks and Colonel Holder in a variety of settings during the last ninety days. This would be tough for me, personally, because I was disinclined to think in the terms of detailed synchronization used in plodding, methodical battle. But if I failed to answer General Franks' apprehensions about the security of his open flanks, the ever-present fear of potentially heavy casualties, and fuel consumption in the tracked tank force, the memo would fail. All of these "take counsel of your fears" matters had figured in every operational discussion and inevitably reconfirmed thinking in the regiment and the corps that supported slow movement, punctuated by repeated halts.

Knowing this to be the case, I tried to fill the memorandum with references to people and events with which Holder, the military historian, was very familiar. All of the events mentioned had a direct application to modern mechanized warfare. It was my way of trying to both reassure Holder and give him "ammunition" for his private talks with Lieutenant General Franks, the corps commander. Somehow, I had to frame the argument in a way that would be persuasive without being abrasive. Eventually, the following words poured on to paper:

In operation Desert Storm, the Corps has the object of its offensive the destruction of that section of the enemy's army whose defeat will result in a decisive victory for U.S. forces. This suggests that unless some important advantage is to be gained from hesitation or by taking each step forward with extreme caution, it is vital that the Regiment reach PL Blacktop no later than 1200 hours on G day. Rapidly gaining Blacktop will compensate for disadvantages incurred in other areas.

Iraqi direct fire weapons will make a slow ponderous advance under fire hazardous and difficult. Yet accurate, direct fire at ranges beyond 1,000 meters is equally difficult, if not impossible, against moving armored forces. During 1942, 30,000 German soldiers led by Rommel advanced 50 miles after crossing the line of departure (LOD) in only 4 hours. . . . [T]his short analysis urges that the Regiment establish the goal of reaching PL Blacktop [PL Blacktop was a line running along an asphalt road, marking a final coordination line for the 2nd Cavalry before turning into the Republican Guard] no later than 1200 hours on G-day. Depending on where the Regiment begins its attack, the distance to be covered in 7 hours will not exceed seventy miles. In the current environment of overwhelming U.S. air superiority, deliberate speed will negate a hundred enemy measures to stop the Regiment and greatly reduce the Regiment's casualties. . . .

In a nutshell I urged that we dramatically increase our speed of advance from the Saudi Arabian border to Phase Line Smash, about 130 miles inside Iraq. PL Smash was the line along which VII Corps would mass before launching its final assault on the Republican Guard.

When I showed the memo to Larson, to my surprise he simply said, "OK, Doug, go ahead, send it." I dated the final memorandum 4 February 1991 and sent it, to start a "paper trail—in writing," as we say, to the 2nd Cavalry's regimental headquarters.

DESTROY THE REPUBLICAN GUARD!

While Cougar Squadron struggled with mundane tactical tasks, the CENT-COM commander in chief (CINC) had his hands full. Secretary of Defense Cheney and General Powell, chairman of the Joint Chiefs of Staff, were scheduled to arrive in Saudi Arabia on 8 February for meetings, and General

Schwarzkopf had to review eight hours of briefings on offensive operations that would be presented to the VIPs. For the most part, the briefings pleased the CINC—all, that is, except the one on VII Corps operation, provided in General Franks' absence by General Yeosock, Third Army commander. General Franks was reportedly busy conferring with his division commanders.

General Yeosock commanded both the XVIII and VII corps, which constituted the Third U.S. Army. As he was the intermediate commander between Schwarzkopf and Franks, the responsibility of briefing Franks' plan for the 110,000-man VII Corps fell to him.

But the more Schwarzkopf heard from General Yeosock about Franks' concept of the operation, the more concerned he became with Franks' excessive caution.

The plan was to advance, stop, regroup, advance again, and so on. Worse, according to Yeosock, General Franks insisted that he needed still another division, preferably the 1st Cavalry Division, the designated theater reserve (emergency backup force), to execute the mission.

Schwarzkopf could hardly believe it. Franks already had three armored divisions, the 2nd Cavalry, and additional artillery and aviation assets, a total of nearly 110,000 men. As far as Schwarzkopf was concerned, the force was more than enough to do the job. Enough was enough, thought Schwarzkopf. It was time for tough talk.

General Schwarzkopf reiterated his view that the enemy was weak and that this offensive should not be a "stop, refuel, rearm, go, and stop again" operation. Schwarzkopf delivered the message to General Yeosock in terms that could not have been clearer: "I do not want a slow ponderous pachyderm mentality. This is not a deliberate attack. I want VII Corps to slam into the Republican Guard. The enemy is not worth a shit. Go after them with audacity, shock action and surprise. . . . Let me make it clear, John. You cannot have VII Corps stopping for anything."[3]

General Schwarzkopf's guidance to VII Corps was unknown to me when I met Colonel Holder during one of his brief visits with Cougar Squadron. Once he was sure we were out of earshot, Holder told me of recent developments at Corps and General Franks' plans for the use of the divisions once we reached the midway point on the march north toward Basra. It seemed this was the ideal time to pop the question. "Sir, did you get the memorandum on rates of advance on G-day?"

Colonel Holder nodded "yes" and said he had received it. I asked him what he thought. He responded it was a good memo but that he would not forward it to Corps. He kept insisting that the intelligence picture was just "too vague," that we would have to move cautiously.

Frankly, I was stunned, and I probably talked too fast in response, but I felt compelled to make the case for the memo. The whole point of having an armored cavalry regiment in tracked armored fighting vehicles was to advance boldly against the enemy, developing the situation and moving as fast and as far as possible, not cautiously inching up to the enemy.

"Sir, one day JSTARS tells us there are thousands of troops in the open desert. The next day, we receive reports that nothing is there. Frankly, I do not think anything is there, and if there is, I doubt seriously that the Iraqi troops who are stuck out there in the middle of nowhere are in a position to present much resistance. Why not just leave everything behind that won't do thirty-five miles per hour and go like hell to Basra? Once we are there it is 'game over' for the Iraqis in Kuwait. Just like Ulm in 1805."

Holder was unconvinced. But when I reminded him of the 1940 British campaign, Operation Compass, during which 35,000 British troops defeated a 279,000-man Italian army in North Africa, Holder seemed a little more amenable.[4] Holder knew the campaign well. I reminded him that Khafji proved we, like the British in 1940, were facing, in Arab form, Rodolfo Graziani's Italian Tenth Army, a force that was smashed in a few weeks. But Holder would still not embrace the notion that the 2nd Cavalry could strike deep into a battlefield environment where our fighter pilots completely dominated the airspace and achieve a strategic fait accompli on the scale of the German advance to the English Channel in 1940.[5]

Holder rebutted me, saying, "What if we are out there without all of our artillery and the Air Force cannot fly? What if we end up with Iraqi forces attacking us from behind, as well as from the front? What if we run out of fuel or ammunition? No. It is just too risky. We do not really know what is out there. We have to stay close to the divisions."

"But sir," I said, "We have more than 1,100 tank-killing rounds in the squadron's first basic load alone. We will never see 1,100 Iraqi tanks in our twenty-kilometer zone. We have the capacity to destroy anything we encounter with direct fire. Anyway, we are a cavalry regiment. It's our job to find out what the hell is out there."

"No. I just cannot do that."

Holder's words were final. I backed off wondering what the hell was happening inside VII Corps headquarters.

WHAT ABOUT THE FLANKS?

Toward mid-February, the 2nd Cavalry's operations officers assembled one more time to discuss the forthcoming offensive. Roughly thirty minutes into the coordination meeting, however, the door of the planning van—a large, wheeled trailer that was part of the 2nd Cavalry's main tactical operations center, where we were meeting—swung open, and in walked the corps commander, General Franks (or "Jayhawk 6," as he was known on the radio).

Right behind him were Holder and Maj. Toby Martinez, General Franks' aide de camp and my predecessor in Cougar Squadron. Toby and I had gone through the armor-advanced course at Fort Knox together during 1980, and we always got along well. I genuinely liked Toby and was glad to see that he was smiling from ear to ear, as always.

General Franks, with his snow-white hair and care-worn face, moved slowly into his place. Toby hastened to make him as comfortable as possible. Then, after Holder made a few introductory remarks to us, we stood quietly and listened to General Franks talk about the situation as he then saw it.

With his gentle and affable nature General Franks seemed to most of us like a man who could get along with anyone. Yet his reputation for caution and slow deliberation had been well established during command-post and field exercises in Germany, long before the 2nd Cavalry deployed to Saudi Arabia.

Pointing to the map, Franks said the Air Force was continuing to bomb the defensive positions along the Saudi–Kuwaiti border and that he was much more concerned about the Republican Guard. As Franks saw it, the operation would be a slow, deliberate attack.

He then talked about the 2nd Cavalry's impending advance around the flank of the Iraqi defensive line and its movement in front of the corps toward Objective Merrell and Phase Line Blacktop. His remarks, however, were hard to follow. General Franks was a very nice person but not very articulate in his speaking style. He had also looked extremely tired as he graciously shook our hands. As I strained to listen, I found his comments revealing.

When asked about the potential use of one of the VII Corps' Apache attack helicopter battalions by the 2nd Cavalry (no Apache helicopters were assigned to the 2nd Cavalry itself) to reconnoiter fifty to a hundred kilometers ahead of advancing troops, Franks talked about the danger to his open flank of Iraqi counterattack out of Kuwait.

The notion that we had hundreds of aircraft, including several battalions of Apache tank-killing attack helicopters, available to pounce on an Iraqi counterattack into our flanks did not seem to register with him. The invaluable intelligence about Iraqi capabilities that we had recently obtained in the defeat of the Iraqi thrust toward Khafji had no influence whatsoever on his plan for a set-piece battle that had been devised weeks earlier.

The possibilities that the Republican Guard Corps might not be the force he imagined or that our undisputed control of the air by a truly massive force of lethal attack aircraft actually paralyzed the movement of significant enemy armored forces did not seem to figure at all in his thinking. The corps commander's obsession with his exposed flank along the northwestern border of Kuwait still dominated the discussion. The formula for success in offensive warfare taught to the world by the master, Napoleon Bonaparte, and repeated often enough by the Prussians, Russians, and Israelis—to ignore threats to the flanks or the rear, to march fast and deep, to throw the enemy off balance—was entirely missing.

When Franks expressed the view that we might still need more than the 110,000 men and 1,100 tanks he already had, it was obvious why any proposal for a rapid advance around the Republican Guard's flank toward Basra was out of the question. At this point, Franks' behavior worried the hell out of me. Worst of all, everyone at the meeting seemed only too willing to adopt his views. It was a confused presentation.

For the first time in fifteen years of service, I began to comprehend the U.S. Army's senior leadership culture. Apart from technical issues, the generals' mentality added up to an unhealthy pattern of caution, indecision, and inaction, primarily for careerist reasons, all of which flies in the face of what history demonstrates is required in warfare. Our electronic intelligence was decidedly imperfect; camel trains became enemy tank columns, electronic anomalies became enemy missiles, and so on. But the senior officers' pronounced aversion to casualties suggested to me that they might not fly forward and see the battlefield for themselves—as generals like Clark, Patton, Gavin, and Wood routinely did in World War II.

Years of sterile, simulated exercises in the Cold War, focused on battles of attrition against Soviet equipment and soldiers, had produced a mentality unsuited to the fluidity and chaos of real war waged by real, thinking humans. This mind-set reinforced the generals' and colonels' tendency to rely on their experiences as lieutenants and captains in Vietnam, where all they had seen was deliberate planning buttressed by top-down control over slow, ponderous masses of infantry advancing behind artillery and air strikes.

It was obvious that Franks had no appreciation for the armored force at his disposal or for the purpose for which it had been designed—to confuse, overwhelm, and, if necessary, destroy the enemy, with its speed, shock, and massive, survivable, and unprecedentedly accurate firepower. Instead, Franks insisted on seeing what he was predisposed to see—a dangerous and capable enemy, one that bore no relation whatsoever to reality. The fact that no Arab army had beaten a European force since the Renaissance made no difference to his calculus.

When I found out after the war that as late as 21 February VII Corps had requested 35,000 TOW-2 missiles and half a million hand grenades, I was no longer surprised. The TOW missile is a highly accurate one-shot/one-kill weapon; asking for such a quantity made no sense.

Fortunately, Gen. Cal Waller had refused, saying, "The enemy only has seventeen hundred or so tanks left in the Kuwait Theater. Not all of them are in the sector where you'll be fighting. Why do you need 35,000 TOW rounds? And hand grenades? This is a mobile armored corps. Where are you going to close with the enemy so that every man in the corps needs five hand grenades? Who in the hell are you going to throw them at?"[6]

General Waller was right, but his common sense and innate courage were not enough to change VII Corps' collective attitude at this late date, and Schwarzkopf did not intervene. In contrast to General Waller, in VII Corps not only was the glass half empty, but action of any kind was unthinkable that did not involve a large, cumbersome mass lumbering on line across the desert behind a continuous air and artillery bombardment.

Though I was disappointed with the tone and character of the meeting, I never doubted anyone's physical courage. A friend serving in the Tiger Brigade, a unit that would distinguish itself in action by rapidly advancing into Kuwait City under the bold and courageous leadership of its colonel, John Sylvester, told me, "Doug, at the staff college, everyone's balls are the size of grapefruits. But in the desert the balls shrink to the size of peanuts." But this extreme caution seemed to have more to do with an acute lack of self-confidence and a fear of failure, failure that would jeopardize otherwise stunning peacetime military careers. But I did leave the meeting fearing that instead of a lightning advance, the corps' methodical leaders, fearful of every potential Iraqi action, real or imagined, would reenact a slow, ponderous action reminiscent of trench warfare.

LET'S FIGHT AND GET IT OVER WITH!

Knowing that we had courageous and competent soldiers, I declined to think any more about what Franks, Holder, and the rest of the chain of command would do when the fighting started. I focused instead on systematically briefing all of the units inside Cougar Squadron on the operation, reassuring them again and again that they would win. These briefings were very important.

Good combat leaders must light a fire in the bellies of their troops and make their soldiers passionate about the fight to come. Passion is such a key part of leading combat troops that if you don't have it, you simply can't lead men under fire. I set out to make my passion for combat infectious, reinforcing confidence in our superior fighting power, lacing my statements with plenty of humor and profanity for effect. The chaplains winced, but the troops loved it. I also made it clear I would be in front of the advancing troops, not behind them. My tactical sign on the back of my tank turret—a square, bright blue field with a diagonal white cross—was easy to identify. It would always be in front, never behind them.

When I finished my briefing the last unit, I returned to the squadron TOC, where I found Tony Ierardi waiting for me inside. Ierardi was seated on a cushion with his legs crossed.

"Tony, thanks for heating the place up. By the way, you missed a truly inspiring meeting at Regiment." After checking the area for scorpions, spiders, and snakes, I decided to lie back on the edge of the ramp that led into the M577 while continuing the conversation. "Yep, we're calculating force ratios."

"They'll get over it, sir," said Ierardi. "Any interesting rumors?"

"Not really. But, come to think of it, the pilots at King Fahd Air Base are supposedly billeted directly across the street from a field hospital that is filled with nurses."

This definitely got Tony Ierardi's attention.

"You mean nurses?"

"What else?" I said.

Our conversation was interrupted by noise outside of the TOC. After nearly wrecking the door while he fumbled to find the entrance in the dark, Hillen entered. Once seated on one of the folding steel chairs, Hillen quickly posed a question.

"Sir, why is it that you always take Burns with you wherever you go? I mean, he is always there."

"John, that's easy," I said, pointing to Burns as he entered the tent. "Because I know Burns will pull the trigger if we get into a fight. And I don't like people around me who like to think about that shit before they shoot."

"You got that right," interjected Burns as he stuck his head out of the neighboring Bradley's rear door, smiling from ear to ear. Lowering his voice a little, Burns added, "My philosophy is shoot first and let God sort them out later."

"See, John, there you have it: The same wisdom I learned on the streets of North Philadelphia," I said, as everyone broke into laughter. "By the way," I turned toward Tony Ierardi and asked, "Speaking of Philadelphia, what sort of exotic snacks do we have from the Ierardi family?"

"Nothing, the mail has sucked lately," answered Ierardi. "Not a damn thing. I think those rear-echelon mothers back at the ports and airstrips are gorging themselves on our food packages."

John Hillen now extracted his *Sports Illustrated* swimsuit calendar from his duffle bag, telling us, "Without this stimulating literature, I would be on the verge of a nervous breakdown."

Ierardi quipped, "If you're not careful, pretty soon you'll wear out that damn thing and have nothing else to look at but sheep and camels."

Before anyone could respond, the TOC shook as several pairs of boots stepped on the gear next to the generator just outside of the TOC.

"Fellas, can I join this august body of men?" It was H. R. McMaster.

"Of course," I said. "What the f—k's happening? You bring us anything to eat?" I asked hopefully.

"Sorry, men," replied McMaster, "only my sparkling personality."

"Shit. In that case," Tony Ierardi groaned, "I'm going to get some sleep."

Burns was still full of energy and just getting started.

"Sir, you know Fox Troop killed another cobra last night."

"What the hell is going on in Fox Troop, Burns?" I was worried that someone would be dumb enough to try and capture the cobra, play with it, and end up severely bitten.

"What attracts the damn snakes to Fox Troop?"

"Trash," said McMaster.

"What?" Ierardi asked.

"Trash." McMaster repeated the word, this time a little louder.

"Yeah, 'Intense 6' [Burns's pet name for McMaster] is right," continued Burns. "You see, the trash builds up, attracting the kangaroo rats. The snakes come around looking for rats to eat, and, well, there you have it."

By now, we were all sitting up, casting our eyes downward toward the TOC's desert floor and looking for any scraps of food that might attract rats. As usual, Hillen couldn't resist pointing out that since I was the one eating all the time, I was the most likely target area for rats and snakes, thereby saving everyone else in the TOC from a terrible fate.

Hillen asked the assembled body if anyone had noticed that Eagle Troop had maneuvered throughout most of the afternoon when the rest of the squadron was in maintenance. None of us knew that, but McMaster began to fidget. I looked at McMaster, shrugged my shoulders as if to ask what the hell Hillen was talking about.

Burns started laughing, so I finally turned back to McMaster and asked, "What's going on, H.R.? I thought today was supposed to be a day of maintenance."

"'Eagle 6' won't tell you so I guess I will," said Hillen.

"No you won't!" yelled McMaster, moving as if to jump on Hillen that instant.

"Oh, yes I will. The major needs to know the true state of readiness to fight in Eagle Troop."

At this point, amidst growing laughter that only I did not seem to understand, McMaster held up his fist, playfully threatening Hillen, but sat back down.

"All right, that's enough." I said, "Damn it, tell me what the hell is going on."

Hillen drew himself up, dusted off his uniform, and related his story: "Jack Waldron [the Fox Troop executive officer] has been getting on the Eagle Troop net imitating Lieutenant Colonel Larson." Hillen looked toward me apologetically. "Anyway, Jack mastered the art of imitating our squadron commander's high-pitched, nasal voice down to perfection. He and Gifford have been pulling this shit on each other for the last week, but today Waldron's performance on the radio was so convincing that half of Eagle Troop scrambled, moved out, and practiced battle drills for thirty minutes before they figured out that it was Waldron on the radio and not the squadron commander."

Over the laughter, Hillen could not resist imitating the squadron commander in his nasal voice screeching, "Eagle 6, I am deeply disappointed, you know that's totally unacceptable."

Other than "Noted, but not with much interest," Lieutenant Colonel Larson loved saying to junior officers "That's totally unacceptable."

"All right," I said with a raised voice, "That's enough. Let's give it a rest. Enough jokes. I can only imagine what the hell you characters say about me when I'm not around."

Undeterred, Hillen immediately quipped, "Sir, you don't want to know."

Fortunately, the laughter died away as Ierardi, Hillen, and I simply faded from sheer exhaustion. The movement to Saudi Arabia's border with Iraq had followed close behind maneuvers, with the result that none of us had really gotten any sleep. I announced to the group that I was sorry but that "I am going to dreamland to see who is there waiting for me."

"What do you mean? Who do you want to see when you get there?" asked Burns. "Not sure. Probably, Elke Sommer, Rachel Ward, or somebody like that."

I chuckled in response.

"You got to be kidding," said Burns "Those broads are over the hill. What about Madonna or Janet Jackson?"

Too tired to respond, I just said, "Not in my dreams, William. Elke never gets old and the two of them do some really miraculous things." With that I got up and started the walk back to my tank, but my departure did nothing to slow down Burns and McMaster, who loved to talk for hours about everything imaginable.

"So," asked Burns, "What's the real deal, sir? When we attack, do we stop on the other side or just drive like hell until we find the Republican Guard?"

"We shouldn't stop. We should just keep going," insisted McMaster. "Speed and position are everything in the desert."

"Well, if Sid Vicious has his way," Burns said (pointing in the direction of my tank), "We'll be in Baghdad by the middle of next week."

Outside of the TOC, the wind picked up just enough to sway the canvas extension in the desert moonlight. Were it not for the occasional camel or sheep, anyone passing by would have thought we were encamped in a field of snow.

A few hundred meters from the TOC a young sergeant in Ghost Troop sat inside his Bradley penning a letter to his father, in Rupert, Idaho. His name was Andrew Nels Moller. Sergeant Moller had a lot on his mind.

19 February 1991
Dear Dad,

I pray every night. I ask to be forgiven for all my sins of mind and act. I ask if killing another human, not out of spite is wrong. I question the right to kill. I hunt. I've slaughtered and killed to stop the existence (of animals), but never a human. I will aim to kill fast and clean. I will defend my crew, myself and my country. Mostly my crew's right to live. It is them or us. I still want a chance to be happy and productive. I see this war as the only obstacle between me and my wish. I have learned little by being told. My hard head prevents good sense and knowledge from entering on first try. So I end by paying the price. I just want God to understand.

Well, I'll write in a couple of days. I need to seal this one up. Don't worry and thank you all for your support.

Love,
Andrew

FOUR

But We've Already Seized the Objective!

One man with courage makes a majority.
ANDREW JACKSON

22 FEBRUARY 1991, ALONG SAUDI ARABIA'S BORDER WITH IRAQ
It was late on a bright, sunny afternoon as the Cougar battle group drove toward Saudi Arabia's border with Iraq.

Within minutes of our arrival near the border, hundreds of artillery shells and rockets were falling into the empty desert on the Iraqi side of the border.

If the Iraqi high command had realized what was happening, the dense concentration of American force in VII Corps moving in packed columns behind us would have offered plenty of targets to Iraqi rockets, missiles, aircraft, and unmanned combat aerial vehicles, if they had had any.

Unfortunately, we crept into Iraq at a snail's pace. For VII Corps, the move into Iraq was not really a combat operation at all but a simple "approach march," an arrangement where the units and vehicles move in columns behind the lead formation—in this case, the 2nd Cavalry.

In war, however, time is always critical. Anything can be regained but time, and this was no time to crawl into Iraq. But there was no chance to reflect. The three cavalry troops were already speeding across the open toward the border, in formation. So I scrambled up the front slope on the driver's side of the tank hull and got into the tank commander's position in the turret on top.

Sergeant Abercrombie watched the remaining fireworks with me. We both looked up into the endless blue sky and were delighted to see two B-52 heavy bombers with streaks of white smoke streaming behind them flying back into Saudi Arabia from a strike on the Iraqi enemy. The sight was breathtaking. I made a point of giving quiet thanks to the U.S. Air Force for America's unchallenged control of the air.

Knowing that our initial advance would be short, we took our time crossing into Iraq. Abercrombie and I rode in open hatches during the movement. Abercrombie had on his black, gold-lettered Georgia Tech sweatshirt, so I commented, "That sweatshirt is not exactly regulation."

Laughing, because he knew that under my uniform I was wearing a red sweatshirt I'd picked up on a trip to Scotland, with the Scottish flag on it, he shot back, "Yes, sir, I wonder where I got that idea?"

We then heard some strange sounds. It was the psychological operations (PSYOPS) team. It played a tape of bagpipe music by the Scots Guards for my entertainment before switching to some very, very hard rock. When the PSYOPS team had joined Cougar Squadron, the team leader immediately asked me for guidance. I thought a minute, then said, "Play whatever you want, but don't play any of that '60s music, you know, the kind of music in which the women sound like they're on drugs and the men have no genitalia."

Though a little surprised by the guidance, the team generally complied. I've never liked that whiny, peacenik crap from the 1960s.

Moving over to Ghost Troop, the PSYOPS team rode with the mortar section, playing Richard Wagner's "Ride of the Valkyries," Tin Lizzy's "The Boys Are Back in Town," and "Hells Bells," by AC-DC. The PSYOPS team was playing requests, and the soldiers in Ghost Troop really wanted to hear AC-DC. Since the eclectic mix would probably have scared the hell out of the Iraqis, I thought it was too bad that there was no enemy to appreciate the concert.

As soon as the artillery preparation ended, Cougar Squadron's three troop commanders went straight for their respective crossing sites like racecar drivers in the Indianapolis 500.

Nobody wanted to be last over the border.

As our tank rolled forward toward unmanned infantry trenches on the other side of the border, Abercrombie kept his machine gun trained on them, just in case. This also gave me an opportunity to watch the troops in action. Subtle differences, already detectable in training, manifested themselves immediately during the border crossing.

Fox Troop's operation was, as I had anticipated, a very deliberate and professional one. Assembling and marching through the existing opening in the sand berm made the crossing fairly easy. T. J. Linzy, a soft-spoken, chain-smoking Kentuckian, had no trouble shooting through an opening in the berm where the Saudi police station stood. He and his platoon burst forward at high speed to their positions out in front of the squadron. Linzy was ideally suited to the task of independent reconnaissance. He had spent years reading about cavalry operations from the Civil War to World War II. When I selected him to lead us across Iraq, he could finally convert his dreams into reality.

For Eagle and Ghost troops, though, the situation was quite different.

For the duration of the breaching operation, our engineer platoons went forward with the cavalry troops. In Eagle Troop, Petschek's scouts covered the engineers by having the armored vehicles fan out, ready to fire on any Iraqis who might try to interfere while they reduced the berm with dozer blades. When the opening was complete, McMaster took his tank, *Mad Max*, through first; once through the gap, Eagle's tank platoons fell into a wedge formation behind him. In Ghost, the engineer vehicles, burdened with earth-scraping and mine-detonation gear dangling from their fronts, found the going a bit rougher. Eventually, Sartiano intervened, telling Garwick's scouts to just push down the damn berm.

After a couple of shoves, the sand barrier fell apart and the *Godfather*, as Sartiano's tank was called led the rest of Ghost Troop into Iraq to the sounds of "Ride of the Valkyries," courtesy, once again, of the PSYOPS team.

Within minutes of crossing into Iraq, the cavalry troops erupted with gun-fire as our soldiers test-fired their weapons, from 7.62-mm medium machine guns to 120-mm tank rounds, making certain that everything worked.

Overhead, OH-58Ds, reconnaissance helicopters capable of designating targets for the artillery. and AH-1S Cobra attack helicopters flew forward in the zone of attack.

We then advanced ten kilometers inside Iraq and halted along Phase Line Becks. After handing over the breach sites to the control of D Company, 82nd Engineers, our own engineers left the control of the cavalry troops and returned to that of Captain Clarke at the squadron headquarters' rearmost position, in the order of march.

Then, everything stopped. At 1630 hours, without our having made any contact with the enemy, Dragoon Base instructed us to advance no farther.

Incredible, I thought, but beyond my ability to influence. After reaching my position at the apex of the diamond vehicle formation, I turned the tank around and drove back to the TOC, where I held a short discussion with Hillen and Scott.

After a brief review of the maintenance posture of all our vehicles and combat equipment, I decided to go back to my tank and get some sleep, knowing that nothing of significance would happen until the coalition ground invasion officially started the next morning. I hoped that sleep would blot out my present frustrations and infuse me with strength for the morning. Reflection on events to this point added nothing except increased frustration with how incredibly timid we were being, and I expected little sleep once we resumed the attack.

By midnight the wind had picked up, and it started to rain though I remained comfortably unconscious throughout most of it. That is, until I began dreaming. Dreams are often triggered by physical stimuli of one kind or another, and the rain falling in my face took me back to the Winter Ranger Course in February 1977, when we had experienced a blizzard during the mountain phase, near Dalonega, Georgia. As I dreamed, I could actually sense the flesh crack on my knuckles and the feeling leave my fingertips. My whole body shivered. Eventually, I woke up in the night shaking with fear.

As I sat up in the rain and wind, looked around, and realized I was in the Iraqi desert, I instantly relaxed. "Thank God, I said quietly, "I am not in the Winter Ranger Course!" I pulled the tarp back over my head and slept for a couple more hours.

At dawn, I thought it rather odd that the rain had left a black, greasy residue all over my one-piece, fire-resistant, green NOMEX uniform. Anyway, I mounted up with my crew and drove forward from the TOC to our position at the apex of the diamond. It was exhilarating, to say the least, to drive forward at thirty miles per hour, passing the combat engineers, the tank company, and platoons from the artillery battery on our way up to the lead position. The word "exhilaration" does not do justice to seeing an armored battle group—forty-three Abrams tanks, forty-one Bradley fighting vehicles, thirty-two self-propelled guns, and three hundred wheeled vehicles—formed and ready to attack.

Half out of the turret hatches of their the tracked, armored vehicles, soldiers, sergeants, lieutenants, and captains waved and shouted as we drove forward through the formation. The scene reminded me of Napoleon's description of the French soldiers forming into their regiments on the morning before Austerlitz after a breakfast of hot coffee and hard bread. I think our food wasn't the only thing better materially today. The moral strength of our soldiers was at least three times better than Napoleon said it needed to be.

At 0700 hours Dragoon Base gave us permission to advance fifteen kilometers farther into Iraq to Phase Line Busch, where we were told we would probably establish a defensive line until the 25th.

Just as we had rehearsed, whenever the battle group halted its movement, Captain Scott drove up next to my tank in his Humvee, jumped out, and briefed me on the latest intelligence. By late morning, however, Scott had relayed the news over the squadron command net that the lead elements of two U.S. Marine divisions had entered the Iraqi defensive belt near the coastal highway and encountered little or no effective resistance. A battle the Marines had expected to last for thirty-six hours was over in less than three. We were elated.

This news meant the main attack on the far left, where we and XVIII Airborne Corps were waiting, would follow soon, with a massive single envelopment of the Iraqi forward defenses. If we attacked decisively and rapidly, I thought, the "left hook" of which Cougar Squadron was a lead element would quickly collapse the right wing of the Iraqi defensive belt and open a clear path across the Iraqi desert toward the Republican Guard, cutting it off in front of Basra.

I waited impatiently for Colonel Holder (known on the radio as "Dragoon 6") to tell us to move forward. Finally, after what seemed like an eternity, Dragoon Base issued orders to attack in zone at 1430 hours, orienting on Objective Merrell.

For the first time, we were attacking in the formation we had practiced in January. In minutes First Lieutenant Linzy was twenty to thirty kilometers out in front, with Fox Troop's mortars just behind him.

Behind Linzy came the rest of Fox Troop and me. Fox Troop led from the apex of the diamond, with Eagle Troop a little behind on the left, Ghost Troop a little behind on the right, and Hawk Company in the center as the squadron reserve. Sam White's howitzer battery moved in the center too, about two thousand meters forward and to the flanks of Hawk, to provide immediate suppressive "fires" (that is, fire missions) as far forward as possible.

Figure 5. Squadron Diamond

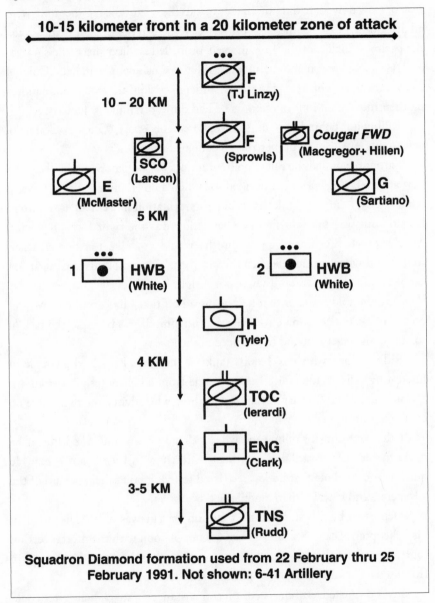

The supporting artillery battalion followed behind, but the three firing batteries fell rapidly behind.

The supporting artillery battalion commander, Colonel Adair, called me to tell me his batteries could not keep up and to press ahead. He said that he would bring the batteries up behind us as quickly as he could. I deeply appreciated Colonel Adair's telling me that. Adair could have pressured me to stop or slow down. He did not. In contrast to the rest of the regiment, we were all determined to make the tank, the fastest vehicle in the Cougar battle group, the pacing vehicle, not the 155-mm self-propelled artillery piece, the slowest.

As the squadron moved in the brilliant sunshine, Lieutenant Colonel Larson started to pop up on the radio in order to critique the troop commanders on their movement in formation, as he had during training in January.

Riding just behind Sartiano's tanks, Larson observed, "Ghost 6, Cougar 6, you are not executing a proper zone reconnaissance, over."

Sartiano handled the call as politely as possible, but knowing that Larson's next stop was Eagle Troop, I decided to launch a preemptive strike of sorts.

Frankly, I did not think that critiquing formation movement at the troop level on our way into our first combat action was the right focus. Knowing McMaster's temperament, I was sure he would not take Larson's criticism well, if and when it came. So I chimed in with, "Cougar 6, this is Cougar 3, I can vouch for Eagle Troop. They've got it right."

Sartiano told me later that he was pissed off that I had gotten McMaster off the hook, but Sartiano also knew that he himself was better at the task of squadron management and hadn't needed the assist.

Riding along with Fox Troop's tanks at the time, I received a couple of interesting calls on the radio. The first came from a helicopter pilot from 4th Squadron, the 2nd Cavalry's aviation squadron, who advised me there were no enemy to our immediate front.

I thanked him for telling me what I already knew and asked him if he could fly farther forward and coordinate directly with Lieutenant Linzy. He quickly informed me that he was restricted to flying no farther forward of the advancing 2nd Cavalry than ten kilometers.

Depressed by this statement, I told him that he was of little use to us in his helicopter, because we already had a scout platoon with the mortar section (our forward reconnaissance element) on the ground twenty kilometers in front of us. He said he could do nothing and flew away.

I was disgusted. At full speed, a reconnaissance or attack helicopter could fly thirty kilometers in a few minutes. A ten-kilometer "leash" on our scout helicopters meant that another cavalry advantage was being squandered, thanks to excessive fear and timidity.

After this disappointing exchange, a much more exciting call came in from our forward air controller, Maj. John Rogler, a very sharp A-10 pilot who always dismissed the generals' fears of the Iraqi military as nonsense. He rode in an M113 armored personnel carrier, packed with ground-to-air radios, that followed close behind Hillen in Cougar Forward. Rogler's call sign on the radio was "Bethel 1."

"Cougar 3, Bethel 1," I heard.

"Bethel 1, Cougar 3, send it," I answered, waiting anxiously for what Rogler might say next.

"The Nails are in the air, do you have any targets?"

The "Nails" were the A-10s flying overhead. What an interesting call, I thought. Now, we have fifteen or twenty A-10 Thunderbolts. Known informally as the "Warthog" because it's armored and agile enough to fly low to the ground and actually see targets, the A-10 is a marvelous ground-attack aircraft.

The problem for me was that we had driven nearly thirty-five kilometers and still hadn't seen any enemy! Our helicopter scouts were leashed and hadn't found any enemy either.

"Roger, Bethel 1. Can the Nails fly up to Objective Merrell and tell us what's there?" Why not, I thought? There was no point in having these pilots drill holes in the sky overhead. At three hundred–plus kilometers per hour the A-10s would be there in seconds. Rogler was quick to oblige.

"Sure, this is Bethel 1, out."

Perhaps sixty seconds later, Rogler called back. With characteristic Air Force precision, Rogler described the scene on Merrell.

"The Nails are over Merrell. They see ten or twelve tanks parked behind trenches and bunkers, with hundreds of little guys running around on the ground. There are fifteen or twenty artillery guns with little guys manning them, over."

Rogler's use of Air Force terminology like "little guys running around" to describe enemy infantry was very endearing.

"This is Cougar 3, do you think you can drop some bombs on them for me? Break, break, alert the pilots to our scout platoon. Make sure they have positive identification of the scouts."

Damn, I said to myself, with everyone listening, you could have been a little more sophisticated with that close-air-support request. Oh well, too late now, the damage is done. A second later, Rogler responded.

"Roggggerrrr. We can do that; Bethel 1, out."

Waiting for something to happen can be more frustrating in war than almost anything else. Probably no more than four or five minutes passed, if that, but they seemed like fifty. I was extremely impatient to know what the A-10 Thunderbolt pilots were doing to the enemy. Then, just as I was about to call him, Rogler was back on the radio, his voice resonant with excitement.

Exultantly he declared, "Cougar 3, Bethel 1, we have positive ID with the scouts. We struck the tanks and the artillery several times. We think that stuff is gone. But the little guys with rifles disappeared into their holes, over."

"Sounds great, Bethel 1. Can they keep it up until the scouts are within five kilometers of Merrell, then cease fire and fly up to Objective Gates, over?"

It seemed reasonable to assume that we would roll over the enemy at Merrell and press on rapidly to Gates. We could easily reach Gates in another hour or so, assuming we executed a squadron refuel-on-the-move in front of Merrell.

"Cougar 3, Bethel 1, Cannon 1 and Cannon 2 are almost bingo on fuel. Will continue for another five minutes, but then they must return to base, over."

I was a little disappointed, but Rogler's response was reasonable. The A-10s had been in the sky all morning waiting for the opportunity to attack, just as we had. Their fuel was low.

"Understand, Bethel 1, please thank them for their good work. Cougar 3, out."

Hearing my discussion with the Air Force on the squadron command net, Tom Sprowls, the Fox Troop commander, informed me that Lieutenant Linzy whose scout platoon together with Fox Troop's mortar section now far out in front of us, recommended a bypass around a field of volcanic rock that he had found. Linzy described the rocks as "boulders the size of bowling balls."

I approved Linzy's recommendation immediately and a few minutes later, the Cougar Battle group moved two kilometers north and then farther east to avoid the obstacle. I said quietly to myself, thank God, Linzy was fifteen kilometers ahead of us. Otherwise, we would have stumbled into the mess, and have had to turn the squadron around to get out. In war, you are fighting the earth itself for room to maneuver not just human enemies.

It was just the beginning of four days during which I would repeatedly give thanks for intelligent decisions made by competent and courageous sergeants and lieutenants.

Figure 6. Cougar Squadron Zone of Attack, 23–25 February

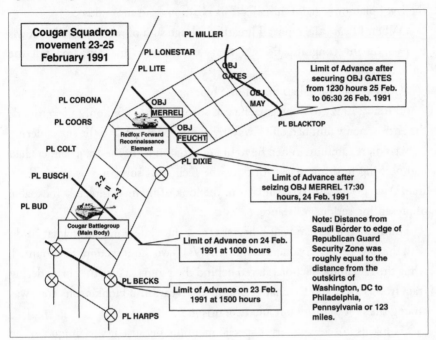

FIRST CONTACT

First contact with the enemy is terribly important to soldiers that have never seen combat. If the first combat action is short, sharp and successful, a soldier's confidence in his abilities, as well as in those of his unit goes through the roof. This was the sort of action we needed to validate soldier confidence and it is exactly what Linzy's scouts gave us.

At about 1530 hours, the Redfox element (First Lieutenant Linzy's forward reconnaissance element consisting of six Bradley fighting vehicles and the Fox Troop mortars) received automatic weapons fire from a small group of Iraqi soldiers. When Sprowls passed the report to me, I made a series of short statements on the squadron net encouraging Linzy's platoon to be confident, strike hard and report. The comments were sincere, but my target audience was the whole squadron battle group. Based on the maneuvers in January, I knew everyone who could do so would tune into the Squadron command frequency and listen to what was happening.

Soon after I made my comments extolling the virtues of our superior equipment and training on the radio, Sprowls passed the report that Linzy's scouts had killed two Iraqi soldiers, with the immediate result that the rest of the Iraqi platoon-sized unit had left its positions and surrendered.

When I heard the report, I breathed a huge sigh of relief. I asked Sprowls to pass on my congratulations. I think everyone in the squadron felt the same way.

Cougar Squadron had drawn first blood.

Initially, Linzy told me later, he was surprised that after only a few rounds the entire enemy unit had effectively given up. So he watched the surrendering Iraqi soldiers carefully. When he found out that most of the Iraqi soldiers had had nothing to drink or eat for days, the feeling of surprise was gone. These Iraqi Arabs were worn out and, from the look of them, completely incapable of presenting serious resistance.

Linzy's scouts were well rehearsed, and they knew instantly what to do with the new enemy prisoners of war (EPWs). Two scout sections dismounted, while the remaining sections stayed behind their guns in case the surrendering Iraqi troops had a sudden change of heart. Sergeant Bill Hopkinson's crew was among the first to dismount and take prisoners.

Hopkinson's crew deserves special mention, because it was unique in the Cougar Squadron. Although all five of the soldiers on Hopkinson's Bradley were American citizens, no two were remotely alike. By that I mean they represented every conceivable racial group on the planet. Staff Sergeant Hopkinson was Samoan; the Bradley gunner, Specialist Gunnet, was your average white guy; the Bradley driver, Smith, was an African-American; Fierro was Japanese-American (from LA); and Fernandez was Filipino by birth and heritage.

In view of this extreme diversity, everybody in Fox Troop referred to Hopkinson's Bradley as "the United Nations," or "UN track" (that is, tracked armored fighting vehicle). Nobody was more confused than the first Iraqi soldiers who surrendered to Hopkinson's scout section. Hopkinson's crew dismounted to secure the prisoners, while Staff Sergeant Hill and his crew stayed mounted, behind their guns, to provide cover. Hopkins motioned to the approaching Iraqi soldiers to drop their weapons, put their hands on their heads, and get down on their knees.

One of the first Iraqi soldiers to fall on his knees, waiting to be searched and disarmed, looked at the mix of soldiers holding him at gunpoint and decided that Hill and his men might not be Americans after all. So he spoke

French, asking, *"Vous êtes partie de la Légion Étrangere?"* (Are you French Foreign Legion?)

Receiving no answer, the Iraqi repeated his question in French until Hopkinson, busy disarming some of the Iraqi soldier's comrades just in front of him, snapped, "Shut up, motherf—ker!"

Smiling broadly from ear to ear, the Iraqi soldier now yelled in English, "Ah, motherf—ker, American, yes, American, American!" Then, in a blast of Arabic, he explained to his fellow countrymen, who were now prisoners of war, that they too were guests of the U.S. Army. Evidently delighted with this news, the Arabs talked cheerfully among themselves.

Frustrated with his inability to shut up the new EPWs, Staff Sergeant Hopkinson shook his head in disgust, repeatedly telling the Arab prisoners, "For Christ's sake, just shut up! Please, just shut up."

While Hopkinson's crew disarmed the Iraqi troops, as quickly as he could, other Bradleys in the scout platoon ran over and crushed the captured Iraqi weapons where the prisoners had piled them up. Whenever weapons were found, they were destroyed under the Bradley tracks. The prisoners were pointed in the direction of the oncoming Cougar battle group and told to walk west.

A few seconds later, Linzy reported to Lt. Jack Waldron, Fox Troop's executive officer, that he was tossing thirsty Iraqi prisoners water and pointing them in the direction of the squadron battle group, about fifteen kilometers behind him. Ever the romantic, Linzy likened the whole experience of collecting Iraqi EPWs to rounding up mustangs on the high plains.

Enormously pleased with Linzy's reports, I turned my attention to the regimental command radio net and so did not immediately notice how much the terrain was changing as we neared an area that Linzy was recommending we bypass.

Fortunately, Abercrombie was paying attention to Ward's driving, telling him not to pivot on top of the large rocks and get stuck or damage a track, to stay on the lower areas and not crest over some of these small hills.

Eventually Abercrombie told him, "The point is to act as if the tank is an infantry squad moving in a wedge." He finished his instructions with the remark, "Just because we are in a tank, we are not invulnerable."

Abercrombie also used the occasion to instruct Ward on other matters. "Ward," he said, "listen up. In a tank, wingman watches wingman. We watch

Cougar Forward and Cougar Forward watches us. The tank commander watches from left front fender clockwise to right rear light with his .50-caliber machine gun while I, the loader, watch from right rear light clockwise to front left fender with the M240. If we take fire on top, we both drop down inside the turret with the loader's hatch shut and the tank commander's hatch closed or in the open protected position. Do you understand?" And so on.

While Abercrombie instructed, I listened to the squadron command radio net. Linzy reported we might encounter a reinforced company-sized element of infantry that he had wisely bypassed. He was right. We did come under fire from a small group of Iraqi soldiers who popped out from behind a small ridge, shot at us with some automatic weapon, and then ducked back into the rocks.

Though the shooting was more of an irritant than a serious threat, I was concerned that the rest of the Iraqi soldiers nearby might suddenly open up on us as we neared their positions instead of surrendering. However, I saw no reason to fire a main-gun round, and my machine guns were not the right weapon for these fleeting targets at 1,500 meters.

So I called Cougar Forward and said: "Shoot that son of a bitch on the ridge before he hurts somebody."

Sergeant Rusty Holloway, the gunner on Cougar Forward, obliged with one round from the 25-mm chain gun, killing the Iraqi soldier, who was firing his AK47, taking his head and upper body off at about 1,100 meters with a 25-mm sabot round. After that, the rest of the Iraqi company surrendered, and the shooting subsided.

This was the first time I had seen a man killed in combat. The experience had an electrifying effect on me and on the troops who watched the event, but not in the way most people would expect. The accuracy and lethality of our 25-mm chain guns was both terrifying and reassuring. Now we knew our guns worked.

Killing was easy.

Farther on, we encountered about a hundred Iraqi troops in defensive positions, and these would not surrender. Recognizing that we had rolled up on an infantry company in dug-in positions, Sartiano directed his scouts and tanks to open up on the Iraqi troops while his mortars executed what Lt. Joe Deskevich, the artillery officer assigned to Ghost Troop fire as the fire-support team leader, liked to call the "Shake and Bake," putting mortar rounds right in front of the advancing Bradleys as they rolled up to the trenches.

Abercrombie watched what was happening and warned, "Sir, there are too many Iraqis surrendering and too many shooting at the same time."

Abercrombie was right. The confusion was dangerous.

Abercrombie kept his M240 trained on all of the new EPWs as we drove by. Then, sure enough, only five hundred meters or so ahead of us and to our left front, three Iraqi soldiers manning a heavy machine gun abruptly decided to open up on our tank. I was on the radio and did not immediately notice until I heard the gunfire and saw Abercrombie drop down inside the tank turret. I looked over at him and asked, "What's wrong?"

"They're shooting at us," replied Abercrombie.

"Well, that's their job," I responded.

Abercrombie looked at me, paused for a second, laughed a little, and went back up to his medium machine gun. Meanwhile I listened to an update from Hillen about what was happening behind us in 1st Armored Division.

A few seconds later Abercrombie's bullets struck one of the soldiers, but unfortunately these Iraqis would still not quit. Hearing our frustration, Sergeant Jones, the gunner, suggested putting a main-gun round into the machine-gun position, which was now only about two hundred meters away.

"No," I said, "We are too close. F—k it. Ward!" I yelled, "Run them over."

"That's what I'm talking about," responded Ward with delight. He hit the accelerator, and the tank jerked so hard into high gear that I was thrown back against the turret wall behind me. Figuring that the problem would soon go away, I turned my attention to a report from Sartiano on the damage he said he'd done on the right flank. My assumption was wrong.

Without any warning, the tank stopped, rocking forward so hard that we nearly put the gun tube into the sand.

Irritated by the sudden, unexpected stop, I yelled, "Ward, Goddamn it, what the f—ck are you doing?"

"Shit, sir," said Ward, in a very low and discouraged voice, "The Iraqis put up a white flag."

Just as Ward was about to run them over, the Iraqis had stopped firing and raised a white flag. Where they had got such an item in Saddam's oppressive army none of us knew. Armies certainly don't issue white flags. The Iraqi action accounted for the sudden stop. I remain amazed to this day that Ward was able to stop a seventy-ton tank accelerating to forty miles per hour, swerve, and miss three Iraqi soldiers less than ten feet away, but he did it.

Ward's gallant action was commendable, but I wanted to get moving again. "OK," I said, "But let's keep moving."

"Sir, we can't."

"Why can't we?" I asked.

"Sir, Abercrombie." Ward hesitated a little. "Well, he's off the tank."

"What?" I replied angrily, "What the hell is he doing off the tank?"

"Sir, he's treating some Iraqi wounded?"

Without a word of warning to me, Abercrombie had pulled out his .45 automatic pistol, grabbed his medic bag, and jumped off the tank.

"What? Give me a f—cking break. We're not the f—cking Red Cross, tell Abercrombie to get back on the f—king tank, *now!*"

Ward said, "Roger!" took off his CVC helmet, the light helmet with integrated radio that soldiers wear inside armored vehicles, and yelled to Abercrombie to get back on the tank. More reports were coming in to me, the rest of the squadron was moving forward, and we were sitting still, babysitting Iraqi wounded. I needed to move out. It's never a good idea to do anything alone, without at least a battle buddy to cover you with a rifle; for a tank, with a four-man crew, to dismount a crewman degrades the crew's effectiveness and puts the tank at risk.

While I alternated between answering reports on the radio and swearing, Abercrombie calmly waved the surrendering Iraqis forward toward our tank. Two of them made it forward easily enough, but the third limped badly and lagged behind. The first two, standing near our tank, pointed at the other's back. The other kept pointed toward his back also.

Baffled by the whole affair, Abercrombie yelled, "What the f—k do you want?" One of the two Iraqi Arabs then turned around. His lower back and right side had been lightly grazed when Abercrombie had reengaged the three Iraqi soldiers with his M240. Abercrombie had apparently managed to shoot the Iraqis who had nearly shot him.

Abercrombie saw that one of the Iraqi soldiers had two minor wounds in his back where Abercrombie had shot him lying on his belly next to the machine gun. Clear ooze was coming out of his back, but the wounds were hardly bleeding. But the third Iraqi's right pant leg from the knee down, including his boot, was soaked in blood.

Abercrombie quickly went to work on the badly wounded Iraqi soldier in an effort to stop the bleeding. He had no surgical gloves on but decided the hell with it and ripped open the Iraqi's pant leg. Abercrombie saw that

Ghost Troop in Saudi Arabia, January 1991.

John Mecca parading captured Iraqi MTLBs past Cougar 3 on the afternoon
25 February 1991

View of Cougar 3's tank halted during Cougar Squadron's move to the Saudi Arabian border with Iraq.

From left to right, 1st Lt. John Gifford, Eagle Troop executive officer, Cpt. H. R. McMaster, EagleTroop commander, and the author, then-Maj. Douglas Macgregor on the morning of 27 Feb 1991. In the background, surviving Republican Guards who surrendered the previous night.

A destroyed Iraqi (Soviet-manufactured) BRDM wheeled recon vehicle along the 73 Easting.

Staff Sgt. William Burns, Cougar Master Gunner, shown in his Bradley (Cougar Forward) from behind a destroyed T-72 along the 73 Easting.

The author, Maj. Douglas Macgregor, shown in front of his tank with his tank driver, Sgt. Ward, just before the ground war in February 1991. Note the reference to "Sid Vicious" on the tank turret.

1630 rs 26 FEB 1991
U 737025

COUGAR 3

COUGAR FWD

Photo of Cougar 3's tank (Major Macgregor's tank) and Cougar Forward (Squadron Forward Command Post in a Bradley led by First Lieutenant Hillen) taken immediately after Cougar 3 halted the attack to the 73 Easting (PU 737025). Eagle Troop tanks are visible pulling up on Cougar 3's right in the weakening sandstorm.

Rendering of Sgt. Nels Andrew Moller1st Platoon Scouts, Ghost Troop
Killed in action on 26 February 1991

Fox Troop XO 1st Lt. Jack Waldron shows how close we came. He stands next to a road sign near An Nasiryah, Iraq.

the man had a hole about an inch and a half in diameter in his calf. As he put a pressure dressing on him, the other two Iraqi soldiers approached. One by one they kissed Abercrombie on his cheek in thanks. The Iraqi Abercrombie treated for the more severe wound suddenly sat forward and kissed him on the cheek as well. Yuck. I was glad I wasn't the "Good Samaritan"!

In the two minutes or so that elapsed, a medic M113 track from Fox Troop pulled up behind us and took control of the Iraqis. Responding to urging from Ward, Abercrombie climbed up and into the tank turret.

He could see that I was not happy. "Don't ever do that again, Rod. Don't ever jeopardize this crew to save a wounded enemy. Got it?"

"Sir, I got it."

"Ward!" I yelled. "Get us the hell out of here, now!"

"You got it, major."

Abercrombie had not really angered me. In fact, I was very proud of him. But we couldn't afford to save every Iraqi soldier we shot. It was just too risky.

In the space of an hour, I had already seen the American soldier at his best. Linzy's courage and intelligence had propelled us forward in the best direction, with renewed confidence and energy. Abercrombie's courage and compassion had filled me with pride and humility. Of course, none of these events stopped the war, and as Ward moved us out at a fast pace to catch up with Fox Troop's tanks, Cougar 32 (Ierardi) passed the message that Regiment had decided to halt again just short of Phase Line Dixie. Referring to my map, I saw that Dixie was the phase line just short of Objective Merrell.

Aware that the minor skirmishes behind him presented no threat to Cougar Squadron, Linzy surged ahead toward Objective Merrell. The sky was overcast. It was now 1600 hours. Linzy was worried.

Linzy had plenty of fuel and ammunition, but he did not know whether or if the A-10s had done significant damage to the Iraqi defenses reported on the objective. Whatever the strength and disposition of the enemy, he wanted to reach the objective before dark. There was not much moonlight to enable human eyes to see, even with image-intensifying night-vision goggles, and Linzy did not want to reconnoiter the Objective Merrell in the dark.

Approaching Merrell from the lower right-hand corner of the objective, or from the five o'clock position, as it was drawn on the map, Linzy's scouts sighted trucks that mounted crew-served weapons of some kind. The Iraqi trucks opened fire on the scouts, but not for long. Twenty-five-millimeter sabot rounds either disabled or completely destroyed the wheeled vehicles.

On Linzy's right flank, Staff Sergeant Hill moved his section toward what looked like a World War I fortification on top of a hill no more than two hundred meters in height. Linzy said it was easy to see that these were primitive trench works, defensive positions that would not have impressed even the Army of Northern Virginia, whose fortifications stopped Grant at Cold Harbor during the American Civil War. But they still presented a potentially dangerous situation to Linzy's scouts, who never knew which trench might contain a crew-served weapon or a team of rocket-propelled grenade (RPG) shooters.

Moving farther forward in the dying light, Linzy fired a few rounds in the direction of the trenches. He had a hunch. Perhaps what had worked earlier in the day would work again. Could these Iraqis be induced to surrender too?

Linzy was partially right. A few Iraqis returned fire and were quickly dispatched with the 25-mm chain gun, but ultimately more Iraqi soldiers emerged to surrender, yelling "President Bush, President Bush!" An odd thing to yell to surrender; had they heard those English words on TV?

Still, while large numbers of Iraqi soldiers were surrendering, others quite obviously were not. Seeing the confusion, Staff Sergeant Hill now swung his Bradley into action and rushed toward the trenches, which were disgorging large numbers of surrendering Iraqi Arabs. Hill's concern at this point was that the surrendering soldiers might become mixed up in the sporadic gunfights that were erupting nearby. The fire was seldom heavy or sustained, but it was dangerous to both Americans and Iraqis. He motioned to the new EPWs to get out of the way.

Linzy was excited over the mass surrenders but ordered his scouts to stay in their vehicles and be prepared to move quickly. The confusing melee of surrendering and fighting Iraqis caused his head to throb: "Red 2, this is Red Fox, make sure you can see the trenches, get some standoff. Red 3 needs to stay mounted, be ready to roll, acknowledge, over."

With orders to dismount as few people as possible, Staff Sergeant Hill had a real problem. Sergeant First Class Miller on his right already had nearly thirty Iraqi prisoners gathered around his track and was in no position to help. Hill decided to dismount with one of his JAFOs (Just Another F—king Observer, or scout) and cope as best he could. When the numbers of prisoners reached close to eighty, Sergeant Miller took the other Bradley in Hill's section and herded the EPWs toward the rear.

Seeing that the situation was well in hand, Linzy called his scouts and told them, "I am going forward with Red 3 to check bunkers and trenches. Red Fox, out."

Linzy moved forward cautiously, worried that a sudden pivot through the broken-up, layered trench lines might cause his driver to throw a track. Linzy began taking fire from five to eight hundred meters on the right, clearly from the first three of the sixty-meter-long trench lines. The fire was inaccurate, but it created serious complications. For every Iraqi soldier who fired at him, dozens of Iraqi soldiers spilled out of the trenches with white flags. A few disappeared into bunkers, shutting the wooden doors behind them. These guys would be troublesome.

Realizing that the overwhelming majority of Iraqi soldiers did not want to fight, Linzy directed his scouts to change their tactic. Instead of systematically killing every Iraqi soldier who returned fire, he told his scouts to unleash maximum firepower from their 25-mm automatic cannons and 7.62-mm machine guns either just in front of or over the heads of any Iraqi troops who fought. Some, like Staff Sergeant Hill, were skeptical at first, but later, when he and other scouts talked to the Iraqi prisoners of war who could speak some English, they found out how prescient Linzy's decision had been. When they were not drinking every drop of water the American soldiers could provide, a few Iraqi soldiers explained in broken English that they had no love for the dictator Saddam Hussein but that they had felt obligated to fire a few rounds to fulfill their promise to defend Iraq.

So shooting over their heads or in front of them in response to what amounted to no more than a gesture on the part of the Iraqi troops meant more prisoners, fewer wounded to treat, and fewer dead to dispose of. The medics in Fox Troop were already overwhelmed with lightly wounded and sick Iraq soldiers. Reducing this burden was a rational act, not just a humane one.

Still, unwilling to risk being shot from behind, Linzy and his scouts in Bradley fighting vehicles decided to stop in front of every bunker. The bunkers had framed doors so new they looked fresh from Home Depot. First, a shot went over each bunker, and then the Bradley commanders demanded the occupants' surrender.

In some cases the doors opened, and more Iraqi troops chanting "President Bush!" emerged. In others nothing happened, and the scouts opened up with the 25 mm, bashing in the doors, after which the Bradley commanders would heave grenades from their commander's hatches into the open bunkers, wait for the explosion of red-hot molten fragments to ignite the enemy ammunition, and then drive on. This was a time-consuming exercise, and it produced lots of prisoners, but it was necessary.

Linzy decided there was no time to lose. It was nearly pitch black except for the streams of orange-red tracer ammunition from the Bradley's 25-mm and 7.62-mm machine guns reaching toward the few resisting enemy positions. Although the squadron was now closing fast behind him, Linzy saw no reason to halt and wait. The A-10s must have destroyed all of the artillery and tanks, because none fired. That meant he had more than enough firepower to either capture or crush whatever enemies remained in their positions on the ridge.

He decided to advance with four of his six Bradleys on line, with, from left to right, Sergeant Schelander and Sergeant Gladkowski ("Ski"), each of whom commanded two Bradley fighting vehicles. If nothing else, Linzy was convinced, this move would flush out the enemy that was left. His tactic worked, and masses of Iraqi EPWs continued to show up in the objective area, but every five minutes or so new firefights would start in some other part of the objective area.

LET ME DRAW YOU A PICTURE!

When Hillen told me Regiment was halting for the night and was planning an artillery strike on the objective tomorrow morning, I was shocked.

"What the f—k is wrong with them? Don't they understand we've already seized the objective? The Iraqis are surrendering," I said. "There is no reason for an artillery preparation tomorrow morning."

"Sir, Captain Ierardi reported that information. Dragoon Base said, 'Just do what you are told. Evacuate the prisoners and wait for tomorrow's artillery prep on Objective Merrell.'"

I was stymied by the whole episode and wondered if I should raise it with Holder. It was day one of the offensive. Was it too early to make the matter of stopping a point of friction with Regiment? In the Army you have to choose your bureaucratic "battles" carefully; as an officer you can only blow the whistle a few times before you are considered a nuisance. Blow the whistle too often, and you will not have the favorable response you need when you really need it.

"John," I said, "I am not going to fight this battle with Regiment tonight."

Hillen was disappointed but nodded in agreement. As it became obvious that we would have no choice but to sit through another pointless artillery strike in the morning, I instantly worried that not all of the cluster bomblets that would be used would detonate on impact. One of our soldiers had already been injured by bomblets and I did not want to lose any more.

"The goddamn bomblets are a catastrophe," I said. "After tomorrow morning's artillery strike on Merrell, dud bomblets will be all over the terrain in front of us. John, please issue new waypoints to Linzy and the cavalry troops to get us around the mess. Let's swing the Cougar battle group wide of the objective area to avoid losing any soldiers or wheeled vehicles to the cluster bomblets." Hillen acknowledged and went to work.

Later, when Hillen was off the radio and could talk, I asked, "John, what's coming over the corps command net?" I knew Hillen loved to eavesdrop on the corps command radio net.

"The division commanders are telling Franks that they need time to stop, refuel, and consolidate for the night. They keep saying that their trains are spread out all over the desert and that they need time to regain command and control of their formations."[1]

"You have to be kidding," I said, shaking my head in disbelief. "Nobody in VII Corps has contact with the enemy but us. For God's sake," I said, "we could drive like hell tonight and pop up behind the Iraqi Republican Guard long before first light. I don't believe there is anything out there that can stop us."

Unfortunately, in our socially stratified army, "support" unit soldiers are too often considered lesser beings. As a result they are not fully integrated into tactical training exercises and are disinclined to move boldly in the wake of combat units. We were now paying for this sin, I thought. The corps support trains were scattered behind us while the enemy potentially slipped from our grasp.

Neither Hillen nor I knew that the decision to halt again had already been made. General Franks had flown forward to meet with Holder after conferring with Maj. Gen. Tom Rhame, the commander of the 1st Infantry Division. Though the 1st Infantry Division's breaching operation had come off without the anticipated lengthy and bloody battle, General Franks remained cautious, holding back the 1st Division when it could have otherwise advanced and joined us in the attack. General Rhame was certainly ready to do it.

Taking in all of this information from his subordinate commanders and reaching the lowest common denominator of conforming his movements to his slowest vehicles and units, Franks decided it was critical to conserve his combat power for the massive strike against the Republican Guard, which he still considered a formidable threat. That was still assuming we could reach the main body of the Republican Guard before it could flee over the Euphrates to central Iraq.

Franks and Holder discussed the situation and apparently decided that there was no reason to "grope in the dark trenches of the forward defensive belt on the night of 24 February."[2] Well, I had no idea what was happening above me, but I would love to have shown them the ridiculous trenches. The trenches were useless for a fight with anyone but a sheer incompetent. Where the hell were the generals getting this stuff?

Supposedly, General Schwarzkopf voiced no objections to the halt, remarking that there would be "plenty of Iraqis around for Franks to attack the next day."[3]

Whether Schwarzkopf understood that the VII Corps would essentially halt and cease operations for thirteen hours is unclear. What we at the tip of the spear knew was that General Franks' methodical timetable for his offensive was unchanged. We moved only fifteen kilometers in the morning and sixty kilometers in the afternoon of 24 February. Of course, in thirteen hours, the Republican Guard, whose destruction was our mission, could retreat—at thirty miles an hour—over three hundred miles (483 kilometers) away from us. But we received no updates on the Republican Guards' position, so it was impossible for us to know one way or the other.

Across Cougar Squadron, the soldiers knew how decisively Linzy had accomplished his advance-guard mission. They also knew that we had yet to encounter any serious opposition, and many, many soldiers wondered what the hell we were doing.

When word went out that we were stopping for the night, more than a few officers were surprised. Some, like Lt. Chuck Correll, who led Fox Troop's 2nd Platoon tanks, were angry and frustrated.

Hearing the halt order over the radio, he pulled off his helmet and threw it down to the desert sand in front of his tank. "What the hell is wrong with us? Don't these guys have a clue? You just don't stop in war unless you are compelled by the enemy to do so! God damn it, who the hell is running this show?"

Correll's soldiers watched, listened, and sympathized with their platoon leader, but there was nothing they could do.

Inside Cougar Forward, Hillen wrote some notes on his *Sports Illustrated* swimsuit calendar. He noted that we had moved only seventy-five kilometers in the last twenty-four hours. The absence of serious opposition induced Hillen to think on a different level, as his questions to me at the time implied.

"Sir, how are these generals going to manage in the days ahead if they haven't even fought a battle and already want to stop, consolidate, and regain command and control?"

He asked, What was going on? Had everyone above us become a control freak? What happened to all that cavalry bravado and talk about initiative? What would these commanders do over the next few days, especially if the president decided to move on Baghdad? These were questions for which I had no good answer.

"John, I don't know," I answered. "The whole thing is depressing. First, we halt in the middle of what is supposed to be an offensive, then we fire more artillery ammunition into an empty desert."

"So, what do we do?" asked Hillen.

"John," I sighed, "we do what we are told. We evacuate the Iraqi troops from Objective Merrell and wait for morning. Get a hold of Jack Waldron and make sure he understands what Fox has to do."

"Roger, sir." John's response was flat. His disappointment with my order was unmistakable. I knew that my answer was not what Hillen wanted to hear. But I felt that obedience was the only possible answer this early in the campaign.

General Franks' huddle with his commanders on the radio was inducing paralysis in the VII Corps, not action. This was not football, I thought. We're really in the middle of a potentially lethal soccer match, where time-outs and huddles give the enemy time to think and react.

But I still had faith in Holder. I was still sure he would press Franks to attack. I had sensed all along that the slow, deliberate advance punctuated by unnecessary halts might characterize the first twenty-four hours, but I hoped the following twenty-four hours would bring us closer to the enemy and change the situation. For the moment, we had broken contact with the enemy, something no armored reconnaissance unit ever willingly does in war. Once again, we were blind.

Lieutenant Colonel Larson now walked up and stood next to me, looking out over the dark desert to our front.

"Sir," I said as I turned toward him, "I do not like stopping when there is no reason to stop. If I were running the show for Saddam Hussein, I would launch everything I had right now against us, sitting on our asses in this open desert."

Lieutenant Colonel Larson was not inclined to question any decision made above him, so I was surprised when he actually agreed with me.

"Doug, I agree, but that is the way it is." Larson paused then and said in a whisper: "Doug, you need to wear the whole chemical suit. You cannot just wear the top and not the trousers. The soldiers are wearing their suits. You need to wear yours too."

It seemed like a strange comment to make at that particular moment, but he was correct. Had Larson not ordered it, I would have kept the soldiers out of the chemical-protection suits until we were much closer to the Republican Guard. The suits do not provide much protection after several days' wear, due to their charcoal lining. They quickly absorb moisture once they are removed from the airtight plastic bags they come in. I had never believed in the exaggerated chemical threat as long as we were in the open desert in a mobile posture in armored vehicles that provide a protective cocoon when hatches are closed. Once we reached the Euphrates River, the threat would become infinitely more serious, especially if we massed near the bridges before crossing into central Iraq. Iraqi artillery on the east side of the river could then pour chemical rounds into us with impunity. But under the circumstances, I simply said, "Yes, sir."

Curiously, Larson then asked, "Doug, what are you going to do now?"

"Sir, I'm going to pay a visit to Ghost Troop. Tom Sprowls is evacuating the prisoners. Major Ruiz is on his way up there with the mess trucks. Eagle is on a quiet flank for the moment, and I am confident that Tom Sprowls and T. J. Linzy have the situation on Merrell well in hand. We are already refueled and ready to roll. Ghost Troop is the one element about which I know nothing, and I want to make sure things in Ghost Troop are in good shape."

"Good idea, Doug. I am going to check in with Major Ruiz."

I was grateful that Maj. Oscar Ruiz, Cougar's executive officer, was on hand to talk with Lieutenant Colonel Larson. Oscar had a calming influence on Larson.

With that Larson moved off to chat with the executive officer, I went over to the TOC, where my lightly armored hardtop M1025 Humvee was parked. I did not want to waste fuel driving the tank around the neighborhood, especially when the enemy was surrendering in droves. A staff sergeant in the S-3's fire-support section volunteered to man the .50-caliber heavy machine gun on top of the Humvee while I rode next to the driver. He also brought along a Global Positioning System unit that would guide us through the open desert over to the left flank, where Ghost Troop was setting up a screen line for the night.

After driving through complete darkness for fifteen minutes, Sergeant First Class McNally, who guided us with the GPS, brought us into position behind Lieutenant Mecca's Bradley. Mecca had known I was coming out, but he seemed surprised nonetheless. Sartiano and Mecca were inside Mecca's Bradley reviewing map positions of the scouts and the maintenance posture of the troop. Lieutenants Garwick and Haines walked in during the visit and described their screen lines and what, if anything was happening.

Ghost was extremely alert, morale was good, and I was satisfied with what I saw. Though Ghost had had no contact with the enemy, the officers were well aware of what was happening in Fox Troop on the left. They also had contact on the right with 3rd Squadron. Given the confusing situation in Fox Troop's zone, a degree of nervousness was understandable, but no one was trigger-happy.

On top of Objective Merrell, where Fox scouts worked to separate the EPWs from the few die-hard resisters, Linzy received word from Lieutenant Waldron that he had to vacate the objective before morning so that the regiment could fire an artillery prep. He was just as furious and disgusted as Hillen and I were.

"Fox 5, this is Red Fox, let me draw you a picture, break!" Linzy paused to take a deep breath and then continued: "We've already taken Objective Merrell. There is no reason for an artillery preparation, over"

"Red Fox, Fox 5, roger, we reported that to higher. Higher says, we have no choice. We have to get off Merrell before morning, over."

"Fox 5, Red Fox, that is the dumbest order I have ever received. We still have POWs here. All they want to do is surrender and live. Doesn't anyone listen to me?"

"Red Fox, Fox 5, roger, I am en route to your location, Fox 5, out."

Linzy, of course, was absolutely right. Fortunately, Waldron was also a superb executive officer. He understood exactly how Linzy felt. And he knew there was no point in discussing it over the radio. Waldron drove forward to where Linzy was inspecting the damage on Objective Merrell and calmed him down.

Not long after Linzy delivered his famous "Let me draw you a picture speech," an antitank TOW missile fired by one of Linzy's scouts must have hit an ammunition storage point; an explosion shook the whole ridge and illuminated the night sky for about fifteen minutes. It was not a bad way to end the fighting on Objective Merrell.

While Sprowls and the rest of Fox Troop's scouts herded the new Iraqi prisoners into some semblance of a holding area, Major Ruiz and Command Sergeant Major Chapman showed up with mess trucks, manned by squadron cooks who had been detailed to handle prisoners. Worried that some of the prisoners might not make it off Objective Merrell in time to avoid the artillery barrage, Linzy was relieved to see Ruiz and Chapman and thanked them both profusely for coming. Now, he could relax. As far as Linzy was concerned, the cavalry really had arrived.

WHO THE HELL WOULD PUT ANYONE IN A PLACE LIKE THIS?

Satisfied that Ghost Troop was in good shape, I drove back to where Cougar Forward and my tank were parked.

On the way back I had the opportunity to see roughly fifty or sixty prisoners lined up and waiting for transport to the rear. Captain Scott was particularly excited, because an Iraqi general officer had been captured, though I am not sure he had much to tell us.

Before returning to my tank, Hillen called me over to Cougar Forward. He said, "You have to hear this."

"What, more good news?" I asked.

"No, but you won't believe it unless you hear it for yourself."

Hillen reached over and turned up the volume on the corps command net. What happened next should probably end up in the *Encyclopedia of Military History*. Maj. Doug Lute, the regimental operations officer, known as Dragoon 3, was talking over the radio to the corps TAC.

"Tell Jayhawk 6 [General Franks] that we are combat critical. Our third basic load of ammunition is stuck thirty kilometers to our rear. Without it, our position is combat critical, I say again, combat critical, over."

War in slow motion was new to me, but I was learning fast.

"John, how long has this bullshit been going on?"

"For about ten minutes."

"You have to be kidding," I said, "How could our situation be 'combat critical,' whatever the hell that means, because our third basic load of ammunition is sitting on trucks stuck in the desert miles behind us? My God, we have not even dented the first basic load and we have another one in our supply trucks."

Hillen was in rare form and had not lost his biting, cynical humor.

"Sir, I just wanted to keep you informed of the dramatic events that shape our lives in the 2nd Cavalry!"

It was too soon to become depressed about this nonsense. I declined to reengage with Hillen on the matter.

"Right, I got it." I paused for a second, then turned to walk away, saying, "Well, let me know what else happens."

A day later, one of the tank commanders in Fox Troop asked me, "Sir, what the hell are they [the generals] worried about? We knew the job was dangerous when we took it."

I had no good answer. I was ashamed to say something like, "Franks and Holder are in charge, they must know what they are doing." I just walked away.

While some of our soldiers were using the time in front of Objective Merrell to catch up on some sleep, Holloway was wide awake. He was looking for the headquarters troop first sergeant. The first sergeant was reportedly making the rounds with some mail. Eventually the first sergeant showed up, telling Holloway, "I got a letter for you. It arrived some time back, but I haven't seen you."

When he handed it over, Holloway could tell before reading the address on the pink envelope that it was from his German girlfriend. He put his finger into the side of the envelope to open the letter, but before he could rip open the envelope there was a large "Whoosh!" in the distance.

Fox Troop mortars had dropped a couple of white-phosphorus rounds on Iraqi positions to "mark the target." The burning phosphorus lighted up the area around it, reminding Holloway of high-school bonfires back home in Kansas. In the distance he could see Iraqi soldiers running in all directions, trying to get away from the illuminated area. They know high-explosive rounds were on the way. Holloway decided to put the letter in his pocket and read it later.

At this point I really needed a little levity, and, fortunately for all of us that night, Fox Troop provided it. Tom Sprowls, who was supervising the evacuation of the prisoners, decided to amuse himself and his Iraqi guests. Keep in mind, these Iraqi soldiers had been forced at gunpoint to enlist and serve as cannon fodder for Saddam Hussein's war. One Iraqi soldier explained in broken

English to Captain Scott how he had been forced by Iraqi Republican Guard troops to join the army. Saddam Hussein's men had broken into his home and threatened to rape and kill his wife and daughter right in front of him if he did not immediately volunteer to fight.

What a recruitment pitch! Of course, this man was exceptional. Most Arabs could not speak English and were poorly educated farmers from the Euphrates River valley who wanted nothing more than to survive and go home.

With no prompting from the chain of command, Fox Troop's soldiers gave these poor souls food, water, and medical attention. Sprowls watched the scene carefully, sensing the fear in the Arabs. He decided to break the tension by leading the captured Iraqis soldiers in what looked like a version of the hokey pokey, a timeless American party classic.

Frankly, I have no idea what the Iraqi soldiers thought, but both American and Iraqi soldiers were laughing and smiling. The sight of the captured Iraqi soldiers trying desperately to keep up with Tom's hand and arm movements is something I wish we had captured for posterity on film or video. It was another lesson in man's capacity for goodness in the midst of the barbarism that is war.

Until 2200 hours, the darkened ridge gave off a pulsating glow, the flickering light of burning vehicles and occasional flashes of gunfire. Fighting on the objective where Linzy's platoon now stood unopposed was over. Linzy was relieved that none of his scouts had even been injured. But a new action was about to commence on the squadron's left flank, where Eagle Troop, anxiously watching Linzy's action on the ridge, was waiting for a chance to get into the fight. Their wish was about to be fulfilled.

Surveying the dark desert to their front, Eagle Troop scouts spotted Iraqi soldiers blazing white with heat in the clear optics of the Bradleys' thermal sights. About twenty Iraqi infantrymen had wisely gone to ground. Knowing they could do nothing to stop the advance of Linzy's Bradleys in daylight, they had hid in what looked like a network of spider holes on the desert floor. Consequently, their presence had gone unnoticed in the sunlight when Eagle Troop rolled to an uneventful stop after a day without enemy contact. Now the Iraqis assumed that they could advance on the American armor to their front without being detected. A few crawled forward as a couple of others opened fire, skipping a few rounds past the Bradleys.

Alerted by Eagle scouts to what was happening, McMaster moved forward in his tank to a position near the scouts. Delighted with the opportunity to draw some blood, McMaster directed the mortars to shell the Iraqi positions with a mix of white phosphorous and high-explosive mortar rounds.

"When the rounds land on them," McMaster told the scouts, "open up and wax them."

Gauging the range was not a challenge for the mortars. Staff Sergeant Taylor and Staff Sergeant Davis were good mortar men. They knew their trade and had laser range-finders. The scouts employed the laser range finder to target the Iraqi positions and provide the experienced mortar men with the distance to the target: three hundred meters.

After a brief interlude, McMaster listened for the dull thud of mortar bombs launching out of their tubes into the empty night sky. A deep pumping sound signaled that the rounds were on their way.

Eyes riveted to their thermal sights, Eagle Troop's scouts waited for the high-angle mortar fire to have an effect. Seconds later, the rounds burst right over the Iraqi positions, and the troops immediately panicked. Jumping out of their holes to avoid the flesh-melting white phosphorous, the Iraqis emerged into the open just in time for splinters and shards of metal to strike their faces and chests.

Some tried to run, others fired wildly into the night, hoping to hit Eagle Troop. Their actions were pointless. A split second later, 25-mm high-explosive incendiary rounds and 7.62-mm machine-gun bullets tore through their bodies, ending their misery. In less than a minute of action, twenty figures fell lifeless where they had planned to fight, heaps of broken bones and seared flesh. For the Iraqi soldiers, first contact was also last contact.

By 0100 hours on Objective Merrell, it seemed like the fighting was once again coming to an end—that is, until Linzy's scouts about sixty meters from the top of the hundred-meter-high ridge began taking machine-gun and RPG fire from still more Iraqis who would not surrender and were trying to escape. Linzy and Hill moved forward, relying primarily on their machine guns until they spotted in their "thermals" a mix of dismounted Iraqi soldiers and trucks mounting machine guns. The group was moving north and east across the open desert.

It was time—as Burns, the squadron master gunner, liked to say—to "bump up!" The expression meant scale up to the next most lethal weapon, in this case the 25-mm cannon. The gunners threw the ammo switches to 25-mm sabot and blasted two of the fleeing trucks, overflowing with fleeing Iraqis. The third truck got away clean.

Shelander and Gladkowski, now on the far left, moved up to clear the last bits of the objective area. Seeing the approaching American Bradleys, a few Iraqi troops in front of them who had been falling back for hours through successive defensive positions started running to the back side of the ridge. When the Bradleys drove over the ridge, they saw that these Iraqis had jumped on board two more trucks and were now preparing to flee.

Linzy told his section to fire a mix of sabot and TOW missiles at them. Staff Sergeant Hill also fired several TOW missiles at what looked like vehicular positions farther down the hill.

When the battle was truly over and most of the EPWs were out of the objective area, Linzy struggled with other matters. His Bradley had thrown a track. There were still prisoners to evacuate. He wanted to try and get some rest, but there was just too much work left to do. In reality, Linzy's most important work was already done. In overcoming any hesitation, conquering his own fears, and exercising common sense in the capture and humane treatment of Iraqi troops, Linzy had put iron into the souls of every soldier in Cougar Squadron.

But Linzy was not basking in the glory of his day's achievement. Once the last Iraqi EPWs were safely evacuated and out of danger, Linzy had one more important task to perform. He drove to the Fox Troop tactical operations center and congratulated Lieutenant Waldron on the occasion of Waldron's twenty-seventh birthday. Linzy brought along a small present, a memento of the battle for Objective Merrell—an Iraqi army black beret.

Jack was thrilled, but seeing how tired Linzy was, he immediately shoved a hot cup of coffee into Linzy's hand.

Linzy walked outside with the coffee into the damp, cold desert air to think. He wanted to comprehend what he had just done. So he asked himself whether he could have handled the initial contacts with the Iraqi troops a bit better. Could his scouts have killed fewer Iraqis and still accomplished the mission? Once his scouts took the enemy's measure, they had managed to induce most of them to surrender, but could they have spared more lives?

Linzy still felt that too many Iraqi soldiers had died pointlessly. After all, Linzy thought, what the hell were these poor bastards doing here? Who the hell would put soldiers in a shitty position like this one and then expect them to achieve anything? Who, indeed?

FIVE

Why Are We Stopping?

All great commanders have come with increasing experience of war
to realize that opportunism is essential in war; that fixed purposes and
objectives are contrary to its nature; and, if rigidly maintained, lead
usually to a blank wall.

SIR BASIL LIDDELL HART, *THOUGHTS ON WAR*, 1944

0600 HOURS, 25 FEBRUARY 1991, ALONG PHASE LINE DIXIE IN IRAQ

Next morning, at 0600, Ward cranked up the engine and drove our tank forward to a position near Fox Troop's tanks at the tip of the squadron diamond.

As the troops watched my tank move forward, they readied themselves for the "battle stations" order to "move out" that would come as soon as the pointless artillery strike on Objective Merrell ended. Most of the squadron assumed this was the day we would come to grips with the Republican Guard Corps, the enemy we had come so far to fight. Everyone with the semblance of a map knew we were at most within three or four hours' drive of the Republican Guard. Perhaps the divisions behind us had moved through the night after all and were now right behind us, ready to strike. We didn't know.

At 0630 hours, the regiment initiated the ten-minute artillery strike on Objective Merrell. Fortunately, there were no Iraqi prisoners on the objective. Fox Troop had evacuated them all in plenty of time. Linzy's thrown track had been repaired, and his platoon had been resupplied. As soon as the guns stopped firing, "Redfox" (First Lieutenant Linzy) blasted forward with his reconnaissance element of six Bradleys and two mortars around the human wreckage of the Iraqi infantry brigade. Ten minutes later, the rest of the squadron followed, swinging wide of Objective Merrell and picking up another twenty-five or thirty Iraqi prisoners on the way, more mustachioed men wearing green uniforms and boots waving little white flags.

In the morning light, scouts in Eagle Troop could also see the results of their short battle the night before. As they drove past the remains of the Iraqi soldiers who had attacked them, the carnage of war was on display for the first time.

One private in Eagle Troop yelled out, "Do you see that f—ker's head? The f—ker's head is half-gone, holy shit!"

Most soldiers said nothing, preferring not to look.

By 1000 hours we were halted along Phase Line Miller, just short of Objective Gates. Although Linzy saw plenty of evidence that Iraqi forces had moved through the area, he reported no enemy contact in zone. Our move north toward Objective Gates was unopposed.

As our standing operating procedure dictated, when we reached the limit of advance we halted yet again and waited impatiently for orders to resume the advance.

Instead of orders to resume the advance, we received light, black rain. Smoke from the oil fires burning across northern Kuwait mixed with the winter cloud cover to create a gothic scene. The gray clouds and light rain reminded me of the Jersey shore in winter, only without the ocean.

Soon after, to our consternation, Dragoon Base directed us to develop a hasty defense along a sweeping half-circle forty kilometers in length, with Ghost tied in on the right flank to 3rd Squadron, Fox Troop in the middle where the half-circle bulged, and Eagle Troop on the far left.

Hasty defense—essentially, digging in quickly—is normally a posture adopted temporarily by attacking units when enemy resistance makes it impossible to continue the attack. In our case it made no sense, because we had met no significant enemy opposition. And time was running out if we were to catch and destroy the Republican Guard.

But orders are orders, and speedily Ghost and Eagle troops were deployed along Phase Line Blacktop. Aptly named, Phase Line Blacktop was an asphalt road running northeast out of Kuwait into Iraq.

By 1230 hours, two hundred more Iraqi prisoners of war had fallen into our hands without a fight.

Figure 7. Hasty Defensive Position of 2nd Cavalry, 25–26 February

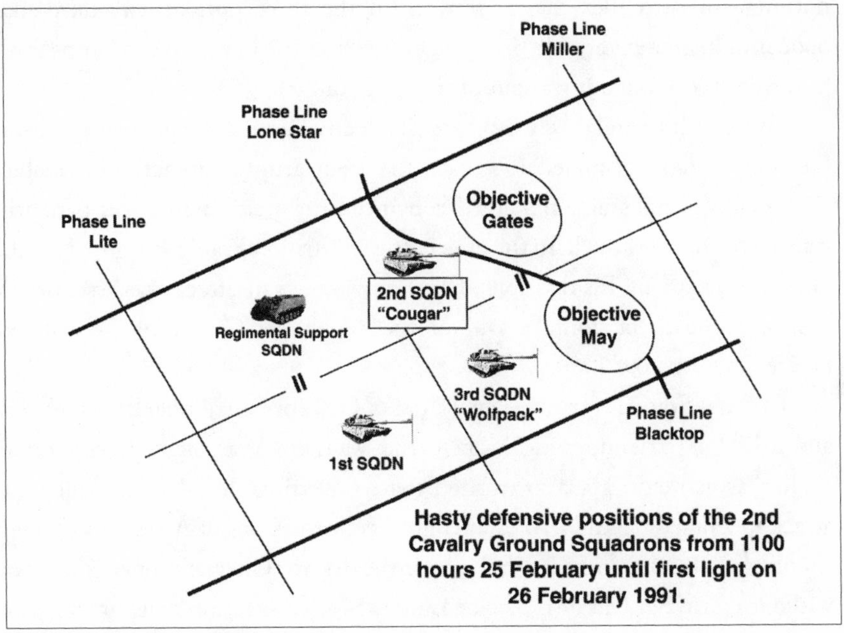

Phase Line
Miller

Phase Line
Lone Star

Phase Line
Lite

Objective
Gates

2nd SQDN
"Cougar"

Regimental Support
SQDN

Objective
May

3rd SQDN
"Wolfpack"

Phase Line
Blacktop

1st SQDN

Hasty defensive positions of the 2nd Cavalry Ground Squadrons from 1100 hours 25 February until first light on 26 February 1991.

Close to noon, Lieutenant Colonel Larson received instructions to attend a meeting with Colonel Holder and the rest of the regiment's leadership. When Larson departed, I asked Hillen to set up a hasty forward command post. Hillen backed Cougar Forward up against the rear ramp of the air liaison section's M113A2 and placed a tarp over the space between the two for some overhead cover. This created some dry space where we could plan without getting wet. Then, we waited.

It was Sunday, though none of us really noticed. While we sat wondering what the hell was happening above us that had made us halt again, Schwarzkopf's staff, far away in Riyadh, Saudi Arabia, was finally figuring out what we in Cougar Squadron already knew. Based on the brief encounters with the few Iraqi forces facing us in the open desert, it was apparent that the only thing the Iraqis had done for the last forty-eight hours was, as the British like to say, "bug out." Schwarzkopf's staff was now talking pursuit rather than deliberate attack—pursuit being a headlong assault to catch the enemy in the middle of his retreat.[1]

As General Schwarzkopf later noted, after Khafji it had always been doubtful that any Iraqi maneuver across the open desert would survive under the crushing weight of American airpower.

Now, it also was obvious to Schwarzkopf that the Iraqi force could do nothing but surrender, die, or retreat. Of the three options, it looked like Saddam Hussein had made the decision to retreat. To Franks' VII Corps staff, however, talk of pursuit was out of the question.

Even with the relatively light and ineffective Iraqi resistance on the 24th, General Franks continued to regard the Iraqi army as intact and capable. Presumably, Franks also remained convinced the Iraqi enemy was patiently waiting for him to attack. In the tank battle of attrition Franks imagined would take place, massing his divisions into narrow zones of attack was essential to success in the direct frontal assault on the Republican Guard that he planned before Christmas of 1990.

Colonel Stan Cherrie, General Franks' G-3 (principal operations officer) and a lifelong friend, going back to the Vietnam War, strongly supported Franks' assessment. He also worried that converting the planned deliberate attack to a pursuit could lead to uncontrolled formations of American soldiers shooting each other in a mad dash across the desert.[2] Cherrie's concern was not without merit, but fear of fratricide is no excuse for inaction when it comes to the overarching priority of attacking the enemy. Predictably, the larger effect of these concerns was to once again halt, not accelerate, VII Corps' movement forward.

In Cougar Squadron, we had no idea that a divergence of opinion on these matters had developed between General Schwarzkopf and General Franks. But Franks must have had some doubts, because now, at 1000 hours on the 25th, he had called his division commanders for advice on whether to continue the advance or to halt.

This was curious indeed. Knowing the criticality of his mission to the larger strategic success or failure of Desert Storm, it's hard to understand why he would ask generals commanding units that had yet to really see action whether he should press the attack or stop. But this is what happened.

The conversation was reportedly similar to what John Hillen and I heard over the VII Corps command radio net on the evening of the 24th. The word "mass" came up again, along with the insistence on equating masses of troops on the ground in restricted battle space with effective combat power, a prejudice that had developed over many years of Cold War peacetime exercises and attrition-based simulations. The idea that the battle was not a question of numbers but of position, tactics, and speed didn't come up.

Once again, General Franks' division commanders thought it advisable to pause for consolidation and refueling. In particular, Maj. Gen. Ron Griffith (later a four-star general and Army vice chief of staff), the 1st Armored Division commander, argued persuasively that an unknown number of Iraqi troops were operating in his rear area from the town of al Busayyah.

Al Busayyah was a very small town of adobe buildings that had served as a logistics base for the Iraqi forces in the nearby desert during the months leading up to the war. The 2nd Cavalry had simply bypassed the town, leaving it in the 1st Armored Division's zone of attack. To this day, I don't think anyone in the regimental headquarters, including Holder, saw much evidence for a significant enemy in al Busayyah, but that is not the way the 1st Armored Division commander saw it.

Surveying the situation from his command post, Major General Griffith had concluded the town represented a major threat. He decided to attack the town deliberately, as though an Iraqi division-sized force held it, when in fact it was very lightly defended. Whether an Iraqi special forces battalion held the town or not is not the issue. Given its size, capability, and striking power, the 1st Armored Division could have run the place over in ten minutes, but Griffith's extremely risk-averse approach dictated hours of artillery bombardment to reduce the likelihood of serious enemy resistance and make the direct-fire battle easier. It also dictated the loss of another day.

Amazingly, General Franks approved General Griffith's plan of attack without hesitation. First Armored Division opened the attack with a night-long bombardment before moving through the town at dawn on the 26th, dramatically slowing down the concentration of force in VII Corps. With each passing hour, this pattern of timidity in the face of extremely weak enemy resistance made mission success less likely.

After the war, General Franks protested that he had actually urged his division commanders to advance without pause. That's hard to imagine, but without the 1st Armored Division, Franks also insisted, it was impossible to attack the Republican Guard. Still, General Griffith's reluctance to advance was not the only reason for Franks' decision to halt his corps for a second time in forty-eight hours.

When Franks asked Holder for his opinion, Holder said, "If we continue to move, you're going to have me into the Republican Guard tomorrow and nobody behind me to mass against them. My recommendation is to hold and resume the attack at first light."[3]

Holder did not protest Franks' predisposition to halt. On the contrary, he, like Franks' division commanders, reinforced it.

Why didn't Holder or anyone in the VII Corps' senior leadership argue for offensive action to shatter the enemy right then and there with the force we had? Was it because decades of experience in the Army teach officers who want to advance to general officer rank to stay in their lanes, focus narrowly on the limited, assigned mission, and never ever "rock the boat"? Was it because generations of four-star generals at the Army's Training and Doctrine Command had decided years earlier that the 2nd Cavalry was doctrinally too light to fight on its own?

If so, this view was erroneous. The eight thousand troops of the 2nd Armored Cavalry Regiment battle group were armed with the same equipment found in the Army's armored divisions. But the 2nd Cavalry was tightly organized into a smaller, more agile, combined-arms team of heavy tanks and armored fighting vehicles, with mobile artillery and attack helicopters, to create combat power disproportionate to its size. With the capability to hit the enemy hard, the 2nd Cavalry was ideally positioned to make first contact, as a sharp spear point that fatally wounds an unsuspecting enemy.

But Colonel Holder's afternoon meeting on the 25th with Cougar 6, Wolf Pack 6, and War Eagle 6 (the three ground-squadron commanders) may well have buttressed Franks' decision to halt. When General Franks asked for an opinion, one of the squadron commanders allegedly warned that heavy rain and darkness would make it very hard, if not impossible, to distinguish U.S. from Iraqi forces. The unnamed cavalry squadron commander allegedly suggested that Iraqi armored vehicles, especially the MTLBs, which resembled M113s, were "tough to distinguish from American fighting vehicles in the rainy darkness."[4] Again, the specter of fratricide was used to justify inaction.

Whatever the reasons, it was hardly the first time in American military history that senior leaders remote from the scene of the battle made decisions to halt at a time when bold, decisive movement, directed from the front, not the rear, was desperately needed.

In August 1944, Patton had Third Army racing to close the gap at Falaise and destroy the German army in Normandy. But orders from Gen. Omar Bradley, the army group commander, to halt made impossible the envelopment of the German army in Normandy that Patton wanted.

Patton's great fear—that most of the best German combat troops and equipment, as well as the leadership of the German army in Normandy, would escape over the Seine River—is exactly what happened. The German army escaped to reconstitute itself and fight again in the battle of the Bulge.[5]

We had no idea, at the time, what was going on above us or behind us, but we suspected that something similar was the case with the senior leadership of VII Corps on 25 February. The result was that we in the 2nd Cavalry would sit idle for another twenty-four hours while the bulk of Iraq's Republican Guard Corps retreated over the Euphrates to safety.

MAY DAY PARADE

With nothing but flat, rainy desert to their front, Cougar Squadron's soldiers watched for signs of the enemy.

At about 1400 hours, an exciting report came up from Ghost Troop. They had contact with the enemy. Lieutenant Mecca reported engaging a company of Iraqi infantry mounted in light, tracked, armored vehicles—MTLBs, the vehicle an unnamed squadron commander had worried we would mistake for M113s. Mixed in with the infantry was a platoon of towed artillery.

Mecca's report made me jealous. I had yet to see really significant action, and I envied Ghost Troop's brief encounter with the enemy—that is, until Mecca called to tell me that after two of the Iraqi troops had been killed in a brief exchange of gunfire, the rest of the Iraqi contingent had surrendered without a shot.

Disappointed with the lack of action but still happy with the outcome, I radioed Mecca, "Ghost 5, good job. Transport for POWs is en route to your location, out."

Thinking that nothing more would happen, I was about to dismount from the tank when Ghost 5 called back to tell me that he had found something really interesting. "Cougar 3, this is Ghost 5, you have to come over and see this equipment. It is all new and in great condition, over."

"Ghost 5, Cougar 3, I cannot leave right now with Cougar 6 out of the area. We have good communications here. If I leave, I may lose contact with Dragoon Base, over."

"Cougar 3, Ghost 5, understand. I will come to your location over."

"Ghost 5, what do you mean, over?"

"Cougar 3, I will bring the MTLBs to your location for your inspection, over."

"Roger, Ghost 5. Look forward to it, out." As I signed off, though, I began thinking. If Mecca brings those Iraqi MTLBs over here, somebody may mistake him for the enemy. Oh my God, wait, I need to warn Hawk Company. They're in the middle of the squadron defense, and they might open up on the MTLBs.

"Battle Stations, Battle Stations, this is Cougar 3, Ghost 5 is moving a group of MTLBs to my location. Do not engage them, acknowledge, over."

Fortunately, all of the stations acknowledged in quick succession, but I continued to worry until I spotted Mecca driving over the horizon in his brand-spanking-new enemy MTLB. Behind him came five more in column. However, as they moved closer to us, Mecca signaled the MTLBs behind him, and a few seconds later the MTLBs were arrayed in two ranks, with Mecca in the center of the front rank. By the time Mecca reached my position, he had wheeled the two ranks of MTLBs around and passed us in review, saluting like a Russian commander at a May Day parade.

This antic brought down the house.

We all piled out of our vehicles, ran over to congratulate Mecca, and began inspecting his lucrative haul of souvenirs. As soon as I saw that everything was new and in superb condition, I turned to Burns and said, "William, listen, you have to pick up some souvenirs for me and my boys, Cameron and Alick."

Burns laughed and said, "Sure, but you can pick stuff out for yourself."

"No, William, I can't. I mean, I'm an officer. For God's sake, officers don't pillage. That's why God created noncommissioned officers."

"OK, sir," Burns continued to laugh uncontrollably, "I got it. Only sergeants who are reformed criminals get to do that shit, right?"

Burns was being a smart-ass, and having a hell of a good laugh at my expense, but he knew what I meant.

"Precisely, God damn it," I whispered. "Now don't give me shit. Just f—cking get some berets and gear for me."

While Burns filled his extra laundry bag with souvenirs, Jones and Abercrombie found a pile of brand-new weapons, including a 7.62-mm medium, belt-fed machine gun fresh from the Soviet factory that had made it.

When Jones showed it to me, I asked whether he thought we could replace my broken .50-caliber machine gun with it. Sergeant Jones was a genius with weapons. If anybody could do it, I was convinced he could.

Jones said he would definitely give it a shot, and by the end of the day he had it firing without any problem from the top of the turret in front of the tank commander's position.

While we entertained ourselves with the captured equipment, the soldiers who could do so, rested.

One soldier, Specialist Jones in Fox Troop, told his platoon leader, Lt. Chuck Correll, "Sir, I'm getting a hell of a lot more sleep than I did in Germany on training exercises."

"Yeah, I know, but maybe they'll let us do something soon," answered Correll. "Soon" was not to be, but something was indeed happening that would change our lives forever.

Back at the 2nd Cavalry's forward tactical command post (TAC), Robinette was sorting through the details of the 2nd Cavalry's anticipated operation when he got a call from General Franks, at about 1700 hours, that Franks was flying in his command Blackhawk (a UH-60 helicopter) to the regimental TAC.

Robinette figured that something significant was up but didn't know what it was.

Franks had been on the radio earlier in the day with Colonel Holder, and Holder had mentioned moving the 2nd Cavalry into a "hasty defense." Schwarzkopf's intervention finally made Franks understand that he could delay no longer. Suddenly, Franks no longer wanted to hear about "hasty defense." Franks had been subjected to more than one white-hot blast of heat through the phone from CENTCOM on the 25th urging him to attack the Republican Guard as quickly as possible.

General Powell had called Schwarzkopf from Washington during the afternoon to find out why VII Corps was not moving. He told Schwarzkopf, "They've been maneuvering for more than two days and still don't even have contact with the enemy. . . . We should be fighting the enemy by now."[6]

Until Franks' heated telephone conversation with General Schwarzkopf on the 25th, Franks' predisposition had been to focus on information about the enemy that confirmed his preconceptions, resulting in a very inwardly focused decision-making process.

Since Franks never went forward to the tip of the spear to talk directly to the soldiers and officers facing the enemy, his preconceived notions about the Iraqi enemy trumped reality. Instead of seeing things as they really were, throughout 25 February General Franks, along with his subordinate commanders, located behind the forward line of advancing combat troops in the 2nd Cavalry, saw the Iraqi enemy they wanted to see, an enemy that did not exist.

Nonetheless, after the discontent that Schwarzkopf registered with Franks' decision to halt the corps on the night of the 24th and then again on the 25th, Franks was now less receptive to his division commanders' desires for halts of any kind. Franks radioed ahead to make it clear he wanted to see Holder as soon as possible.

As always, Robinette was one step ahead. As soon as General Franks indicated he was en route to the regimental TAC, Robinette informed Holder on the radio that Franks was on his way. Franks wasted no time getting to his command post and actually arrived before Holder did. Colonel Stan Cherrie, the corps G-3, was with Franks. The two men stepped out of the Blackhawk and walked straight over to Robinette.

Wiping the sand from his brow, General Franks asked Robinette, "What's this about hasty defense?"[7]

Because he had not recently listened to the VII Corps command radio net, Robinette wasn't sure how to respond. He was unaware that Holder had mentioned to Franks moving the 2nd Cavalry into a hasty defense, he did not need a picture drawn for him to figure out that Franks wanted nothing to do with it. Defense was Holder's idea, and it was no longer what Franks wanted.

Robinette quickly assured Franks that the 2nd Cavalry was ready to resume the advance if that was what Franks wanted. A few minutes later, when Holder arrived, Franks, Cherrie, and Robinette were standing outside of the TAC. Franks was still agitated about Holder's use of the words "hasty defense." When Holder joined the group, the four men quickly walked into the regimental command post, making a beeline straight for the map.

Cherrie told Robinette that VII Corps was coming out with FRAGPLAN 7. A "FRAGPLAN" is, literally, a fragmentary plan, as opposed to a complete operations order. Until the commander directs it to be implemented, the fragmentary plan is treated as one that *may* be implemented.

Cherrie said that FRAGPLAN 7 would detail the forward passage of the 3rd Armored Division on the 2nd Cavalry's left flank. Then Cherrie and Robinette turned to the map and determined what ground Robinette and Cherrie thought the 2nd Cavalry should take. The FRAGPLAN was, in fact, consistent with the original plan devised months earlier. Pursuit, not deliberate attack, was called for; the idea of racing ahead with the 2nd Cavalry to catch the Republican Guard, pulling the divisions into battle behind it, does not seem to have occurred to Franks or Holder.

While Cherrie briefed Robinette on the FRAGPLAN, Holder and Franks discussed what the 2nd Cavalry would do before it was executed. What intelligence sources were telling Franks and Holder was that the Tawalkana Division, a component of the Republican Guard Corps, reinforced by some Iraqi army formations, was now in defensive positions covering the movement of the main body of the Iraqi Republican Guard as it retired north toward Basra. In view of this development, Franks intimated that the 2nd Cavalry would have to lead the divisions forward, then, as previously planned, halt and let the divisions pass through in their attack to destroy the Republican Guard. Once the divisions passed through, the 2nd Cavalry would become part of the VII Corps reserve, available for new missions.

In essence, this plan called for the 2nd Cavalry to bump up against the Republican Guard, then politely back away, pausing until the divisions came up and attacked. This impractical scheme presumed, of course, that the Republican Guard Corps was still waiting to be attacked and would cooperate with the maneuver.

When the meeting broke up, Cherrie indicated that FRAGPLAN 7 would be issued some time after he and Franks returned to the corps TAC. Cherry said that Lt. Col. Dave McKiernan (later four-star General McKiernan), who was serving as the officer in charge of General Franks' TAC, would keep the corps TAC far enough forward to stay within FM radio range (ten to twenty kilometers) of the regiment's TOC and TAC.

Around 1745 hours, after Franks and Cherrie departed, Robinette and Holder compared notes, since the two men had talked separately to Franks and Cherrie, respectively. Robinette understood what needed to be done and set to work developing instructions for the 2nd Cavalry, instructions that would not reach Cougar Squadron until the next morning.

WAITING FOR BATTLE

While we waited in the desert, I worried. All I could think of was another U.S. Army commander, Gen. "Fighting Joe" Hooker. He had made a similar decision to pull up and wait on the first day of May in 1863.

Hooker halted his army, nearly 134,000 troops, including eleven thousand cavalry and 413 guns, poised to slam into the Confederate rear and potentially end the Civil War. Against this force, General Robert E. Lee had less than half the number of troops at Hooker's disposal; sixty thousand troops, including three thousand cavalry and fewer than 220 guns. The situation was so bleak for Lee and his Army of Northern Virginia that Sir Winston Churchill would write of it: "Nothing more hopeless on the map than his position on the night of 30 April can be imagined, and it is this which raises the event which followed from a military to an historic level."[8]

When General Hooker decided to halt his advance on 1 May and fall back on a defensive line constructed in front of Chancellorsville, Virginia, Hooker's voluntary surrender of the initiative convinced Lee to attack precisely where Hooker least expected it. As is well known, 25,000 Confederate troops eventually took the Union army's defensive positions from behind while an entire Union corps contented itself with an irrelevant attack on Lee's front. General Hooker's vastly superior Union force was defeated and retreated, having accomplished nothing of strategic value for the United States.[9]

Based on what we had seen to this point in the war, it seemed unlikely the Iraqis would act as Lee had at Chancellorsville. There was always the remote possibility that some desperate Iraqi commander might deliver a punishing blow while we sat doing nothing. But as I thought about our situation on 25 February, an Iraqi retreat during the night seemed much more likely.

For the first time in the campaign, I began to lose faith in the chain of command from the 2nd Cavalry to Washington, D.C. I wondered whether, if the Iraqi army retreated fast enough, the generals would not simply hold back the corps' 100,000 men, 1,000 tanks, and 1,100 armored fighting vehicles and let the Iraqis do it.

Sometime between midnight and 0200 hours in the morning of the 26th, word came from Lieutenant Colonel Larson that he was returning from his meeting with Colonel Holder and the other ground squadron commanders with a change in orders. The warning of Larson's return gave me time to summon the troop, company, and battery commanders to a quick meeting inside the makeshift command post that had been established with Staff Sergeant Burns' Bradley, the air liaison officer's M113A3, and my tank.

By the time Lieutenant Colonel Larson walked into the command post, Cougar Squadron's troop, company, and battery commanders were assembled and ready for whatever new orders would be issued. Everyone who walked in looked tired. In some cases, it was obvious that the captains had not slept more than a few hours since we crossed into Iraq. The captains' olive-drab, fire-retardant NOMEX uniforms were soaked with the black, greasy residue of the oily rain that had fallen, off and on, for several hours. I looked at the troop commanders; they looked at me. No one spoke a word.

Lieutenant Colonel Larson strode into the squadron's forward command post confidently, almost excitedly. He was quick to break the news. We would now go into reserve, Larson said. "We've done our job. It's now the mission of the divisions to pass through and take on the Republican Guards."

Although we did not know it, Franks was actually no longer preparing to move the 2nd Cavalry into reserve, but those had been the last orders Larson received from Holder.

Larson also added that 6-41 Artillery, the direct-support artillery battalion that had followed Cougar Squadron to this point on its march across southern Iraq, was preparing to move to the 1st Infantry Division (Mechanized) immediately. This was especially depressing. When you lose your supporting artillery to another unit, it is because you are no longer the main attack.

Larson explained that engineers would come with digging equipment to dig defensive positions for our tanks and Bradleys. With that numbing prospect, Lieutenant Colonel Larson ended the meeting and walked out of the command post.

For the troop commanders and me the disheartening news that the 2nd Cavalry would now move into a hasty defense without having fought a significant battle was too terrible to contemplate. Joe Sartiano stared at me for a second, then turned and left in silence. Dejected, H. R. McMaster got up and walked out in a controlled fit of anger. As usual, Tom Sprowls kept his own counsel and quietly departed with the rest of the commanders. They were all tired, and the news did not fill them with new energy.

After a quick breath of fresh night air, I walked back into the command post. Hillen was on one side of the post, while Sgt. T. K. Wightman took inventory of our radios. Unknown to me, T. K. had already changed out several radios, but the speed with which he worked made the matter transparent to me. Thanks to Wightman's superb work, our communications system, both within the squadron as well as with Dragoon Base, had performed without a hitch.

I decided to sit down on the ramp of the Bradley across from Hillen. I was tired, but really more demoralized than tired. My despair was so intense that I nearly broke down. But I didn't; I could not afford it. Most probably VII Corps would eventually fight the Iraqis, but it would do so as though it was

1944, we were in Sherman tanks and half-tracks, and the enemy was German, not Arab.

For a split second, we both stared at the photograph of Rommel that Hillen had attached to the outside of the turret wall separating the gunner and driver from the compartment where normally scouts or infantrymen ride. Hillen then looked across at me and saw that I was transfixed by the photo of the old field marshal staring down at me.

Hillen asked me what I thought Rommel would have done. I let out a long, deep breath before saying anything. I had to be truthful. Hillen knew me well enough to sense any lack of absolute frankness in my voice.

"John, you can be Goddamn sure there would have been no halt from the time we crossed into Iraq," I grumbled. "Hell, we probably would be in Basra by now, because he would long ago have shown up at the front with us to see for himself. That is something our generals just don't do."

Hillen was no longer surprised by events. Neither was T. K. Wightman. Neither of them bothered to react to my statement. Hillen reached into his pack for his *Sports Illustrated* swimsuit calendar. It was time to make another notation.

He wrote in the block marked 25 February: "We moved about 70 km in the morning. A few hundred more enemy prisoners of war and the enemy recon destroyed/captured."

Subsequently, General Franks insisted that he was surprised to see that Cougar Squadron and the 2nd Cavalry had not moved farther forward during the night of 25–26 February in order to maintain pressure on the enemy.

He would say, "I had left the tactics up to Don Holder. Don had used the time for local actions to block the Iraqis and to get orders out appropriate to the change of mission I had given him. Given the terrible weather that had cancelled the aviation strikes, and the change in mission, I supported his choice."[10]

Though Franks' postwar claim hardly seems plausible, if it's true, Holder's choice was to dig in Cougar Squadron along with the rest of the 2nd Cavalry and not move until the next morning.

Why? One reason was that no one in command at the regimental or corps levels bothered to go forward and see the real situation on the ground. There was no one in the VII Corps chain of command above us like Col. John Sylvester, commander of the 2nd Armored Division's Tiger Brigade, who was to lead his brigade to Kuwait City from the turret of his tank.

Figure 8. Lieutenant General Franks' Plan for 2nd Cavalry on 25 February

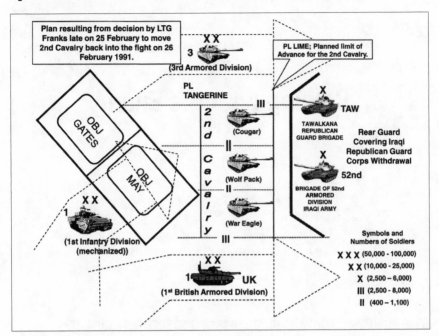

For God's sake, Cougar Squadron hadn't seen anything yet that could be honestly characterized as an effective enemy. Handfuls of Iraqi troop carriers (the MTLBs) and half-assed infantry wandered into us and surrendered or were quickly sent to paradise, but nothing worthy of the designation "enemy" had really been encountered.

These depressing circumstances were not to last, however. Divine providence was taking a hand. The ninety-degree turn, the final phase of Schwarzkopf's "Hail Mary" maneuver, the plan briefed by General Franks to Secretary Cheney, General Powell, and General Schwarzkopf in early February, would now belatedly be executed.

But would Iraq's Republican Guard Corps wait for VII Corps to make its attack? Its units had been withdrawing forces for almost a whole day. How much of the Republican Guard would be left to fight by the time we attacked?

SIX

Closing with the Enemy

To move swiftly, strike vigorously and secure all the fruits of
victory is the secret of successful war.
MAJ. GEN. THOMAS JONATHAN "STONEWALL" JACKSON, JANUARY 1863

0530 HOURS, 26 FEBRUARY, CLOSE TO IRAQ'S BORDER WITH KUWAIT

On the cool, damp morning of 26 February, Cougar Squadron awoke to orders
that moved the 2nd Cavalry out of reserve and back into the fight.

When the word came to us, you could practically hear the adrenalin surge
through the men.

General Schwarzkopf's phone call to General Franks reversed the
decision to move the 2nd Cavalry into reserve. Instead, the 2nd Cavalry was
directed to prepare for further combat operations. In response to new orders
from VII Corps, Dragoon Base issued a new fragmentary order (FRAGO)
around 0522 hours to the regiment: "2nd ACR [Armored Cavalry Regiment]
attacks East to fix Tawalkana Mechanized Division; on order, 1 ID [1st
Infantry Division] passes through 2nd ACR to continue the attack East and
fix the 17th Armored Division. Second ACR reverts to corps reserve and
consolidates in Assembly Area Spur. New graphics [referring to maps and
diagrams indicating assignments] in effect, acknowledge, over!"

From its position almost ninety miles inside Iraq, the 2nd Cavalry would
now advance eastward to fix the main body of the Tawalkana Division, but
the idea was to do it while avoiding decisive engagement. Simultaneously,
the regiment would prepare to pass the 1st Infantry Division (Mechanized)

through its lines while the 3rd Armored Division swung into action along its northern flank, where Cougar Squadron's zone of attack was.

When it was my turn to respond to Dragoon Base for Cougar Squadron on the radio, I answered: "This is Cougar 3, acknowledged, over."

That was it! We were back in the war. My heart began to pump a hell of a lot faster. I was elated. Finally, I thought, we would get a chance to fight the vaunted Iraqi Republican Guard.

The black, greasy rain no longer mattered. The cold dampness went unnoticed. The air of misery and gloom that had hung over us all night vanished in seconds. But where would we find the enemy? What did the orders really mean?

The answers were not straightforward. But to me, artillery and air strikes alone would not suffice. "Fixing the enemy" in war always entails engaging the enemy with direct fire in sufficient strength to prevent the enemy from either maneuvering to advantage or escaping. Somehow, Cougar Squadron would advance directly into what was presumably the Republican Guard Corps' security zone, establish a blocking position, and, at some point, allowing the follow-on divisions to drive through. This operation entails marking lanes that guide the soldiers and equipment of the follow-on units through us.

Rhett Scott had briefed me more than eighteen hours earlier that the Republican Guard's security zone was probably somewhere between the 60 and 65 Easting grid lines, with the main defense some five to eight kilometers beyond. We both wondered the day before why anyone in command would halt so close to the enemy and do nothing for twenty-four hours.

When the order came in to advance into the security zone to an unknown point on the ground and stop, however, Scott questioned the sanity of halting Cougar Squadron in an area that was probably covered with minefields and preplanned targets for artillery.

Scott was right. Security zone forces consisting of observation posts, forward reconnaissance screens, or delaying positions provide warning to the main body of the defending forces behind them that they are about to be attacked. A one-word radio message from a forward observation post would be enough to sound the alarm across a defending force and bring holy hell down on our heads. The whole idea of halting under such circumstances was nuts. How do you halt a freight train halfway down a mountain? But I was relieved that Cougar Squadron would get back into the war; I was too ecstatic to voice any objection.

To this point, we had led the VII Corps nearly a hundred miles and had yet to see the kind of fight for which we had trained and prepared. The long, pointless halts imposed on us from above on the 23rd, the 24th, and again on the 25th had been more than irritants. They had downright demoralized us. In the middle of a war, moving is always better than sitting still, even if the directive seems strange.

When Hillen issued the warning order to the squadron over the radio, however, Cougar's junior officers began wondering whether I had lost my mind.

Until now, Lt. Chuck Correll in Fox Troop, one of my former students at West Point, told me the squadron's lieutenants were confident that I would never ask them to do stupid or pointless things. But now the lieutenants began to seriously wonder about me. Cougar Squadron's junior officers were smart, and they had good reason to question my judgment on this occasion. The notion of stopping short of the enemy's defensive positions, but very much in range, was more than just ridiculous. It was downright dangerous, and the junior officers knew it. However, the "junior partners" in this venture also knew that the premises behind many orders are set by higher headquarters and are handed down over the commonsense objections of their immediate superiors.

When orders are received that seem irrational but must still be executed, it is important not to blame the stupidity on higher headquarters, in a knee-jerk reaction. It's better to make the best of a potentially bad situation. Inject some sanity and tactical common sense and make the outcome as beneficial as possible. In short: find a way to win. That is exactly what I set out to do.

While I responded to further instructions from Dragoon Base, Hillen worked up a warning order for immediate transmission to the Cougar Squadron battle group, and Specialist Wightman, with the help of the crews from my tank and Cougar Forward, hastily dismantled the command post and readied the vehicles for action. It was neither time consuming nor difficult. In wars of movement, the staffs of armored forces seldom bother to camouflage their command posts with elaborate nets and poles. We were ready to move in minutes.

When at 0530 I informed Lieutenant Colonel Larson of the new orders, he said he had heard the traffic on the regimental command net. Hillen later said Larson seemed very worried. Anyway, I told Lieutenant Colonel Larson that we would have to move in the box formation, to give the lead troops five thousand meters of space to maneuver and fire, and that I would work up the squadron's scheme of maneuver.

"OK, Doug," is all Colonel Larson said. He did ask whether the squadron had been refueled, and then, hearing that it had been, he walked back to his tank.

Hillen thought the encounter was amusing and said sarcastically, "Surprise, surprise, the ball is entirely in your court."

I certainly hoped so. Decisions would have to come fast and furious.

My first task, though, was to get out of the screwy defensive position in which we had been sitting for an entire day. We were deployed in a half-circle, with Ghost on the far right, Fox on Ghost's left, and Eagle on the far left, with the tank ("Hawk") company and our own artillery battery ("Caisson") deployed near the center. I laid out my map on the front slope of my tank where Hillen and I could see it in the pale daylight.

A sandy wind came up and lifted the map, but the blast of cold air was actually refreshing to me after a long, frustrating night in the rain. I had no doubt that the sixty-degree weather would fall like a blessing from heaven on our soldiers, in their heavy and hot chemical suits. I could not imagine how terrible fighting in 120-degree heat would be in Iraq's blazing summer. Weather was not my greatest concern. Our new zone of attack *was* a concern, though.

The 2nd Cavalry's new graphics gave the squadron a ten-kilometer front, or half the frontage we had on the way up from Saudi Arabia. McMaster, Sprowls, Sartiano, and I had discussed the box formation in the weeks of training during January before moving west toward the neutral zone.

None of us liked the box. Configuring the squadron in a box, without any forward reconnaissance element, meant we would unavoidably crash like a Napoleonic column into the enemy. It also prevented the majority of Cougar Squadron's tanks and armored fighting vehicles from being employed quickly when we did make contact.

"John," I said, "We're screwed. We cannot deploy into the diamond inside a ten-kilometer zone."

"You mean, the damn box?" John asked.

"Yes," I said. "Unfortunately, the least desirable formation for a maneuver battle, but the only one that will give each of the two lead troops five-thousand-meter fronts. Otherwise, our soldiers will be so hemmed in, they may accidentally shoot themselves. But that's not all," I replied, pausing to take off my helmet and goggles to scratch the matted hair on my head. "We also won't have a reconnaissance element like Linzy's scout platoon out in front of us. Regiment is forcing us to move in mass. Instead of making contact with the smallest element first, we've got no early warning at all."

The only good thing that could be said about the current situation was that the width of the ten-kilometer attack zone still gave each of the lead troops five thousand meters to maneuver in the flat, open desert. Based on our training in January, I was afraid that anything less than five thousand meters per troop would produce fratricide. When I learned after the war that other divisions had crammed attacking brigades into ten-kilometer attack zones, I was not surprised by the incidents of fratricide that occurred there.

"You know," said Hillen, "Wolf Pack will shove three troops abreast into that narrow zone."

"Yeah, I know. Well, that's stupid," I answered, "They will end up shooting themselves. Two troops in the lead are enough."

John agreed, smiled, and said: "It's time for Eagle Troop, right?"

"Hell, yes," I answered, "Eagle Troop has been in the bull pen long enough."

Though I did not learn about it until much later, McMaster had had a very tough night. When engineers showed up in his troop area to dig in his M1A1 Abrams tanks and Bradley fighting vehicles with their dozer blades,

Figure 9. Cougar Squadron in the Box on 26 February

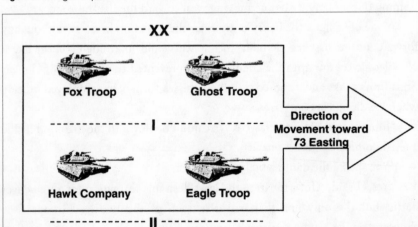

so they would sit half-buried in the ground like pillboxes—the antithesis of mobility—he was depressed beyond words and rolled over onto his back and practically died from disgust inside the Eagle Troop TOC.

What I did know, though, was that the prospect of real action would reinvigorate McMaster. Eagle Troop was ready to lead Cougar Squadron in the attack. I had promised McMaster his shot. Now it was time for me to keep that promise.

"John, my only concern at this point is whether or not there is anybody on the Iraqi side watching us." Hillen agreed, saying, "We have to assume someone over there is paying attention."

"Right," I said. "What about moving Ghost over, then, swinging Eagle around up behind and next to Ghost, after which Fox Troop and the tank company can move in behind Ghost and Eagle troops?"

The positioning of Eagle Troop and the tank company was not accidental. I had promised McMaster in January that if and when the time came, I would bring forward the tank company and ensure that the devastating fire of Hawk Company's fourteen tanks would combine with that of Eagle Troop's nine tanks and mine to break any serious enemy resistance.

Knowing that Eagle Troop's scout platoons were composed of highly intelligent and capable men, I had great confidence they would have no trouble coordinating this maneuver with the tank company, if necessary. We had practiced this maneuver in January, and I knew we could execute it.

"Having Eagle on the right flank with 3rd Squadron will make my life much easier," quipped John. "I know I can count on Eagle's scouts to keep me up to date on where they are and where 3rd Squadron is. But shouldn't we use Fox alongside Eagle?"

"Not this time," I told Hillen. "Fox is just too far out of position. Moving Fox is a dead giveaway to the enemy, if any enemy is watching. Fox will have to cover the open flank behind Ghost."

What I did not say was that I also thought Fox Troop needed a break from taking the lead. Fox Troop had done a great job, but it needed a rest.

Hillen seemed a bit puzzled. His wrinkled brow was a familiar indicator of discontent, and I fully anticipated a longer discussion on this matter. From his time in Eagle Troop as a scout platoon leader, Hillen knew the scouts in Ghost and was concerned about their readiness to take the lead. I pre-empted him.

"John, I know what you are thinking, but Sartiano's got the mission. I am confident he can execute it." My expression of confidence in Sartiano was probably not enough for Hillen, but he saw no reason to belabor the point.

"Roger," was all he said in response. I then asked John to work up the new boundaries and to let Dragoon Base know what we were going to do, while I mounted up and issued the order to Cougar Squadron. John nodded his head, adjusting his goggles to keep the sand out of his face.

"John, let's mount up and get the f—ck out of here. I am f—cking sick of this f—cking place."

Hillen smiled and said, "Sir, do you think you can find a way to get f—ck into that sentence just one more time?"

"If I try f—cking hard enough? F—ck yes!"

We both laughed. We were nervous, but we knew the time for deliberation was over. It was the time for action, not for second thoughts.

It was 0600, and we had put in twenty-four very boring hours. Both of us were relieved to be on the move again. Hillen went off to plot and issue the six-digit grid coordinates for our troops' projected locations to Cougar Squadron's troop executive officers. While he plotted contact points on the empty desert floor of southern Iraq, I climbed up the front slope of my tank and got into the turret. As usual, Rod Abercrombie was already up in the loader's hatch, waiting for me. As soon as I slipped my CVC helmet over my head, Abercrombie spoke.

"Is this it?" he said referring to the probability of a battle. I decided to be cautious in my response.

"We will see, Rod. I think it is. I mean, I think this is the fight we've been looking for. Why? What makes you think we're headed into action?"

"Sir, you are f—king happy as hell!"

"Does it show that much?" I asked.

"Hell yes, it shows!" said Abercrombie.

Like any good professional soldier, Abercrombie's feelings were mixed. On the one hand, he wanted to get into the fight. On the other, he knew what that meant. Even under the best of circumstances, your luck can run out: the enemy can get lucky and kill you.

"Well, Rod," I mused, "I wouldn't worry too much. I think these Arabs are a hell of lot more worried about the future than we are."

Abercrombie just let out a long sigh that finished with a quiet but conclusive: "Shit."

Without uttering another word, he dropped down inside the turret and checked the ammunition storage area, reemerging to recheck his M240 7.62-mm medium machine gun on a sliding skate mount. While he was busy with the machine gun, I spoke to Ward, our tank driver.

"Ward, crank this monster up and get moving."

"You got it, Major." Ward instantly hit the start button, while I spoke to Sergeant Jones.

"Dewey, Eagle will probably battle-carry sabot, so let's battle-carry HEAT." I meant high-explosive antitank ammunition, versus the uranium-depleted warheads preferred in tank battles. Based on our actions to this point, I anticipated as much mechanized infantry as armor in the coming battle.

"Roger, sir."

While the gunner, Sgt. Dewey Jones, talked to Abercrombie about pulling out a heat round, I pulled my "ski" goggles down over my eyes around my helmet and told Ward to move out, with a half-right turn. The tank jolted forward with the characteristic whine of the turbine engine.

While I listened to the traffic over the regimental command net via my helmet's "spaghetti cord," connected to the vehicle's intercom system, Rod directed Ward to a position from which I could see Eagle and Hawk pass by on their way forward.

As the tank moved, I searched anxiously through the sandstorm for a glimpse of Eagle troop and listened for any report of enemy activity that might come in over the command net. I would not relax until we had completed our move into the box without enemy interference. It's one thing to come up with schemes on paper but another to translate them into reality with men, machines, and the weather interacting, before making contact with the enemy.

Great, thick, swirling clouds of sand and dust now spiraled up into the skies above while the last lingering bits of brilliant sunlight fled, reducing the flat desert to monotones of shimmering gray and tan. With visibility in the storm varying from a hundred to two hundred meters, it seemed unlikely to me that the Iraqis in their defensive positions would detect our move to reposition; but I continued to monitor the net closely for any evidence of enemy contact.

Looming up like mythological beasts out of the gathering sandstorm, first Eagle Troop and then Hawk Company moved forward. Eagle's tanks swarmed past me like phantoms, veering off through the sandstorm to their respective positions in the squadron box formation.

As Eagle's flank scouts drove past, a few saw me and waved. More than a few shouted to me as they passed. I could not see under their goggles and face masks, but it was obvious these soldiers were looking for a fight.

The shark was ready to eat, I thought.

I began breathing an immediate sigh of relief. Sitting still is a bad thing for an armored force; sitting still robs the force of its mobility, its sense of purpose, and the inherent additional security that comes from maneuvering aggressively. An armored force in motion is both harder to target and much harder to hit, yet it is better placed to position itself at speed to destroy the enemy. The Air Force has a saying: "Speed is life." The principle is no less true when applied to armor.

In what seemed like an hour but was probably no more than ten or fifteen minutes, the squadron's troops began moving into position. All over the squadron, decisions were being made to expedite movement into position for what everyone figured would be a fight. As soon as Lt. Jeffrey DeStefano, 4th Platoon leader in Eagle Troop, got the word that the squadron battle group was preparing for a new mission, he canceled an earlier order to evacuate his platoon sergeant's tank to the squadron resupply trains.

DeStefano, a five-foot eleven-inch West Point graduate of slender build, was quiet, contemplative, and unflappable. Most important, DeStefano was an armor officer of high competence. He was intimately acquainted with his tanks and the men on them. Details of any kind, from tank maintenance to the birthdays of his soldiers, never escaped his attention. He strongly encouraged initiative in his sergeants and soldiers, all of whom respected and trusted him without question.

When Eagle 41, Staff Sgt. Henry Foy's tank, had proved to be losing four quarts of oil for every thousand meters of travel, DeStefano had had to decide whether to send the tank to the rear for repairs or keep it in the fight. With or without an oil leak, Foy was determined to stay in the fight. Now, when DeStefano signaled the change in mission, Staff Sergeant Foy grabbed forty quarts of oil to get him through. Foy knew instinctively that every tank would be needed now.

While the troop, company, and battery commanders readied their units for action, I received word from Dragoon Base to move forward. I directed the battle group to advance into the developing sandstorm, or *shamal,* as the Arabs call it, until we reached the 50 Easting. Most of the time, the soldiers moving their vehicles into the box formation could see only the first two vehicles behind them, and it was only through the heavy use of radio that we could keep all the troop elements together.[1] In fact, other than occasional hot spots in the thermal sights, after 0730 hours none of us could see much farther than 100 or 150 meters, and the weather continued to deteriorate.

On the arrival of Ghost and Eagle scouts along the 50 Easting, at 0741 hours, I called Scott for an intelligence update.

Rhett Scott had surprisingly little that was new to tell us, but he did confirm one more time the probable location of the enemy's security zone between the 65 and 70 Easting grid lines.

Meanwhile, the lead scouts in Ghost and Eagle troops continued to reconnoiter by fire, sending 25-mm high-explosive incendiary rounds into anything that looked suspicious. There was no return fire. Ghost Troop reported finding some abandoned Iraqi equipment, while Eagle Troop assumed its new obligation to quickly establish contact on its right flank with 3rd Squadron.

Our howitzer battery of eight self-propelled 155-mm guns had moved a short distance and was once again ready to shoot. Thanks to Captain Rudd's good work, the combat trains were lined up in column behind us, and Master Sergeant Vera kept our refueling assets ready to come forward at a moment's notice and quickly top off the fuel-hungry tanks if needed. By the time the electrifying order to prepare for action went out over the radio, the shark was swimming at full speed toward the enemy.

Despite the intensifying storm, Eagle and Ghost troops deployed along the 50 Easting, scanning the desert in front of them for any enemy that might be lurking behind the wall of sand blowing in their faces.

Both troops knew they would be the first to meet any enemy we encountered.

Around 0800 hours, Ghost and Eagle troops got their first taste of what turned out to be an appetizer before the main course. Three Iraqi armored personnel carriers, MTLBs, which must have become disoriented in the sandstorm, drove directly into Eagle Troop's path.

Staff Sergeant Patterson was the first to engage the vehicles, marking the target area with his 25-mm for the rest of the troop. When McMaster heard Patterson's contact report and the firing, he lost no time in coming forward with his tank and blasting one of the MTLBs with a 120-mm sabot round.

For once, however, the Iraqi soldiers reacted quickly. The remaining two MTLBs sped away, fleeing north before Eagle Troop could inflict any more damage, only to find Ghost Troop waiting in ambush for them. Most of the twenty Iraqi soldiers inside the MTLBs dismounted and seemed at first ready to surrender. But when they spotted Ghost Troop's scouts, three of the Iraqi soldiers jumped back into the vehicles, while the others fired their AK47 assault rifles wildly in the direction of the scouts. The Iraqi MTLBs had machine guns mounted on top of them, but to fire accurately the vehicles had to be stopped. This made the Iraqi MTLBs perfect targets for Garwick's Bradley gunners.

Lieutenant Keith Garwick, a Californian, led Ghost Troop's 1st Platoon scouts. Along with Lieutenant Correll in Fox Troop, Garwick was one of the few West Point graduates in Cougar Squadron whom I had known before I arrived in Bamberg. Garwick had the dubious honor of having suffered with me through West Point's rather boring core course in American government and politics. In class, he was always bright, imaginative, and energetic. After graduation, he was just as energetic, although a bit erratic at times. The 1st Platoon scouts liked Garwick and certainly appreciated his willingness to move quickly and decisively on short notice, but his scouts sometimes wondered what reality he operated in. Garwick erased any doubts on 26 February.

In what would be a series of brilliant actions throughout the day, Ghost's 4.2-inch heavy mortars were the first to open up, dropping high-explosive rounds right into the top of one of the two remaining MTLBs. Lieutenant Garwick, Ghost's 1st scout platoon leader, finished the job with a TOW antitank missile. Nothing survived.

It may have seemed like overkill at the time, but the importance of preventing the Iraqi elements from using their radios to alert their comrades in the security zone made any other course of action imprudent.

Private First Class Jason E. Kick, from Pembroke, Georgia, summed it up this way: "All I can say is better them than me. That sounds cruel, but it's true."[2]

When Garwick's scouts drove forward to inspect the damage, they noted Republican Guard markings on the Iraqi MTLBs.

The fate of the Iraqi MTLBs also serves as a reminder that every armored vehicle in a fighting force must be able to fire on the move with automatic cannon. This allows the force to break contact if it bumps into a superior force or to destroy the enemy quickly. For mortars to be effective at reaching fleeing targets, they must be able to fire immediately from their tracked vehicles, and fire accurately. Ghost Troop's mortars were damn good.

While Garwick finished off the MTLBs, Caisson, our howitzer battery, together with four guns from 6-41 Artillery, answered a call for fire from Lt. Joe Deskevich, Ghost Troop fire-support team leader.

Lieutenant Deskevich, a North Georgia Military College graduate, was a tough hombre. He had worked under the previous troop commander and like Mecca was a strong source of support for Sartiano. There was something else, too: Joe is Ukrainian. Having grown up with several Ukrainians in north Philadelphia, I can attest to the toughness, determination, and absolute integrity of this remarkable people. Joe Deskevich exemplified toughness.

At Deskevich's direction, the guns hammered some suspected enemy targets to the northeast with a "battalion 2," slang for forty-eight rounds of dual-purpose improved conventional munitions (DPICM)—little bomblets that scatter all over the target area. This time, the sixteen operational guns, eight from Caisson and eight from 6-41 Artillery, fired thirty-two rounds.

Deskevich, however, was not pleased. He estimated that 25 percent of the bomblets had not exploded and alerted the combat trains behind the advancing combat troops to the danger that the unexploded bomblets presented. As we had discovered on Objective Merrell, bomblets that do not explode on impact can disable wheeled vehicles. It turned out that the target area had been full of abandoned vehicles and equipment, but the action was an inspiration to the artillerymen, who had yet to see much indirect-fire action (that is, where they could not see the target) in a war dominated by tanks and air strikes.

Around 0830 hours, when I was confident that the squadron battle group was in its new attack formation, Ward turned our tank northeast in the direction of Eagle Troop. For a time, I felt like I was at sea. Standing in the turret during a sandstorm was like operating in the conning tower of a partially submerged submarine.

When we reached Eagle Troop's formation, we pulled in next to Lt. Mike Petschek's scouts on Eagle Troop's left flank. Petschek was a graduate of Georgetown University. Slim, blond, and good looking, about five feet nine inches, and very articulate, Mike Petschek was Eagle Troop's resident gentleman. He seldom if ever raised his voice, and he always led by personal example. His humor was a bit challenging for some of his peers to grasp, but no one, least of all his soldiers, ever questioned his competence or skill as a scout platoon leader.

With Petschek's scouts on the left flank of Eagle Troop, I would try to keep an eye on Ghost's right flank scouts—no small challenge in the worsening weather. After scanning as much of the formation as I could through my thermal sights, I asked everybody on board the tank to stop talking on the intercom long enough for me to speak externally to Cougar Squadron over the squadron command net.

I was careful to speak on the radio in the same even tone I used in training: "Battle stations, battle stations, this is Cougar 3. Eagle Troop is now the main attack. Squadron will key its movement on Eagle Troop. I will move with Eagle Troop, break."

I paused for a few seconds to let this statement sink in with the troop, company, and battery commanders. Then, I continued: "Ghost is the supporting attack. Hawk follows Eagle in support. Fox Troop follows Ghost in support. Cougar Forward will issue waypoints. Acknowledge, over."

Like the static electricity in the air that presages a thunderstorm, there was an unmistakable atmosphere of impending action that everyone listening could feel over the squadron command net.

All of the battle stations acknowledged my transmission in short order. Lieutenant Colonel Larson, who had been having trouble with his radio, broke in and asked Tony, "Cougar 32, say again all Cougar 3's instructions, over."

Tony obliged, and Lieutenant Colonel Larson signaled his approval over the radio.

On Cougar Squadron's right flank, Lt. Tim Gauthier, referred to as "Blue 1" inside Eagle troop, had the mission to maintain contact with Wolf Pack (3rd Squadron), and he now sent Staff Sergeant McReynolds, one of Gauthier's section sergeants, to make contact with Iron Troop at a predesignated coordination point in the desert. Gauthier hailed from West Hartford, Connecticut. He was also a distinguished military graduate from Arizona State University Reserve Officer Training Corps program. Gauthier looked physically tough enough to be a prizefighter. Gauthier was no shrinking violet when it came to expressing opinions. He was generally unimpressed with most of the captains and majors he met. I knew him better than the rest of the scouts and respected his opinion on everything. Gauthier was one of the first officers to whom I turned for honest appraisals of what was right and what was wrong in Cougar Squadron. His answers were not sugarcoated, and, as I found out quickly enough, they were very much on target.

At the contact point with Wolf Pack, McReynolds found a nervous scout platoon leader from Iron Troop with lots of questions and concerns about the mission. While McReynolds conferred with the lieutenant over the map to coordinate movement, the coaxially mounted M240C 7.62-mm medium machine gun in the lieutenant's Bradley accidentally discharged a burst of bullets directly over McReynolds' head.

The incident scared the hell out of McReynolds. When he drove back to personally report the incident to Gauthier, he said: "Please, sir, don't make me go back there again."[3]

Informed of McReynolds' experience on the flank with Wolf Pack, McMaster decided to fill the temporary void of information from Rhett Scott and me with an update on the radio over the Eagle Troop command net. To make sure his officers understood what was ahead, he made a point of saying, "Contact is imminent."

Hearing his troop commander's statement over the troop net, Tim Gauthier responded with, "What kind of contact, over?" Perhaps he was thinking a Steven Spielberg–type ET was nearby. Who knows?

"Enemy contact, over," answered McMaster. Gauthier shot back an immediate reply:

"Good, that's the best kind, over." Gauthier had sent the message Mc-Master wanted everyone in Eagle Troop to hear: Gauthier's men were ready and anxious to fight.

Scott broke in shortly after 0900 hours with a quick intelligence update. Scott said that what was left of the Iraqi Republican Guard's armor, the Hammurabi and Medina divisions, remained in place, with some elements moving northeast toward Basra. At the time, I was surprised that the whole Iraqi force had not exploited our inactivity during the last twenty-four hours and escaped entirely. But I had other concerns.

Visibility continued to decline as the weather grew worse and worse. At 0950 hours, P Troop, one of the aviation troops in the regiment's 4th Squadron, reported that it could not launch its aircraft due to poor visibility.

As the sandstorm enveloped our movement, I realized that we were unlikely to get much air support, but I thought that stopping was far worse than continuing to move forward into the unknown. The lack of visibility hurt the enemy, who lacked advanced electro-optical or thermal sensors, much more than it hurt us.

It was at this point that we began a series of slow, deliberate moves to a succession of lines that Dragoon Base designated "limits of advance." Between 1000 and 1200 hours, the squadron received orders to move first to the 52 Easting, then the 55 Easting, then the 57 Easting, a process over which I had no influence from the turret of my tank.[4]

Time dragged while we crawled forward. As we reached the successive limits of advance, the Ghost and Eagle executive officers had to endure my relentless calls for immediate frontline "traces," marked-up maps, showing where all of our lead combat elements were on the ground.

Mecca's slow reporting on Ghost Troop's movement made me nervous. For some reason, Mecca just seemed unable to provide information quickly enough. Dragoon Base was impatient with me, and as the saying goes, "Shit rolls downhill." What I did not know was that the delay in Ghost Troop's reporting was the result of one lieutenant's excessive enthusiasm.

Lieutenant Paul Haines led Ghost Troop's 3rd Platoon scouts. Paul was a West Point graduate and the hapless victim of a Cougar Squadron tradition. Every Easter in Bamberg, one lieutenant had been selected to don an Easter Bunny suit and provide entertainment during the Easter-egg hunt on the parade ground for the small children of the squadron's soldiers, sergeants, and officers. Haines was a very kind and gentle person and an instant hit with kids, so he was stuck with the duty in two successive years, permanently earning for himself the sobriquet of "Easter Bunny." As the day wore on, though, the 3rd Platoon scouts would watch as "Easter Bunny" kicked some serious ass.

Leaping from phase line to phase line, Haines thought he had a personal obligation to provide GPS coordinates for each Bradley in his platoon. Haines either walked or drove to where each of his scouts was temporarily halted, collected the GPS data, and sent it to Mecca. Mecca waited impatiently for Haines' frontline trace every time the squadron was halted; why it was so time-consuming was a mystery to him. Finally, he could wait no longer and told Haines to call him on the admin-log net, the radio frequency reserved for matters pertaining to administration and supply only. When Haines explained what he had been doing, Mecca made it clear that he did not need to provide a six-digit grid coordinate for each of his vehicles. Left, right, and center of mass vehicle grids would suffice. After that, the reporting process speeded up somewhat, making all of our lives a little easier. Haines' exuberance, however, would soon find a positive outlet along the 73 Easting.

While we struggled to establish accurate frontline traces for our scouts, Sergeant First Class Newman, Ghost Troop's mortar section leader, picked up some Iraqi prisoners—eleven soldiers, three lieutenants, and one captain. The Iraqis were in bad physical shape and seemed relieved that our soldiers treated them with kindness. The Iraqi troops appeared to be totally uninterested in fighting, but Newman drove his mortar carriers over the captured weapons, just to be sure. Then the Iraqi captain, who seemed to be in charge of the little group of officers, spoke up, requesting permission in perfect English to check on the well-being of his lieutenants, from whom Newman had separated him. When Newman determined that the four Iraqis presented no threat, he turned them over to the first sergeant and moved back up with the scout platoons.

While Sergeant First Class Newman was taking prisoners, General Franks was in his command post, some twenty kilometers to our rear, watching the JSTARs picture from the Air Force converted Boeing 707 airliner, full of electronics, sweeping over the corps area.

With electronic intelligence at their disposal, Franks and Holder felt confident they could exploit the radar to move Cougar and Wolf Pack squadrons to points on the ground just out of harm's way. Whenever they detected moving-target indicators, they halted us.

Unfortunately, the surveillance radar mounted in the Air Force aircraft was unable to distinguish friendly forces from Iraqi forces in the sandstorm. Worse, the radar picture exaggerated the danger and reinforced the 2nd Cavalry and corps commanders' predisposition to see Iraqi tanks and armored fighting vehicles everywhere. It was the worst of all possible outcomes for us. It was also a graphic demonstration of the dangers of trying to direct an attack in detail from a headquarters in the rear.

Staff Sergeant Lawrence, the senior scout in Eagle Troop's 1st Platoon, noted afterward, "You could feel the tension through the troop at being held back again and again. We couldn't believe they stopped us when we weren't hitting any contact."[5]

Creeping forward and stopping just short of where the moving-target indicators were on the radar screen may have seemed like a good idea inside the regimental and corps command posts, but it played hell with us.

When Dragoon Base signaled permission to move, we started running into sporadic enemy artillery fire, probably directed by the Iraqi outposts detected earlier by Ghost Troop. But thanks to the rapid destruction of the enemy outposts by our scouts, the Iraqi artillery shells tended to burst well over our heads, presumably for the purpose of driving us down into the tank turrets and slowing us down by restricting our vision, or wounding us if we remained exposed. Like the artillery fire on 24 and 25 February, however, the impacts of the artillery rounds on the desert floor did not move with us; they just pounded sand. Iraqi artillerymen could not adjust their fire fast enough to keep up with our movement toward them.

With each successive jump to a new grid line, a new "Easting," I received near-continuous requests to strike targets to my front with rocket artillery, when we could find no evidence of enemy concentrations that would warrant the use of either rocket artillery or air strikes. I saw no evidence for the intelligence reports streaming in about enemy to our front. Each time we moved through an area where the enemy had been reported, we found either nothing or abandoned enemy equipment.

All of this came at a time when I had to personally confirm the positions of the troops, using exact coordinates for the left, right, and middle of the lead troops. This was hard on me, but much harder on the troop executive officers, who, as we've seen, had to badger the scouts in Ghost and Eagle Troop for their locations roughly every five or ten minutes.

In time, I became quite annoyed with the whole affair. So I check-fired (stopped) the artillery missions I felt were counterproductive. When I refused to approve one fire mission in particular, Cpt. Jack Millar, Cougar Squadron's fire-support officer, warned me that an enemy artillery battery was in position to take us under fire. Millar was obviously under pressure from the supporting artillery brigade commander to clear the targets it had presumably received from JSTARS.

Having had so many erroneous reports based on inaccurate radar readings of moving-target indicators, I did not like the implied threat. I was convinced it was phony and told him "no" repeatedly. My refusal to approve his latest request resulted in another warning. If I prevented the artillery from attacking this mysterious enemy artillery unit to our front, he said, we could face serious trouble.

Listening to my irritating exchange with Captain Millar, McMaster suddenly broke in on Cougar Squadron's command net and offered to confirm whether there really was an enemy artillery position to our front, noting that the alleged target was less than a thousand meters to our front.

Without hesitation, I told McMaster, "Execute!"

In less than a minute McMaster confirmed that he and his scouts had gone forward to the location given by Dragoon Base and found no evidence for anything there other than sand and sheep shit, let alone an enemy artillery battery.

When I reported to Dragoon Base on the regimental command net that Eagle Troop's scouts were forward and confirmed that there was no enemy at the location, I received a punishing call from Holder, some ten to fifteen kilometers from where I was, telling me on the regimental net to "use bullets, not soldiers."

The tension in Holder's voice on the radio was so thick you could have cut it with a knife. (Sometime later, Holder turned to Major Lute, the regimental operations officer, and said: "If the enemy is getting out of Kuwait, why die for it? We don't want to bloody ourselves if we don't have to." Holder added. "I'm not going to impale this regiment for the sake of body counts or glory.")[6]

Under the circumstances, it made sense for me to simply say "Roger" and wait for permission to resume the advance. But firing artillery bomblets, many of which would not explode on contact, into an area through which our soldiers would soon have to advance was just stupid. I was acutely sensitive to the dud rate experienced with DPICM munitions near Objective Merrell and would not approve any fire missions unless I was confident they would confer some real advantage on our advance. Moreover, why, I wondered, would Holder urge us to rely on artillery fire in a sandstorm, when most of the time we couldn't see farther than a couple of hundred meters? How were we supposed to target the enemy in this soup?

Meanwhile, Iraqi artillery rounds continued to burst overhead and around us without effect, only a few rounds exploding in the sand. None of us had ever been on the receiving end of so much artillery, but I found the experience of being under artillery fire in a tank moving at twenty or twenty-five miles per hour singularly unimpressive. One round hit perhaps one hundred meters to our front, white smoke rising in the air after the explosion. But the airbursts were so high as to be completely ineffective. As before on the 24th and 25th, Iraqi artillery was registered fire, aimed at preset map coordinates, and had little effect.

A couple of days later, I discovered that an artillery round had detonated near the left front slope of a Hawk Company tank and that its eighteen-year-old driver, Private Byrd, in an open top hatch, had been injured by the blast. One of his legs had been fractured by the concussion. Otherwise, we sustained no losses and no injuries. To its lasting credit, Hawk Company did not miss a beat. The advance continued without interruption. Surely, the M1A1 Abrams tank was an astonishing moving fortress. Nothing the enemy threw at it seemed to have any effect. But it was really the character and the courage of our soldiers that made the tank seem invincible.

As the white smoke from nearby explosions drifted off to our left, some of the scouts in Eagle Troop looked toward me to see if I had put on a protective mask. I did not mask. I was up in the hatch, my upper torso partially exposed, so it was easy for the soldiers to see that I was not wearing a protective mask. I saw no evidence for chemical munitions, and 1st. Lt. Swen Erickson, the squadron chemical officer, who was monitoring the air as best he could in the sandstorm, reported he had not detected anything.

Rodney Abercrombie was less certain. He looked nervously in my direction for some signal that the smoke was just smoke and not some Iraqi chemical cloud. When an Eagle tank to our right drove through some dissipating smoke and no one masked, Abercrombie finally relaxed.

With the rapid loss of their forward outposts, the Iraqis could not shift their artillery rounds to keep up with us, nor could they adjust the rounds' bursting height. We simply drove around or through the artillery fire at twenty-five miles per hour. I should say the fire had "almost" no effect, though, because our wheeled vehicles were less successful in following us.

The desert floor was strewn with antipersonnel mines, and several trucks were disabled when their tires were blown to pieces. Our trucks and Humvees lost tires, radiators, and, occasionally, engines to these mines, which were quite lethal if you were not mounted in a tracked, armored fighting vehicle. Fortunately, with the exception of a battery commander in our supporting artillery battalion, who was mounted in a Humvee, there were few serious injuries to our soldiers. However, when 50 percent of even a heavy, mechanized unit is mounted in vulnerable, wheeled trucks, the risk that men could be killed or wounded is high.

In one battlefield incident, an artillery battery commander from 6-41 Artillery had the misfortune to drive over an antipersonnel mine in a Humvee. The mine pierced the sheet metal beneath the compartment where he was riding, and a piece of shrapnel struck him in the groin. He was immediately evacuated. When he returned to us a couple of months later and was asked whether the injury to his groin had done any lasting damage to his private parts, he replied, "Don't think so, but I can't wait to get home and perform a function check!"

As the artillery fell intermittently among the advancing armor, Ghost Troop reported finding and destroying Iraqi outposts in the billowing sand. That definitely marked the beginning of the so-called security zone, but otherwise, an eerie quiet settled over Cougar Squadron's command net as we waited for permission from Dragoon Base to continue our movement forward.

Sartiano moved back and forth in his tank between Ghost Troop's scout platoons in an effort to maintain coherence in the poor visibility. Simultaneously, Sergeant Hunnicut, Mecca's gunner, kept telling Mecca what he could see through the thermal sights, helping Mecca to keep track of where the scout platoons were.

On the 57 Easting, I was able to hear Dragoon Base again. FM communications are notoriously bad in complex terrain, but for some reason—perhaps it was the weather, or the growing distance between our position on the regiment's northern flank and the regimental command post—I could not always hear the regimental command net.

This time, however, I did hear the signal from Dragoon to advance to the 60 Easting. I came up on the Cougar Squadron command net and said, "Battle stations, battle stations, this is Cougar 3, move to the 60 Easting, out."

When we finally resumed movement, I listened for more traffic on the regimental command net. Holder's attitude remained a mystery that I could not solve. After my last rebuff, I certainly was not interested in saying much on the regimental command net—just then. But I wanted to glean from the information on the radio what the larger picture looked like.

At roughly 1400 hours, Scott passed a report to me from Dragoon Base of eighty moving target indicators, suggesting the presence of enemy vehicles, presumably T72 tanks, BMPs, and other armored fighting vehicles, near grid reference point PU 6405.

As I looked at my map, I realized that this point was only two and a half miles to our front! My heart beat faster as I strained over the next fifteen minutes to hear more information that would provide me with a glimpse into thinking at high levels. Finally, I picked up a transmission from the Wolf Pack commander to Colonel Holder:

"Dragoon 6, Wolf Pack 6, over."

"Dragoon 6, over," answered Holder.

"Dragoon 6, we are taking artillery fire. Request permission to fall back, over."

Now, I waited for what I was sure would be a blast of white-hot flame through the radio to Wolf Pack 6. There are good reasons for not stopping. Not only is armor designed to resist such fire, but hesitation itself is a potentially fatal mistake during an attack. Timidity not only puts the mission at risk but affects morale and not infrequently results in higher casualties.

In the instructions to his officers during World War II, Patton wrote, "In battle, small forces—platoons, companies, even battalions—can do one of three things, go forward, halt or run. If they halt or run, they will be an even easier target. Therefore, they must go forward. When caught under fire, particularly of artillery, advance out of it; never retreat from it. Artillery very seldom shortens its range."[7]

Patton's words echoed in my mind. Speed, resolve, and sheer momentum are the attacking armored force's strong suits. In the back of my mind, I also worried that the sharp cracking sounds of our tank tracks might alert the Iraqis to our approach, but I was comforted by the thought that the deepening sandstorm made that unlikely.

When I heard "Wolf Pack 6, you have permission to fall back" over the command net, I was stunned. It made me question my own judgment.

Moving in our tanks and Bradleys, we hardly noticed the artillery rounds landing near us. Had it not been for the splashes of sand that added smoke and debris to the thickening sandstorm, most of the detonations would have gone undetected. But maybe I was underestimating the danger.

Burns and Abercrombie had warned me more than once on the 24th and the 25th that I was so preoccupied with the battle I frequently missed the danger around me. Maybe they were right. So I called Ghost 6 and Eagle 6 and asked the troop commanders on my right and left for their opinions.

"Wolf Pack reports artillery fire on their location and is falling back. What is your assessment, over?"

Both McMaster (Eagle Troop) and Sartiano (Ghost Troop) confirmed to me that the artillery fire was indeed ineffective. At worst, it was a minor nuisance that caused us to maneuver around the places where the registered artillery fire continued to strike.

My response was simple and direct: "Roger, continue to advance, out."

From the commander's hatch on top of my tank turret, I could see in every direction soldiers in Abrams tanks and Bradley fighting vehicles driving forward through blowing sand and periodic artillery fire. Every pair of eyes was riveted on the storm to the front. Tank guns scanned to the left and to the right, searching for the elusive Iraqi enemy.

My God, I thought, these men are professional combat soldiers of the highest caliber. There is not enough money in all the banks of the United States to pay these soldiers what they are worth. What an honor to be with them on this day, I thought. It was hard not to feel strong emotion as I expressed the hope in my mind that my own sons would grow up to become men like these soldiers. It was both humbling and inspiring to be surrounded by so much courage and competence.

Were the soldiers at the sharp end of the spear afraid? Of course they were. So was I.

All sane men fear battle, but months of discipline and training had suppressed any trepidation or doubt. Every soldier, sergeant, lieutenant, and captain was focused on the unseen enemy. The soldiers could see that their officers were out in front. There were no backseat drivers in this outfit.

If our senior leaders could witness the moral and physical courage of the soldiers they had the honor and the privilege to command, I thought, there would be no halts, no hesitation, and no apprehension. But remote from the action in their electronic command posts behind the advancing troops, too distant to have a true sense of the fight, the senior leaders seemed more concerned with avoiding defeat than with winning a battle.

As these thoughts and emotions washed over me, I resolved to minimize the possibility that we would be stopped on our way forward. I spoke to Tony Ierardi on the Cougar Squadron command net so that everyone in the battle group would understand precisely what I was thinking and what I wanted to achieve.

"Cougar 32, Cougar 3, over."

"Cougar 32, over."

"Cougar 32," I said very slowly and deliberately, "be careful what you report to Dragoon. Be accurate, but don't give Dragoon Base an excuse to stop us, over."

Ierardi wasted no time in responding.

"Cougar 3, this is Cougar 32, roger, over."

"This is Cougar 3, thank you, out."

I relaxed. Tony Ierardi knew precisely what I meant. I could depend on him to handle the delicate task of reporting to Dragoon Base. Ierardi had already done a great job of reporting our movements and keeping us in touch with the regimental command post and headquarters all afternoon, but his excellent reporting could easily be confused with the Wolf Pack reports about the enemy situation, which my instincts told me were exaggerated. So Ierardi understood me well enough to know exactly what to do.

Now that the shark that we had worked so hard to build had been launched, I was determined that nothing would stop it.

By 1300 hours, however, General Franks' order that the 2nd Cavalry was to halt along the 60 Easting, pass the 1st Infantry Division through, and become the corps reserve seemed to make the matter academic.[8] We were halted again without having made serious contact with the enemy.

Again, my instincts told me that we were finally closing with the enemy we had come so far to fight. If we advanced again, I was confident we would find the enemy and destroy him, too fast for the regimental or corps commanders to stop us from doing it. Having made the point over the Cougar Squadron command net so that everyone in the battle group could hear it, I thought that if we resumed the attack to the east there would be no question in the soldiers' minds about what I intended. No more nonsense. I was tired of regimental and corps headquarters overreacting to reports, imagining conditions on the battlefield that did not exist.

Apparently, I was not alone in my frustration with the slow pace of our painful "movement to avoid contact."

At 1520 hours, the mission changed again. Suddenly 2nd Cavalry headquarters reversed its earlier directive to establish a hasty defense along the 60 and gave us permission to advance to the 67 Easting. For a change, the distance to the new limit of advance was a seven-kilometer stretch of desert. Robinette relayed Franks' decision over the 2nd Cavalry command net.

Robinette was always Holder's primary link to General Franks whenever Holder could not talk directly to Franks himself.

Throughout the morning and the afternoon of the 26th this link became extremely important as the squadrons of the 2nd Cavalry moved forward, with the mission of finding and fixing the Republican Guards.[9] Finding was easy, but fixing required decisive engagement to prevent whatever remained of the Republican Guards from fleeing.

So when Franks told Robinette that the 2nd Cavalry was to "go to 70 Easting, but don't become decisively engaged," even Robinette, though always optimistic, could not ignore the element of unreality in General Franks' directive. When Robinette passed the instructions to Holder on the 2nd Cavalry command net, he emphasized Franks' point that the 2nd Cavalry was to enter the security zone but not become decisively engaged, adding, "I do not know how to do that, but that is what he said, over."

It was like poking your opponent in the nose and then waiting for him to counterpunch.

Not long after Robinette passed the message, far to the rear in Riyadh, Saudi Arabia, General Schwarzkopf told his executive assistant, Col. B. B. Bell (later a four-star general), to get General Franks on the line.

Schwarzkopf knew from intelligence intercepts that an order to withdraw from Kuwait had been issued to Iraq's forces still south of the Euphrates. If VII Corps did not get moving soon, there was the danger that a cease-fire would be called before the Republican Guard Corps was even attacked, let alone destroyed.

Colonel Stan Cherrie, the VII Corps G-3, was in the VII Corps TAC when a call came through from CENTOM headquarters. Franks' corps command post was really nothing more than two armored personnel carriers filled with communications gear. Colonel Bell was on the line. Schwarzkopf wanted to talk to Franks, but Franks was not there. He was off talking to Maj. Gen. G "Butch" Funk, the 3rd Armored Division commander.

When Schwarzkopf heard this, he lost patience. He grabbed the phone and told Cherrie, "I want to keep pushing. We got a full-court press on. I want the Bobby Knight press. You know who Bobby Knight is? Keep moving!"[10]

Having made his point (Knight, of course, was a famously volatile college basketball coach, since retired), Schwarzkopf hung up the phone abruptly without revealing his real desire: to fire Franks and get on with the war. His aggressive words would have been an inspiration to the soldiers of Cougar Squadron, struggling as we were with the sandstorm and the 2nd Cavalry's palsied movement to contact. But we knew nothing about Schwarzkopf's frustrations. We just pushed forward into the clouds of sand and dust.

In Ghost Troop, Sartiano was busy herding his cats, sending his scouts forward in their Bradleys while holding his tanks in reserve. I knew that

Ghost Troop was on my left, but I rarely saw any trace of Sgt. Rick Michalec, who, in his Bradley, Ghost 36, was maintaining contact with Eagle Troop's 1st Platoon scouts. Michalec had the mission of maintaining contact with Eagle Troop. Sartiano had complete confidence that if any scout in Ghost Troop could maintain contact in the terrible weather, regardless of enemy action, Michalec was the man.

Michalec was a junior noncommissioned officer at the time. He was very smart and despite his youth, totally unflappable. When the Ghost Troop master gunner was relieved for drinking one too many beers in Germany and reassigned to Eagle Troop, Michalec, a qualified Bradley master gunner, had to assume his duties. This assignment would normally have gone to a more senior staff sergeant or sergeant first class, but I not only approved of Sergeant Michalec's selection for the job but personally urged it. His performance under fire now fully justified my confidence in him.

The relatively light contact to this point was frustrating to me. We knew there were more enemy soldiers out there, but we could not be sure of how many or where they were. As is frequently the case in war, much happens that is not reported, and that was the case with Ghost Troop's movement to the 65 Easting between 1530 and 1600 hours. Sartiano was all over the place, continuously moving back and forth between his flank scout platoons to ensure that they maintained contact with each other, as well as with Eagle Troop. But it was always touch and go.

When Sergeant Michalec, on the right flank with Eagle Troop, reported receiving fire at 1540 hours from two BMPs, which he destroyed with automatic cannon fire, Sartiano concluded that serious enemy contact was not far off.

Somewhere beyond the 66 Easting, Michalec's driver, Private First Class Parker, noticed that the Bradley was sitting among some square objects that looked like explosive devices.

Michalec instinctively halted the vehicle. Struggling to see clearly through blasts of wind and sand, Michalec dropped down inside the Bradley switching his gun sight to high magnification. As soon as the young sergeant saw that the green square objects had yellow writing on them, he directed the crew to put on their gas masks and gloves in order to fully protect themselves from what could be chemical mines.[11]

Reporting the situation along with a detailed description of the mines, Michalec leaned out of his hatch and looked over the right side of the Bradley.

Moving forward was out of the question. Somehow, he had driven miraculously over and around two mines without detonating either one, but to the left and to the front the desert was covered with them.

A minute later, Haines called back saying that the engineer on board his Bradley was insisting that "they are not chemical mines. They're some kind of plastic explosive, though, over."

Haines now faced a new dilemma. Should he hold back the whole scout platoon until Michalec's Bradley was out of the minefield or press ahead to keep up with the rest of Ghost Troop, now moving up on his left?

Haines didn't like the idea, but he decided to move the rest of the scouts forward, saying that he'd be back once they were on the 70 Easting.

Michalec acknowledged Hanes' decision over the radio, drew in a deep breath, and decided to test the engineer's theory. Using his 7.62-mm machine gun, he blasted two of the mines in front of his Bradley, causing an explosion but, thankfully, no yellow cloud of poison gas. The explosions, however, were powerful, certainly powerful enough to rip apart the tracks on his Bradley fighting vehicle if he drove over a mine.

Michalec told his crew in a raspy voice, "It's clear. No chemicals, thank God. Now, here's what we're going to do. We'll blast the closest mines, then, back the f—ck out."

With rivers of sweat pouring over his forehead, Michalec now guided his driver, Private First Class Parker, out of the minefield. First one mine, then another exploded until a path was opened and the Bradley could get out.

Hearing on the radio that Michalec was blasting his way out of the minefield, Haines continued to the 70 Easting. But less than fifteen hundred meters later, Haines caught sight of a massive object half-concealed in the sand about three hundred meters ahead of him.

As he approached it, a long barrel poked out at him. It was one of three Iraqi tanks, but in the blowing sand it was impossible to tell if any of the tanks were manned or whether anyone in them had seen him or the rest of his scouts.

Despite the repeated delays, and thanks to the sandstorm, Cougar Squadron seemed to have achieved complete surprise, but Haines took no chances.

He halted his Bradley, swallowed a few times, erected his TOW missile launcher, and fired two missiles in quick succession directly into two of the Iraqi tanks, using the vehicle commander's override, a hand control device that allows the armored fighting vehicle commander to take immediate control of the weapon system.

Specialist Varney, a scout observer in the back of Haines' Bradley, nervously reloaded the TOW launcher, as quickly as he could. But before Haines could send another missile into the third Iraqi tank's turret, the Iraqi crew bailed out, disappearing into the sandstorm. Just to be sure, Haines put another ten rounds of 25-mm high-explosive rounds into the smoking tank.

Haines now moved out as fast as he could to get a closer look. The rest of his section pulled up with Deskevich, who was just behind Haines in his M981 fire-support vehicle, manning his M60 medium machine gun just in case anything inside the smoking tank suddenly came to life. Once Haines realized that he was on line with the rest of the troop, he doubled back, in time to discover that Sergeant Michalec's scout section had blasted its way through the minefield and was headed east at high speed to rejoin the troop.

A few hundred yards away from Michalec, frustrated with a lack of hard information from Dragoon Base, I called Tony Ierardi and asked him for an update, because I was receiving the regimental command net *only* sporadically. I figured we were too far forward of Dragoon Base. But Ierardi could add little to what we knew. He said he would relay permission to move forward when it came in from Dragoon Base. I thanked him, returned to the Cougar command radio net, and called Cpt. Rhett Scott for a quick intelligence update.

Scott said we were headed straight for the enemy and outlined what elements of the Republican Guard he thought were in front of us. I was not really surprised by what Scott said, but I was frustrated with my inability to do much about it.

Growing impatient with the start-and-stop routine, I decided to push my tank forward with Eagle Troop's scouts, looking for enemy through the sandstorm. To my front, I could make out a slight rise obscuring my field of vision, but I did not immediately appreciate its significance. In the desert, a rise or fall in elevation of *even* ten feet over a distance of five hundred feet is militarily significant, but, hell, it was my first desert war. I was still learning.

Growing somewhat bored with the situation, Hillen turned around and looked through the vision block of Cougar Forward. He noticed a slight rise to our front, was just tall enough to obstruct our view of what was on the other side. He also noticed that my tank and his Bradley were out in front of Eagle Troop's scouts.

"Burns," asked Hillen, "What the hell are we were doing out in front of Eagle Troop's scouts?"

"Staying with Cougar 3," replied Burns, "What did you think we were doing?"

"Well, don't you think this is a little risky, I mean, scouting with a tank?"

"You know Sid Vicious. He's tired of the waiting game."

Burns was right. I was impatient and nervous. Something was in the air. I could sense it. Something significant was finally going to happen now.

The 2nd Cavalry's scout helicopters were still grounded due to weather, with the result that our ground scouts had to go farther forward to reconnoiter. In any event, Regiment's limits of advance prevented them from going forward to where they could actually confirm the enemy's main defensive positions. All they could do was report the heat signatures they detected with their excellent thermal sights. The situation was disconcerting but not without possibilities.

We knew the Republican Guard Corps was somewhere to our direct front. What we did not know was exactly how many Iraqi troops, tanks, and armored fighting vehicles would face us or in what condition we would find them.

At 1525, not long after they arrived along the 68 Easting, the visibility improved enough for Gauthier's scout platoon screening the Cougar Squadron's flank to spot what looked like a small village complex of adobe buildings, with a derelict oil derrick. Simultaneously, one of Petshek's scouts reported, on Eagle Troop's 1st Platoon net, seeing a couple of ZSU-23-4s (Soviet radar-guided antiaircraft 23-mm guns on tank chassis) in the vicinity of the same complex.

This was a disturbing report, of which I was completely unaware. Eagle Troop's tank platoons were still echeloned in depth behind the scout platoons. If any of the antiaircraft guns opened fire, Eagle scouts would be in real trouble. A burst of fire from these high-velocity antiaircraft guns would certainly tear apart an early-model Bradley fighting vehicle, without today's A3 model's heavier skirts and plating.

Unlike T. J. Linzy's platoon, which had fought its way across Objective Merrell on the 24th, and Ghost scouts, who had engaged a mechanized infantry company on the 25th, the scout platoons in Eagle Troop had seen very modest action on the 24th and no action whatsoever on the 25th. Consequently, Tim Gauthier wondered if his men would kill without hesitation in a situation where hesitation might be fatal. Gauthier did not have to wait long to find out, but his first action did not commence with the sort of explosive fight he had expected.

Before a shot was fired, out of nowhere came four Iraqi soldiers with white flags. They were about eight hundred meters in front of Gauthier's position near a group of adobe buildings.[12] Seeing that the prisoners were waving frantically, Staff Sergeant McReynolds, the Bradley commander of Eagle 32, did not wait for instructions but raced forward to pick them up. McReynolds knew the risk. His heart raced, but within seconds McReynolds searched the Iraqi soldiers, policed them up, and sped toward the Eagle Troop supply trains, the Iraqi prisoners hanging on to the front slope of the Bradley. Watching as McReynolds drove by, Tim Gauthier recalled that the Iraqi troops looked like the happiest guys he had ever seen.

Sergeant Harris, Bradley commander of Eagle 33, noticed gunfire coming from the village complex. When Gauthier received the report, he concluded that the prisoners had probably been bait, designed to lure his platoon to within range of the defending Iraqis weapons. But that was academic now. As the gunfire intensified, Gauthier's scouts waited anxiously for the order to open fire—something green troops frequently do.

It was at this point that Gauthier issued a textbook order that any Army or Marine officer graduate of the Cavalry Platoon Leader's Course at Fort Knox, Kentucky, would immediately recognize: "F—king kill them, over!"

Gauthier's scouts instantly "hit the kill switch" and poured copious amounts of 25-mm cannon shells into the buildings. If anyone thought of hesitating, the volume of fire disguised it. Of course, all hell broke loose inside of the buildings.

Meanwhile, Petshek's right flank section joined in, sending two TOW missiles down range into the same target area, while Sergeant Hovermale, Gauthier's gunner, cut down defending Iraqi troops near a BTR60-S (a Soviet-manufactured, eight-wheeled armored car that resembles today's Stryker) at the corner of the building complex faster than Gauthier could report them to Gifford in the troop TOC. Gauthier's platoon fired one TOW missile into the buildings to mark them for the tanks, then shifted its fire to enemy armor off to the right flank.[13]

McMaster was keen to join the fight but quickly decided that it would take more than his tank to terminate the action in and around the buildings to his front. No point in half-measures now, thought McMaster. Briefly discussing it on the radio, Gauthier agreed with McMaster's assessment. There was a problem, however. My tank and Cougar Forward were obstructing the movement of his tanks. We were where McMaster judged his tanks should go.

McMaster called Eagle 5 (John Gifford) asking him what I was doing up there. Gifford said he would go higher and resolve the matter. Within seconds, Gifford called me to tell me that McMaster wanted to maneuver his tanks into position to fire on the village complex but that my tank was in the way.

Gifford said, "Cougar 3, this is Eagle 5, Eagle 6 says you are masking our fire, over."

Gifford's message surprised me a little. I was less impressed with the small-arms fire from the village complex on my right than Eagle Troop was, but I figured that engaging the enemy would be a useful warm-up for Eagle Troop's tank platoons, which I knew were itching for a fight.

Frustrated, I asked on the squadron net, "Why the hell are we stopping? There is nothing up here!"

According to Abercrombie, the squadron's soldiers could hear the firing in the background as I spoke and laughed quite a bit over my comment. Still, I knew that like the rest of us, McMaster and his troops were frustrated and anxious to fight. Since I saw no evidence for civilians in or around the buildings, I told Ward to back us up and move to the left about fifty meters.

As I moved out of the way, McMaster called his tank platoons and said, "Green come up on my right, White come up on my left, battle carry HEAT, one round HEAT, village, direct front, frontal, at my command, ready report."[14]

Unable to move his troop forward because of the restriction imposed on us by Regiment, McMaster now undertook whatever he could to get Eagle Troop ready for the fight he was sure was waiting for us in the sandstorm.

Going to "tanks lead," in a wedge formation with McMaster's tank at the center, was the right decision. Our Abrams tanks could engage and destroy enemy tanks using large-caliber main guns without having to stop, as Bradleys did when they employed their TOW antitank missiles. Eagle's nine tanks now moved to the front, just to my right, and they immediately let loose with two volleys of eighteen high-explosive rounds. These tank rounds blasted through the walls to destroy the machine-gun positions that Eagle's scouts had been unable to eliminate. If anyone in the buildings survived, they kept it a secret. The fire stopped.

Always mindful of his mission to maintain contact on Cougar Squadron's southern flank with 3rd Squadron, Gauthier (Blue 1) broke in on the Eagle Troop command net to report that Iron Troop had come on line with Eagle Troop. Both troops were along the 68 Easting. Meanwhile, Gifford kept sending reports from the scouts to Ierardi and Hillen of enemy armored fighting vehicles to Eagle Troop's right front.

In an engagement that signaled how much the situation had changed, a barely visible T72 tank about eight hundred meters to the right of Gauthier's scouts fired a round that exploded short, directly in front of Gauthier's position, but close enough to definitely get Gauthier's attention.

For the first time, Cougar Squadron was exchanging fire with enemy tanks.

Gauthier yelled, "Driver, stop! Gunner, missile, tank!"

While Sergeant Hovermale elevated the TOW missile launcher, he found the target in his sights and called back, "Identified."

A few seconds later, Gauthier yelled "Fire," and a TOW missile howled through the air like a firecracker straight for the Iraqi tank on the right flank.

Red 3, the right section of Petchek's platoon, now joined in the fight, launching a TOW missile in the same general direction. Lt. Danny Davis, Eagle Troop's fire-support team leader, watching the engagements, remarked on the troop command net that flames were shooting twenty feet into the air as the T72's turret exploded.

Listening to the traffic, McMaster knew it was time for his tanks to take the lead. He called Eagle Troop, "Battle stations, go to tanks lead. Cease fire, Red. We're going to tanks lead."

Blue elements ceased fire, but not all of the 1st Platoon scouts (Eagle Troop's Red elements) got the message. Eagle Troop's 1st Platoon scouts were too busy blasting away with 25-mm at the barely recognizable revetments, built for T72 tanks, that were beginning to emerge in the distance as the sandstorm dissipated.[15]

Frustrated, McMaster repeated his order loudly over the radio: "Damn it, Red 1, goddamn it, cease fire!"

Cowed by McMaster's harsh tone on the radio, 1st Platoon finally responded, "Red 1. Roger, understand cease fire."

"Damn it!" said Eagle 6, "We're going to tanks lead. Follow my move."

McMaster now moved forward in his tank. In the heat of the moment, however, McMaster began reporting the destruction of five enemy armored vehicles by his tanks on the troop command net, thinking that he was talking to Hillen. It did not matter. John Gifford, Eagle Troop executive officer, immediately relayed the reports. Anyway, we could see most of what was happening to our right.

At 1618 hours, Tony Ierardi came up on the squadron command net to relay permission from Dragoon Base for Cougar Squadron to advance, announcing the 70 Easting as the new limit of advance. Lieutenant Colonel Larson, who had spent much of the day struggling with communication problems at Eagle Troop's TOC, broke in over the command net to remind Ghost and Eagle troops to maintain contact on their flanks. Larson's point was valid, but the matter would shortly become academic.

As soon as I heard Ierardi announce the new limit over the radio, I acknowledged it on the Cougar Squadron command net and said, "Cougar elements continue to move, Cougar 3, out." Then, I told Ward to drive straight ahead and keep well to the left of Eagle's tanks so we did not inadvertently mask their fires.

To my right, Eagle Troop now moved off with McMaster at the apex of the Λ-shaped shaped wedge formed by Eagle Troop's tank platoons.

A couple of thousand meters away, listening to the Cougar Squadron command net, Sartiano concluded we were going into action. He decided to tighten control over his scouts and Abrams tanks. Visibility in Ghost's zone of attack still varied between fifty and three hundred meters. Naturally, Joe worried the troop might be too widely dispersed if it slammed into the kind of tank threat that seemed to be emerging in front of Eagle Troop. All of Ghost Troop's scouts were reporting hot spots to their front in their thermal sights.

He told Mecca, "Ghost 5, I have a strange feeling, break. Let's get the tanks up on line with the scouts before we move out."

Ghost Troop moved out of the troop wedge with scouts in the lead into a line with tanks in the center and scouts on the flanks.

Inside Cougar Squadron's armored command and control tracks, bouncing over the desert, Tony Ierardi stood holding the radio mount with one hand while chewing on some hard, stale bread in the other. It was a good way to suppress the tendency to worry. Ierardi whispered to himself, "No point worrying about this shit now anyway."

As the M577 headquarters vehicle accelerated to keep up with Cougar Squadron's combat elements, Ierardi wondered if a new phase in the campaign to find and destroy the Republican Guard had really begun. Already enervated from straining to hear the regimental command and fire-support nets over the whine of the vehicle's diesel engine, he turned to the status board and map to check the reports of the last hour from across the squadron front. Ierardi knew that we had penetrated the security zone.

Meanwhile, Sergeant Major Catchings jumped out of an armored Humvee to check on the driver of one of the tactical operation center's M577s to make sure nothing was wrong.

Lots of soldiers with lumps in their throats stood or sat behind their guns wondering what would happen next. The driver was fine, just understandably nervous. After reassuring the young soldier that all was in order, Catchings ran back to the Humvee. Catchings would do this repeatedly throughout the battle, ensuring that Captain Ierardi and Lieutenant Scott had everything they needed.

Inside Cougar Forward, Hillen sat nervously on top of two Kevlar-armored flak jackets. Burns dropped down inside to look around and when he saw Hillen sitting on the flak vests. Burns smiled, asking, "What the hell are you doing sitting on those flak vests, lieutenant?"

"Protecting the family jewels, what the f—k do you think I'm doing? I want to make more Hillens when this thing is over," answered Hillen. Still unmarried, John Hillen wanted to make sure his capacity for reproduction would survive the war, no matter what happened next. Burns gaffawed some more, a good thing for a soldier to do on his way into battle.

Hillen's next report to Dragoon Base was simple, direct, and prophetic: "Now moving to 70 Easting, Cougar Forward, out."

None of us realized it just then, but the battle we had prepared for months to fight was just beginning.

SEVEN

Action Front!

In war, valor is superior to numbers.
FLAVIUS VEGETIUS RENNATUS, *MILITARY INSTITUTIONS OF THE ROMANS,* AD 378

1618 HOURS, ALONG THE 68 EASTING INSIDE THE
TAWALKANA DIVISION'S SECURITY ZONE

Racing forward in his tank, McMaster yelled over the troop net: "Contact, five armored vehicles direct front! Three more off to the left!"

McMaster's gunner, Sergeant Koch, spotted Iraqi tanks in prepared defensive positions, some of them traversing their guns in the direction of the advancing American tanks.

Koch pushed the button on his laser range finder until 1,420 meters popped up on his sight picture; he belted out, "Identified!"

Specialist Taylor, the gunner, screamed "Up!"

McMaster yelled, "Fire, fire sabot!" and the 2nd Cavalry began its first major tank battle since 1945.

Koch sent the HEAT round that was already in the gun tube toward the T72 while Taylor pulled a sabot round out of the ammunition storage, slammed it into the breech, and screamed "Up!"

The first HEAT round found its mark, and fat plumes of smoke and fire rolled out from beneath the T72 tank. Three seconds later, the sabot round shot like a meteor through the second T72 tank, sending its turret into the air while secondary explosions ripped the tank apart as though it were made of cardboard.

Pushing forward over the rise that had obstructed my view during the now-waning sandstorm, I looked to the right as a two-meter-high cloud of sand and dust rose up next to McMaster's tank, moving in the shimmering light of clearing skies. Then, another dust cloud exploded near the right front of his tank. Unable to hear anything over the howling tank engine and the radio chatter in my ears, I wondered if this was not more enemy artillery falling.

Sergeant Jones, the gunner, who had a better view through his sights, shouted, "Sir, look at this!"

I dropped down inside the turret, looked through my sights to where Sergeant Jones had aimed the main gun, and said quietly, "Holy shit." My heart jumped up into my throat.

Tanks, tanks, and more tanks sitting behind neatly piled mounds of sand stretched off to the right. We did not know it then, but the 140 men, nine Abrams M1A1 tanks, and thirteen Bradley fighting vehicles of Eagle Troop were on a collision course with the Republican Guard. Waiting for them were thirty-nine tanks, fourteen BMPs, and forty assorted other armored vehicles and trucks, together with two hundred infantrymen sitting in the defense just southeast of the buildings where we had first come under fire.

Driving like mad toward the first ten T72s in defensive positions to his front, McMaster suddenly wondered where his tank platoons were.

"Are you guys with me, over?" he asked on the troop net.

They were. Cresting the rise, the two platoons pulled up on either side of McMaster's tank and made a half-turn to the right, firing as they advanced, following *Mad Max* (McMaster's tank) directly toward the enemy. Eagle Troop was punching right with a vengeance.[1]

A couple of seconds later, the air was shattered with the concussion of more explosive cannon fire as Lt. Mike Hamilton's four tanks opened up simultaneously with two volleys at roughly 1,100 meters. Hamilton, a sturdy, six-foot two-inch dual U.S-Canadian citizen from Burlington, Vermont, was a graduate of Norwich University's ROTC program. He was also a natural fit with the confident, aggressive mentality that McMaster worked hard to cultivate in Eagle Troop.

Before leaving Bamberg for the Persian Gulf, a lieutenant from an infantry battalion in the 1st Armored Division had tried to butt in line ahead of everyone else, saying, "Sorry, but I need to get through the vaccination line. It's important."

Hamilton said nothing, just put his arms around the offending officer's chest, picked him up and carried him out of the line. Surprised, the lieutenant said, "Why the hell do you think you can do that?" Hamilton focused his gaze on the lieutenant and said loud enough for everyone to hear, "Because I can kick your ass!" After a pause of two or three seconds, the infantryman decided to beat a hasty retreat amid the laughter of everyone within earshot.

Hamilton's tank commanders were just as aggressive and confident as he was. They fired sabot rounds that struck with the power of freight trains. Nothing survived the impact. When DeStefano's four tanks added to the chorus of destruction, letting loose a torrent of shells at the defending Iraqi tanks, very few Iraqi tanks managed to return fire.

Inside Eagle Troop's tanks, ammunition doors opened and shut with perfect precision while loaders slammed home the long 120-mm sabot rounds, yelling "Up!" and waiting for the inevitable explosion that followed the words "On the way!" Metal smashed against metal inside and outside of the turrets as round after round after round flew into the Iraqi tanks and BMPs. Gunners' eyes glowed with delight as they watched the enemy's defenses collapse in ruins.

First eleven, then fifteen Iraqi T72 tanks exploded into flame under the impact of Eagle Troop tanks' concentrated cannon fire. Enemy tank turrets flipped like bottle tops twenty, thirty feet into the air while burning debris pinwheeled in all directions, infusing the American tank commanders and their gunners with a sense of impending triumph. Any lingering doubts or fears dissipated.

As Eagle Troop's tanks moved through the first set of enemy positions, black smoke streamed from holes in destroyed Iraqi tanks. Simultaneously, secondary explosions of fuel and ammunition cooked off, ripping apart what remained of the enemy tanks and bunkers. Eagle Troop's tanks were cold-cocking the Iraqis with cannon fire and when necessary driving over the Iraqi defensive positions, crushing them.

Not knowing precisely what was happening, Gifford felt obligated to remind McMaster on the troop net of the 70 Easting limit of advance. McMaster answered quickly, "We can't stop, tell them we are in contact, tell them I'm sorry, out."

I was unaware of McMaster's comment, but he was right. The whole matter was academic. Talk on the radio was minimal. We were too busy fighting. But watching the Eagle Troop tanks charge into the Iraqi defenses, I came up on the squadron command net and said, "Battle Stations, this is Cougar 3, continue to move, out." Until there was nothing left to destroy, stopping was out of the question.

As Eagle Troop's tanks closed with the Iraqi tanks in defensive positions, steel fragments flew in all directions. With the reduction in range to the enemy's defenses, the violence simply escalated. When four tanks and BMPs suddenly blew up simultaneously no more than five hundred meters in front of him, McMaster gasped in amazement at the destruction. Taken by surprise, Iraqi troops were swept away in salvos of tank fire that broke like tidal waves over their fighting positions.

Now Gauthier's scouts swung wide and to the right of Eagle Troop's tanks, spotting another ZSU-23-4, only this time the lethal Soviet air-defense guns were firing in the general direction of the advancing Bradleys. Gauthier's scouts halted and immediately returned fire with two TOW missiles, blowing up the antiaircraft guns and collapsing the bunker next to it.[2]

Farther to the right of the smoking antiaircraft guns, an Iraqi T72 tank fired a sabot round at Gauthier's Bradley. Despite the short range, perhaps only six or seven hundred meters, the tank round struck the desert floor in front of the Bradley, throwing sand and gravel into the air and into Gauthier's face.

Inside, Gauthier's gunner, Sergeant Hovermale calmly guided his aim point on to the Iraqi tank and fired a TOW missile. Seconds later, the T72 went up in flames. Gauthier's advance continued.

DeStefano's tanks did not miss what had happened to Gauthier. The fact that several of the destroyed Iraqi tanks were already burning furiously did not conceal the depth of the U-shaped defenses from DeStefano's tank commanders. As DeStefano's tanks emerged from the line of burning tanks and BMPs, the gunners could see that roughly two thousand meters to their front, seventeen more T72 tanks were parked in a "coil" (tanks were positioned the way a snake coils its body), presumably as a reserve to deal with any penetration of the defense. It did not matter.

The Iraqi armored vehicles vanished in one explosion after another. The so-called Iraqi tank reserve was demolished in seconds, but amazingly, the enemy's fire did not slacken much. Seeing almost no letup in the small-arms fire on Eagle Troop's right flank, Gauthier's gunners rushed to reload more high-explosive-round belts into the feed trays of their 25-mm guns, while scouts in the rear compartments popped the top hull hatches to reload their TOW missile launchers on the left side of their Bradleys' turrets under small-arms fire from the defending Iraqis.

Inside the Bradley designated "Eagle 35," Sergeant Digbie, one of Gauthier's toughest and most experienced scout leaders, yelled his lungs out at Sergeant Cooper, the gunner, to fire a TOW missile, but Cooper was so busy mowing down Iraqi troops with his 25-mm—each blast a reverberating boom—that he couldn't hear Digbie.

Cooper kept saying, "You want me to—*boom! boom! boom!*—shoot 'em with a TOW—*boom! boom! boom! boom! boom!*—OK." Cooper then answered Digbie. "Stand by." A second later, Cooper yelled, "On the way!" But no TOW missile fired. Instead, Cooper struck the target with more 25-mm high-explosive rounds, causing a massive explosion.

"Whoa, did you see that f—cking shot? That motherf—cker is gone."

Sergeant Digbie was not impressed and repeated his order, "Goddamn it, Cooper, shoot 'em with a TOW."

This time Cooper got the message and moved the turret to the TOW load position, which takes a few seconds, and sent the 25-mm barrel to maximum elevation, leaving the Bradley temporarily defenseless. Aiming and firing the 25-mm cannon means pointing and shooting; the TOW missile is different, because after it is fired, as it "flies," it unreels two thin guidance wires that receive correction signals as the gunner looks through his sights and keeps a crosshair on the target.

Thus, to switch from firing 25-mm cannon to TOW missiles, the gunner has to switch his control inputs from the 25-mm gun barrel and engage them to the TOW missile launcher box. With a maximum effective range of 3,750 meters, TOWs can have a twenty-plus-second flight time. In combat no one likes to spend precious seconds tracking a missile all the way to the target while the enemy is shooting at you.

But there was a problem. Digbie's crew had already shot their first two TOW missiles; their launcher box was empty. When Bertubin and Frazier, the two soldiers riding in the back of Digbie's Bradley, tried to open the cargo hatch in its hull ceiling to load more missiles, the lever broke, jamming the hatch. Digbie was furious, started swearing and cursing in one long stream of invective, but nothing the two soldiers in the back of the Bradley tried solved the problem. In what was the first of many instances inside Abrams tanks and Bradleys over the next few hours, American soldiers would meet the unexpected with courage, imagination, and panache.

Frustrated, Frazier ripped off his CVC helmet, opened the ramp door in the rear of the vehicle, and jumped outside.

"F—k it," said Frazier, "Just f—k it."

Bertubin handed Frazier two TOW missiles from inside the vehicle, then climbed out and up onto the back deck, saying, "If you can't raise the bridge, then . . ."

Tapping Sergeant Digbie on the shoulder, Bertubin yelled, "Get Cooper to put it on TOW-load!" The TOW launcher had to be angled and the turret turned to the left so missiles could be inserted into the rear of the launcher from the top rear hatch, popped open only as far as necessary to allow soldiers to reload missiles from the safety of their vehicle. But unable to open the hatch at all, Bertubin had to do it the hard way—exposed.

Eyes bugging out of his head, Digbie could not believe his loader was standing on the back deck trying to load TOW missiles in the middle of a firefight. For the first time in a long time, Digbie was speechless, almost frozen in place.

Seeing the confusion in Digbie's eyes, Bertubin screamed again, "Get him to put it on TOW-load!"

Digbie nodded "yes," and Cooper complied while Frazier calmly lifted one missile at a time up over the side of the Bradley to Bertubin. Bertubin wasted no time. Bullets were striking the sand in front of the vehicle, and he knew it. He loaded the missiles into the launchers as quickly as possible, jumped off the rear end of the Bradley, and yelled "Get in!" to Frazier, who instantly dove into the back of the Bradley.

Bertubin grabbed a CVC helmet, turned the radio/intercom switch on his earpiece, and screamed, "TOW up!" just as Frazier closed the door behind them. A second later, Cooper launched the TOW missile.

With the crashing sound that a racecar driver in the Indianapolis 500 would recognize in a straightaway, the TOW flew like an ICBM toward its target some 1,500 meters off to the right, presumably a tank or some other armored vehicle—the visibility made it hard to tell.[3] The gunner had just aimed in the direction of the firing black silhouette in the distance. When the warhead on the missile struck its target, however, the explosion it caused looked like a mini–Fourth of July celebration.

Iraqi troops started running into the waist-high trenches or into the deep bunkers next to the burning tanks. The smoke and flame added a certain amount of confusion to the battle, but it did nothing to stop or slow Eagle Troop's advance.

Eagle's tanks just roared forward through the enemy's positions, turning the troop's right punch into platoon and section fights. Scout sections on Eagle Troop's flanks fired TOW missiles to augment the fire from the troop's tanks, while the inner tank and scout sections concentrated on the destruction of enemy infantry, light armor, trucks, and bunkers that the tanks had passed on their way into the depth of the enemy defenses. It was a frenzied scene, with all the barbarism and savagery of close combat.

The battle was moving so fast that Cpt. Jack Millar, Cougar Squadron artillery officer, with call sign Cougar 13, under pressure all day long from Steel 6, the regimental artillery officer, to employ artillery, popped up on the squadron's fire-support net at 1646 with a plea for fire missions from the fire-support teams in Eagle and Ghost troops: "This is Cougar 13, all 13 elements, this is Cougar 13, break—just whenever you can, send up some indirect. We need to get into this fight, over."

Cougar Squadron's howitzer battery and supporting artillery would have their chance, but not now.

Russia's great Marshal Suvorov is alleged to have said: "Hard on the training ground, easy on the battlefield."

Eagle Troop's nine tank crews validated Suvorov's philosophy. The tactic of extreme violence delivered at speed that Eagle Troop practiced relentlessly in field training throughout the month of January was now administering a shock to the defending Iraqi troops, a shock from which they would never recover. In a matter of minutes, firing roughly sixty-three 120-mm main-gun rounds, Eagle Troop's tank crews eliminated all thirty-nine of the defending Republican Guard tanks from the fight.

With the Iraqi tanks out of the picture, Eagle Troop's tank commanders now turned their attention to other targets of opportunity. Tank gunners began firing main-gun rounds at BMPs, MTLBs, and any other vehicles they could find. The surviving mass of Iraqi armored vehicles and trucks positioned in depth behind the Iraqi tanks now disintegrated in a series of thunderous explosions at ranges of less than three hundred meters. An Iraqi soldier burning from head to toe who had miraculously survived a sabot round through the turret died in a hail of machine-gun bullets from one of the advancing tanks as he climbed out of the turret on to the back deck. Tank gunners were now dropping Iraqi infantry all over the battlefield with their machine guns. To Hamilton in particular, the enemy soldiers seemed like ducks, dropping one after the other, as if in some horrific amusement-park shooting gallery.[4]

As the smoke partially cleared from the burning tanks dispatched by Eagle Troop, McMaster and his tank commanders, still in a state of semishock at the scale of their success, perceived the depth of the enemy's formation. This was no company strongpoint. Eagle Troop had struck the center of a much larger force, part of which rested beyond the line that divided our attack zone from 3rd Squadron's.

From my turret, I could see fortified trenches, sandbagged bunkers, T72 tanks, and BMPs in depth, along with several dozen Iraqi infantry running madly around the positions.

"Stay left," I told my driver, Ward. "Don't get in front of Eagle Troop's tanks. Just stay with them on the left."

Ward, always a man of few words, said, "You got it, Major."

He hit the accelerator and moved us out at high speed. At the time, I figured that if we kept moving straight ahead I could stay in touch with Ghost Troop on the left, as well as Eagle Troop on the right. Simultaneously, the weather was definitely clearing, and the intensity of Iraqi tank, antitank guided-missile, and machine-gun fire directed at us from the Republican Guard's positions began picking up. Thinking that I could maintain control was delusional. Control went out of the window with the first tank rounds. We would have to fight through the enemy until there was no more enemy to kill.

As Ward put pedal to the metal, Sergeant Jones uttered the following: "Sir, look, I mean look right, look in front of us!"

I dropped down and looked through the gun sight and saw exactly what the gunner had seen: I could make out T72 tanks in defensive positions to my right front.

Mesmerized by the sounds and sights to my front and flanks, I had not looked at what was directly in front of me. Perhaps I was also riding a little higher in the hatch than I should have been to fire the Soviet souvenir machine gun that Sergeant Jones had fixed up for me the day before. Who knows? But when my machine gun stopped firing, I worked frantically to fix it and completely missed the mines.

The scouts behind me and on my flanks were more alert. They did not miss the mines. In fact, let's be honest: everybody behind us saw them, even though we did not. Later I found out that a call had gone out on the Eagle Troop command net alerting everyone to avoid the mines. As I was trying to talk on the squadron command net just then, I missed the warning.

Watching through the gunner's sights of Cougar Forward my tank move forward, Holloway pointed out to Burns that I was headed toward a minefield.[5]

"Is the major about to do what I think he's about to do?" asked Holloway. Burns chuckled and said, "Yep, the crazy bastard is driving right into a minefield."

Holloway was incredulous. "We better get up there. Macgregor has no idea where Ward is taking the tank."

Burns grunted back, "Yep. Better get ready to shoot." Burns then snapped at Hank Wells, "Driver, move out!" Over the intercom, as he drove Cougar Forward into position behind my tank, Wells mumbled, "I was afraid you were going to say that."

Later in the day, Ward would take enormous crap from Eagle Troop's scouts for driving through what was a hasty minefield in front of an Iraqi tank platoon's position. Behind Burns came Staff Sergeant Patterson, one of Petschek's scout section leaders. He carefully maneuvered his Bradley into the deep tracks made by the accelerating tank and followed us straight through the minefield. That's when the lights went out.

A huge cloud of sand, black smoke, and burning debris rose beneath the right track of the tank in what felt like an earthquake. To the scouts behind us, the intensity of the noise and the fireball from the blast that swept over the tank looked like an erupting volcano. The scouts weren't wrong. I was thrown down with enormous force as the explosion rocked our seventy-ton tank up and sideways.

Picking myself up off the turret floor, I figured it must have been one hell of a big mine, but I had no idea what kind of a mine it had been. Even Ward, who was rarely impressed with anything that happened on the battlefield, felt the force of the blast and asked me, "What the f—ck was that?"

Sitting on top of two Kevlar vests inside Cougar Forward, Hillen had the satisfaction of being warmly congratulated by Burns and Holloway on having the foresight to sit on additional protection. Everybody on the Bradley with

Hillen now scrambled to do exactly what Hillen had done—sit on additional protection!

Not really knowing why but extremely grateful that we were still moving, I told Ward, "Just another f—king antipersonnel mine, don't worry about it."

Miraculously, though the explosion blew off the external parts of two track blocks, the inside portions, including the end connectors, held, and so the track held. I said a quick prayer of thanks for the thoroughness of the men in Detroit who had built this monster. I repeated it later when I saw the enormous hole blasted out of the desert floor where the Chinese antitank mine had detonated under us.

Not more than five hundred meters away, as my tank emerged from the minefield, Sergeant Jones, the gunner screamed: *"Tank!"*

Immediately, Abercrombie yelled "Up!" while Jones placed his sights on the nearest of two T72 tanks and said, "Sir, identified."

Why the hell Dewey Jones decided to be so damn polite at this point was odd, indeed.

I yelled back "Jones, for Christ's sake, fire!"

With the words "On the way," Jones sent the HEAT round low into the tank's hull. The absence of any discernible effect left him nervous, but I said, "Traverse left, left tank, fire!"

Jones swung the gun over to the left-hand tank and blew the turret off.

"Good f—cking job, Dewey," I yelled, "now get the other one."

"Roger that, Sir," but as the young Floridian started to say, "On the way," Abercrombie screamed, "Wait!"

The second HEAT round was not yet fully loaded into the breech. For some reason, the 120-mm HEAT round did not fit properly and the breech did not close.

I said, "Whatever you're going to do, do it f—king quick." Abercrombie didn't wait for instructions. He reached up with both arms and grabbed either side of the loader's hatch and, hanging like an Olympic gymnast from the rings, lifted up both legs, kicked the base of the HEAT round hard, and shoved it straight into the breech. "Up!"

"On the way!" was the next thing I heard, and Jones repeated the first engagement.

The second round obliterated the Iraqi tank. It just disintegrated.

With the two Iraqi tanks to my immediate front gone, I turned my attention back to the battle on my right, yelling again and again, "Keep firing, fire at will."

Jones kept firing, relying mostly on his machine gun to engage trucks and infantry. This left Abercrombie free to go topside and man his own machine gun, just in time to deal with Iraqi troops popping out of all sorts of places as we drove through the maze of bunkers and equipment.

Machine-gun rounds pinged off the turret, while an occasional rocket-propelled grenade slammed with a dull thud into the side of the tank. In truth, we never noticed the RPGs. We just kept moving.

As soon as we were through the mines, Burns and Holloway moved up, slaughtering several pockets of Iraqi infantry that focused their fire on my tank. Again, I was unaware of what happened behind me. These actions happened within the first minutes of our move out of the minefield during Eagle Troop's tank assault. Moreover, static from the radio was going full blast in my ears as I watched Eagle Troop pound the hell out of everything on my right. The sandstorm was dying away, and events moved at breakneck speed. Predictably, my calls for an update on Ghost Troop's status went unanswered.

Meanwhile, moving up behind the curtain of tank fire, Eagle Troop scouts drove between and around the burning Iraqi tanks, past the secondary explosions, only to find that the farther they moved, the more the defending Iraqi troops seem to wake up.

Iraqi troops surged out of the bunkers and burning vehicles. In some cases, Iraqi troops who had played dead until the tanks passed by now came to life. Grabbing their rifles and RPG launchers, the Iraqi soldiers who survived the onslaught of Eagle Troop's tanks either ran for vehicles that promised the hope of escape or sprang into firing positions near or behind the destroyed T72 tanks and BMPs.

Amazing things began to happen as the fighting raged at very close quarters. Eagle scouts fell like an avalanche on the surviving Iraqi infantry and remaining light armor. Gauthier and Petschek ruthlessly exploited the destruction of the Iraqi armor with their platoons, weaving in and out of the bunkers and burning tanks, cutting down the defending Iraqi infantry with machine guns and 25-mm cannon fire, tossing grenades into the armored infantry carriers and bunkers as they drove by the burning wrecks to ensure they could not be used against us.

For Staff Sergeant Patterson this was the moment he savored most. Patterson was the noncommissioned officer who had gotten into trouble in the summer of 1990 for celebrating too much during a gunnery rotation in Germany and had been reassigned from Ghost to Eagle Troop. His reassignment now proved a godsend to Eagle Troop. Not satisfied with the usual complement of weapons on board his Bradley fighting vehicle, Patterson placed an M16 rifle with several clips of ammunition inside the vehicle commander's hatch.

Just below his gun sights, Patterson also assembled a reserve of grenades. While his gunner blasted the Iraqi infantry and trucks with 25-mm high-explosive rounds, Patterson rose up out of his hatch to shoot Iraqi soldiers waiting in ambush as the tanks and Bradleys passed. After shooting them, Patterson did exactly what Linzy's scouts had done on Saturday, the 24th: he threw a grenade in the same direction to ensure complete annihilation.

It looked as if there was nothing the Iraqis could do to halt our onward rush, a matter more of instinct than command. One by one, the Iraqis were destroyed; every tank, BMP, MTLB, truck, and bunker erupted in flame. A single tank or 25-mm sabot round went through two or three Iraqi vehicles at a time. Men were cut in half right in front of our eyes, and at the time, we thought nothing of it. I watched as 25-mm high-explosive rounds burst open human chests, releasing what in the thermal sights looked like clouds of steamy heat into the atmosphere. But everyone was inured to the images. If anything, the sights and sounds whetted the appetite for action and spurred the soldiers on.

Though astonishingly ineffective against our tracks and armored hulls, the volume of enemy small-arms fire hardly slackened. It continued without much interruption. Even as blood splashed and splattered over the dismembered remains of Iraqi soldiers struck by 25-mm high-explosive rounds and 7.62-mm machine-gun fire, the enemy kept firing at us.

Worried that if our scouts dismounted to clear bunkers they could be injured by the small-arms fire, the numerous antipersonnel mines lying on the ground, or secondary explosions from burning vehicles, I quickly made a net call prohibiting anyone from dismounting until we had completely destroyed the enemy: "Battle Stations, this is Cougar 3, no one dismount, I say again, no one dismount, out."

Nice gesture, but like so many orders in the heat of battle, it had little effect.

Not far from my tank from which I was transmitting the directive over the squadron command net, driving through the bunkers, Lieutenant Petschek was about to do exactly what I hoped to avoid. As he drove forward through the enemy positions, Petschek happened to catch sight of something through the open door of one of the bunkers. What he saw was pallets of ammunition lying unprotected and exposed.

Petschek decided that the store of ammunition was too dangerous to ignore, as it could be used against us. He stopped his Bradley and told Sgt. Shane James, a combat engineer from the 82nd Engineer Battalion attached to Cougar Squadron, and Spec. Terry Shiflett, an Eagle Troop scout, to dismount and destroy the ammunition.

In a very risky move, Petschek dropped the rear ramp, and the two soldiers jumped out with plastic-explosive satchel charges. They sprinted to the bunker door, placed the charges against the stacks of ammunition for demolition, set the time fuses for a short delay, pulled the rings to start the powder in the plastic tubes burning toward their blasting caps in the plastic-explosive blocks, and abruptly jumped back into the track.

As soon as the two soldiers were inside, the driver engaged the motor to raise the ramp, only to discover that it would not close beyond the halfway mark! Why they had not gone out the simpler door in the ramp is a good question; the rear of the Bradley was now half-exposed to the explosion that was timed to go off any second.

Petschek kept his cool and told the soldiers to examine the hinges and space between the ramp and the vehicle. A couple of seconds later, Specialist Shiflett discovered a spent 25-mm shell casing stuck in between the ramp door and the chassis.

He removed the obstruction, yelled "Close it!" and just as the ramp door sealed shut, a deafening explosion rocked the Bradley.

"Close call," Petschek said. "Let's get the hell out of here."

Back on my tank, Abercrombie kept blasting away at Iraqi troops with his 7.62-mm medium machine gun on top of the turret when we drove past a burning armored vehicle, a BMP, I think.

The armored vehicle abruptly exploded as we passed, and the blast sent both of us crashing down into the turret for a second time. I felt like my eardrums would explode. Abercrombie asked if I was OK.

"Roger," was about all I could blurt out.

Being slammed into the turret floor a second time behind the gunner was enough for me. I stood up and adjusted the turret hatch above me to the "open protected position." That still allowed me to poke my head up high enough to see what was happening outside but made it less likely that I would be shot through the head, as often happens to tank commanders in close combat. There was considerable risk of that—we kept hearing the splash of small arms punctuated by occasional thuds that we figured were RPG hits. My Soviet-manufactured machine gun had quit working after the mine strike anyway.

After we went to the open protected posture, none of the crew on my tank could see much to the left or right as we passed through the remaining Iraqi positions. We tended to look ahead, where the enemy was, not behind us. We actually missed the numbers of Iraqi troops darting out from behind bunkers and vehicles who attempted to shoot us with RPGs and machine guns from behind.

Fortunately, either Staff Sergeant Burns or one of the Eagle Troop scouts near us cut down the Iraqi infantry before they could inflict any damage. This pattern was repeated throughout Eagle Troop as the tanks led the attack through the enemy's defensive positions.

During the initial advance, I doubted that anyone at Regiment was aware of the intense battle we had just fought. But I was wrong. The thunder of tank and TOW missile fire over the horizon had not gone unnoticed. The convulsive battle that began at 1618 hours actually brought Colonel Holder out of the M113A3 that served as the 2nd Cavalry's forward command post.

Looking toward Cougar Squadron's zone of attack where our gunfire illuminated the darkening sky like lightning in a thunderstorm, Colonel Holder told the regimental operations officer sitting inside the M113, "Something is happening over there in Cougar Squadron. Maybe we should go over and see what's going on."

Eyes riveted to the JSTARS screen displaying electronic blips, or moving-target indicators, like a very expensive "light brite" set, with the regimental scheme of maneuver overlay on top of it, Major Lute, the regimental operations officer, cautioned Holder to stay put.

"Sir, General Franks expects you to stay in constant contact with him right now. If you move, the corps commander will not have the communications link with you he needs during this critical phase of the operation."[6]

Holder reconsidered for a moment. Then, he climbed back inside the M113.

Suddenly, the shooting slackened.

I looked around and saw nothing to my front but open desert. I told Ward to slow down. Eagle's tanks were coming back into view on my right.

McMaster's charge through the enemy in the form of a right punch had been brilliantly executed, and the engagement left us in complete control of the desert as far as we could see in every direction. Somehow or another, despite the fact that I had attacked generally straight ahead while Eagle's tanks had punched right into Wolf Pack's (3rd Squadron) zone of attack, then left back into Cougar Squadron's zone of attack, McMaster and I had ended up right next to each other.

WHERE THE HELL ARE WE?

According to my watch, when I stopped my tank only about eighteen minutes had passed since the first tank rounds were fired. I lifted myself completely out of the hatch and looked around.

To the front and to the flanks I could see nothing but an empty, flat, featureless desert in the gray, failing light. It looked like we had simply run out of enemy to kill.

Behind us, the scene was horrific. Eagle Troop's attack through the Iraqi tanks, mines, and bunkers had left the Republican Guard Brigade of the Tawalkana Division badly smashed up. All of the Iraqi tanks, along with countless other armored vehicles, trucks, and an undetermined number of Republican

Figure 10. Cougar Squadron Attack to 73 Easting

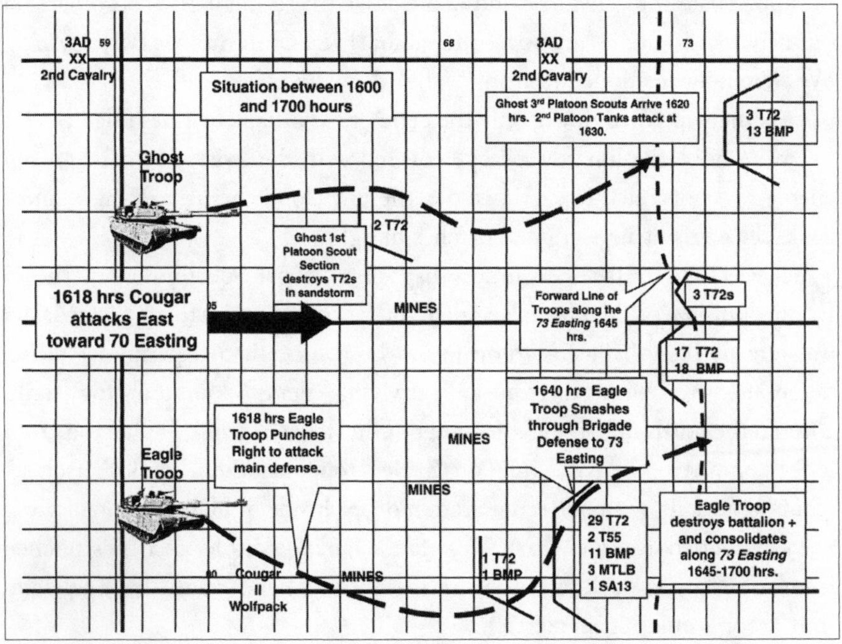

Guard troops, appeared to be destroyed. On the left, just out of sight in the dissipating sandstorm, Ghost Troop reported moving forward, engaging Iraqi outposts in the security zone. We were now facing northeast as the punch, which had started from an eastward advance, had taken us through the enemy and off our initial course. Mecca called to update me on Ghost Troop's progress, and both of us expressed the concern that Eagle Troop might now actually be in front of Ghost Troop. That was not the case, but it seemed a real possibility at the time.

Ultimately, Ghost Troop's position concerned me less—I was confident that Mecca and Sartiano would keep a tight rein on Ghost Troop scouts if they did in fact roll up behind us—than the possibility that our advance had carried us to some new unappealing destination.

It was about 1640 hours. I called McMaster, ordered a general halt, and asked where the hell we were. McMaster had no more idea than I did but said he would ask his GPS-equipped scouts.

While I waited for a precise answer on our location, I called for a combat-power report: "Battle stations, battle stations this is Cougar 3, combat power, over."

To my amazement, each station in rapid succession reported 100 percent combat power. We had blasted through the enemy's defenses without a scratch! I dropped back into the turret and wrote down the six-digit grid coordinate for our new location as it came over the radio: "Papa Uniform [for PU] 737025." We were now positioned in front of the 73 Easting.

As the wind died down, only the eerie drone of tank engines filled the air. We were now in a lunar landscape covered with the twisted remains of our enemy and not much else. Above me, the low clouds began to vanish, and I could see occasional pale, small patches of light.

It was time to issue new orders disposing Cougar Squadron along the 73 Easting until we could inform Regiment of the action we just fought. McMaster was already organizing his troop into a horseshoe-shaped perimeter facing due east to deal with fire from any surviving enemy. Hamilton's four tanks covered the north side in the direction of Ghost Troop, while DeStefano's four tanks completed the half-circle on Eagle Troop's southern flank. Petschek's scouts were split, with one scout section on each side of Hamilton's tanks and one section tied into the rear of Destefano's tanks. Gauthier's scouts stretched from 4th Platoon back to a point in the desert where, eventually, Eagle and Iron Troop would regain contact.

Then I called McMaster to find out whether his scouts had contact with Ghost's flank scout platoon or 3rd Squadron. McMaster told me that Petschek's scouts were already looking for Lt. Paul Haines' platoon and that Tim Gauthier's platoon was on its way to make contact with Iron Troop, 3rd Squadron's left flank cavalry troop. Tim Gauthier had last seen Iron Troop around the 69 Easting, now more than two miles behind us on the right. Tony Ierardi was tracking 3rd Armored Division, keeping Fox Troop informed of when and where 3rd Armored Division's cavalry squadron would make contact.

Confident that McMaster's scouts would soon find Ghost Troop's right flank, I asked Hillen (who was on my flank in Cougar Forward) to tell Dragoon Base that we had just encountered and destroyed a large enemy formation, including an unknown number of enemy tanks and armored fighting vehicles. As usual, Hillen was already on top of things. Meanwhile, my head was swimming.

I felt like I had just drunk a bottle of twelve-year-old single-malt scotch without pausing. It seems strange to say it now, but the surreal experience of driving through the enemy, engaging enemy tanks at five hundred meters and killing enemy troops at ranges as close as fifteen meters, was intoxicating. It was also macabre.

For a moment, I had the eerie sensation that we were bit players in one of Arnold Schwarzenegger's action films. Everything around us had exploded or died, but we, like film characters, had miraculously survived. It was not a macho moment. It was just the realization that death surrounded us on every side but, thankfully, had passed us by.

But it was no time for contemplation. I had to suppress the urge to think about what had just happened. As I regained communication with the troop, company, and battery commanders, John Hillen scrambled to report events to Dragoon Base. To my left, however, another action, of which I was as yet unaware, was getting under way.

Ghost Troop had encountered scattered enemy elements between the 60 and 70 Eastings, but not the large concentration of enemy that Sartiano was sure was lurking somewhere to his front. Sartiano figured that the short, sharp engagements on the way up to the 73 Easting undoubtedly represented encounters with forward outposts for larger, defending enemy forces.

Whenever possible, Sartiano directed Ghost Troop to engage the enemy with both mortars and indirect fire. Now, as he moved forward to come on line with Eagle Troop, he told his gunner to engage whatever looked potentially hostile with 7.62 machine-gun fire. With the weather clearing, it was finally possible for Sartiano to see more than just hotspots in the thermal sights. Listening to the troop net, he and Mecca both knew that Garwick's 1st Platoon scouts still had no contact in the north and that Haines' 3rd Platoon scouts on the southern flank were busy regaining coherence.

As most of Ghost Troop rolled to a stop just short of the 73 Easting, sometime between 1630 and 1640 hours, Sartiano told his gunner to put a HEAT round into what looked like a tank 548 meters to his front. Sartiano laid the gun on the target, released the controls to his gunner, and waited until the gunner said "Identified," confirming that he had found the target. As soon as "Up!" came out of the gunner's mouth, Sartiano yelled, "Fire!" and the gun went off. The target blew up, but not much happened. Sartiano repeated the engagement against what turned out to be another BMP, only this time the results were spectacular fireworks.

Seeing the secondary explosions, Sartiano called Mecca and said, "Ghost 5, Ghost 6, just destroyed two targets to my front."

Acting as Sartiano's wingman, Mecca was able to see the engagements and report them to Cougar Forward before Sartiano even mentioned them. However, remembering how Captain Scott, our intelligence officer, became furious whenever reports from the cavalry troops failed to provide exact vehicle descriptions, Mecca decided that he needed more details from Sartiano,

"Target description, over," asked Mecca.

"Ghost 5, I have no f—king idea, they could be tanks, they could be BMPs, hell it could be a truck convoy for all I know, but they're smokin' now."

That was enough for Mecca, whose response was limited to a single "hooaah"—the Army's ubiquitous remark for "Yes, I understand," a war cry, and everything in between.

Sartiano's position at this juncture should be familiar to anyone who has ever been to war. Although the sandstorm had diminished to the point where visibility now reached out beyond a thousand meters, the smoke and fire from recently destroyed enemy equipment more than compensated for the disappearance of the sandstorm.

Visibility in war is never perfect. Battlefields are not tidy, and desert fights are no exceptions, as we would repeatedly discover over the next several hours.

EIGHT

Danger Close!

A favorable situation will never be exploited
if commanders wait for orders.

HELMUTH VON MOLTKE, 1866

1630 HOURS, ADVANCING TO THE 73 EASTING WITH GHOST TROOP

Ghost Troop was now approaching the 73 Easting disposed in a loose line, with the two scout platoons on either flank and the tanks in the center forming a lazy wedge—Lt. Andy Kilgore's tank platoon a little to the left and behind Sartiano and Mecca.

A little to the right and behind Sartiano's tank in the center was Kinsley's (not his real name) tank platoon, in reserve. Lieutenant Kinsley, a West Point graduate, had joined Ghost Troop just before the squadron deployed to the Combat Maneuver Training Center (CMTC) at Hohenfels, Germany, and was learning the proverbial ropes when war came. Very young in appearance, Kinsley was the archetypal kid in John Wayne's World War II movies.

Kilgore, an athletic and aggressive University of Tennessee graduate, arrived just in time to take over the 2nd Platoon tanks and deploy with Ghost Troop to Saudi Arabia. His previous service with a tank battalion in 1st Infantry Division (Forward), the 3rd Brigade of the 1st Infantry Division (Mechanized), the rest of which was stationed at Fort Riley, Kansas, was cut short when his battalion was disbanded. Disappointed with the prospect of filling some bureaucratic position in Germany, Andy Kilgore begged to be assigned to a fighting unit that would deploy to the Gulf, and the chain

Figure 11. Ghost Troop Actions on 73 Easting

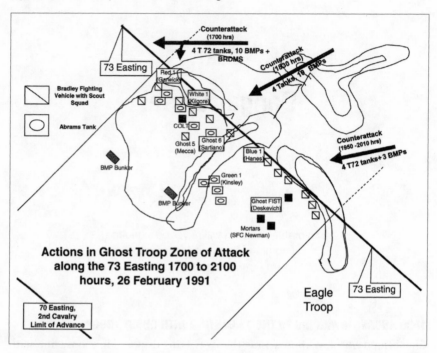

of command finally granted his wish. Despite his short service with Ghost Troop, Kilgore fit in well with Sartiano's relaxed, caring, but demanding style of leadership.

Curiously, the middle of Ghost's zone, just ahead of where Ghost Troop's tanks were concentrated, was bisected by a rise that ran east to west, with small spurs of one or two meters in height leading off to the north and south. As the night wore on, these modest terrain features, together with bowl-like depressions in front and north of Ghost Troop, would shape the conduct of the fight that was to come.

Staring at the cloud of smoke from a burning BMP blowing across his front, Andy Kilgore decided that sitting behind the growing smoke screen made no sense. Patience was not one of Kilgore's virtues. He called Sartiano for permission to move his tank platoon forward through the smoke: "Ghost 6, White 1, request permission to move forward through smoke, over."

Sartiano's response was quick and to the point.

"White 1, Ghost 6, make your move, over."

"White 1, roger, out."

As Kilgore's tanks moved forward through the smoke, Sartiano looked at his watch and saw that it was now about 1630 hours. He concluded, shit, this is dumb. Why not send all of the tanks forward? Nine tanks moving forward would be better than four. So Sartiano got on the radio and said, "White 1, Ghost 6, halt on the far side of the smoke. I will bring up the rest of the tanks, over,"

Thinking that Kilgore had heard his command, Sartiano watched patiently as Kilgore's four tanks disappeared into the smoke on his left. While he waited for a call from Kilgore that his tanks were halted and ready to fire, he prepared to move the remaining four tanks up on line with Kilgore's tanks. But the call never came. Then, to put it bluntly, all hell broke loose.

Kilgore's tanks moved forward. Kilgore opened fire first, yelling, "Enemy tanks direct front, direct frontal fire!" Firing their main guns as they advanced, tearing T72 tanks and BMPs to pieces, the drivers, gunners, loaders, and tank commanders were all filled with that strange emotional mixture of apprehension and elation that is inseparable from offensive action. Yes, they were scared, but they were also ready to kill, nonetheless.

In a few seconds, Kilgore's four tanks broke right into the Iraqi defensive positions, ripping a big hole in the middle, turning through and around the bunkers that stood near each of the tank and BMP fighting positions.[1]

Thanks to the smoke of the burning BMPs, along with the suddenness and force of Kilgore's assault, his four tanks achieved complete surprise. By the time Kilgore's tank commanders had finished off the dozen or so BMPs and two T72 tanks in the company strongpoint, the Iraqi defenders had fired no more than two or three main-gun rounds and no antitank guided missiles at all.

Kilgore was relieved. His tank commanders looked around, waving excitedly at each other.

"What a rush," Kilgore said quietly under his breath while streams of sweat poured over his brow.

But the action was far from over. In the midst of the wrecked and burning motorized rifle company, an amazing event now occurred.

Large numbers of green-clad Iraqi infantrymen suddenly jumped up from the surrounding bunkers and defensive positions and began firing RPGs and AK47s from less than twenty meters away, directly at the four American tanks. While Kilgore's tanks tried to return fire, a couple of Iraqi troops managed to get into a BMP that wasn't burning and man the 73-mm cannon in the turret. They got off a round, but it flew too high and just missed Kilgore's tank.

Realizing that the Abrams tanks were too close to engage with main guns, Kilgore told his tank commanders to maneuver their tanks to bring their machine guns into action as best they could against the masses of Iraqi infantry running and firing at them from all directions. What had started out as an orderly advance now disintegrated into pure chaos.

Unable to see the battle that was raging on the other side of the smoke clouds, Sartiano called Kilgore on the radio. Suppressing the feelings of concern and apprehension he knew must be detectable in his voice, he controlled his temper and repeated, "White 1, Ghost 5, report, over."

"White 1, this is Ghost 6, answer, goddamn it, over"

"White 1, this is Ghost 6, what is your status, over?"

"White 1, Ghost 6, answer the goddamn radio, over!"

It was hopeless. Kilgore's radio had slipped off the Ghost Troop frequency. Kilgore couldn't hear anything and even if he did, what could he do? He had a battle to fight. Fight the battle, then report. That was Kilgore's thinking, and he was right.

Sergeant Macom, Ghost Troop's communications chief, hearing the frustration in Sartiano's voice, dropped down to Kikgore's platoon net in an effort to figure out what was happening. Upon hearing the chaotic radio traffic on Kilgore's platoon net, he told Mecca, "Sir, Kilgore's platoon is in some serious shit. Better tell the old man."

Hearing the tension in Macom's voice, Mecca immediately reported to Sartiano that Kilgore was engaging an unknown number of Iraqi troops at point-blank range and was too busy to report.

Sartiano felt that hollowness in his stomach that comes with the realization that for the moment events were beyond your control. He stopped trying to reach Kilgore over the radio. Angry and a little frightened, he kept saying to himself, over and over again: "What the f—k do I do now?"

Pushing forward into the smoke and confusion could make things worse, even cause fratricide. No, Sartiano concluded, Kilgore would have to figure it out.

Kilgore was figuring it out. He knew that his tactic wasn't working. Neither he nor the rest of his tank commanders could get rid of the attacking Iraqis. They swarmed closer through the bunker complex, partially hidden by the smoke from the burning vehicles in their midst, piling on with their automatic weapons and RPGs.

Kilgore's tank crews were spraying machine-gun fire from every available weapon to the left and right of the tanks ahead or next to them in order to keep the Iraqi soldiers from reaching the tracks, but it was getting damn dangerous, and there was no time to think.

With his own .50-caliber heavy machine gun Kilgore was cutting to pieces Iraqi soldiers who were now no more than fifteen meters away. Body parts were flying everywhere. The sight sickened Kilgore, but any slackening of fire, and he knew that the Iraqis would be on them.

But soon it became clear that the tank commanders and the gunners inside the turrets could not depress their guns low enough to kill the Iraqi infantry that was now "danger close." If any of the Iraqi troops crawled up next to the tanks, Kilgore thought, they could probably plant charges on the tracks without ever being seen. Without more standoff, he and his tank commanders simply could not reach the Iraqi troops with their streams of 7.62- and .50-caliber bullets.

"Back up!" Kilgore yelled into his mike at the top of his lungs, "Everybody, back the f—k up now, over!"

Nobody answered, and for a split second Kilgore experienced the anxiety that Sartiano had been feeling. But Kilgore's men got the message. In a few seconds, the tank drivers slammed their transmissions into reverse and backed up. As the tanks jerked backward, they threw up great clogs of sand and gravel behind them like warships reversing course to avoid running aground. While the tanks moved backward, the gunners fired their machine guns without pause. Iraqi troops unlucky enough to end up behind the retrograding tanks either ran or crawled out of the way or were pinned under the tracks of the Abrams tanks and crushed.

Kilgore recalled seeing one Iraqi soldier whose legs had been completely blown off. He was propped upright and waving at Kilgore who was bearing down on him in reverse. Seeing that the man was still alive and now in the direct path of his right track, Kilgore tried to steer the tank around him, but there was not much he could do. It was a tragic moment that for a split second filled Kilgore with sorrow and empathy, but it changed nothing. Moving the tanks back as quickly as possible took priority.

No more than thirty seconds later, Kilgore's tanks were on line about a hundred meters to the west of where they had stopped. Now, salvos of red-hot tracers from the tanks' .50-caliber machine guns poured like water from high-pressure fire hoses into the Iraqi infantry. Despite the senselessness of it all, the remaining Iraqi troops kept coming. Did they think they had driven off the tanks and were winning the battle? Kilgore and his tank commanders had no idea. They just reloaded their 7.62- and .50-caliber machine guns and fired, fired, and fired.

Sixty seconds later the battle was over, but Kilgore wasn't taking any chances this time. He searched the desert in all directions thoroughly for any more Iraqi infantry.

Iraqi armor continued to burn like giant flares marking an accident on Interstate 95 between Baltimore, Maryland, and Washington, D.C. In front of the four tanks, Kilgore finally concluded, nothing lived anymore. Where once green-colored uniforms had darted in and out of bunkers, there were now only heaps of corpses. The Iraqi soldiers had been blown to pieces. The Republican Guard company strongpoint was now a heavy-metal graveyard.

Other than the blowing wind, the only thing the tank commanders could hear was the sound of their own blood humming in their ears.

When no more Iraqi soldiers appeared, Kilgore leaned back in the commander's hatch. His eyes filled with tears of relief. Then, Kilgore began wondering, where the hell is the rest of Ghost Troop? He realized he needed to report what had happened. Seeing that the tanks were back on line and in good condition, Mecca beat Kilgore to the punch. He called Kilgore on his platoon frequency, prompting him to report to Sartiano.

Kilgore instantly dropped down inside to check his radio and discovered that he was not on the Ghost Troop frequency. He knew exactly what that meant; "F—k," he said. When the attack began, Kilgore figured, his right knee had struck the radio switch on the junction box inside the tank, where his "spaghetti cord" to his CVC helmet connected, and had cut communications with his troop commander.

Thanks to Mecca's call, he dialed up the right frequency and moved the switch on his CVC helmet. Kilgore was almost out of breath when he spoke into the mike:

"Ghost 6, this is White 1, report follows, over."

"This is Ghost 6, where the f—k have you been?"

"Sir, I mean, Ghost 6, engaged and destroyed a dozen BMPs, tanks, and unknown number of enemy troops, over."

"White 1, understand. If you ever do that again, I will shoot you myself, goddamn it!"

In retrospect, Sartiano's comment may seem a bit over the top, but Kilgore knew he'd screwed up. But he was also happy. He and his tank crews had killed the enemy without dying in the process. Not much else he could say at this point, so he kept his response short.

"This is White 1, Roger, sir, uh . . . over."

Kilgore's charge into the Iraqi position had taken the initiative completely away from the defending Iraqi soldiers. It was in Sartiano's words a truly great action. How great it was, neither Sartiano nor I would realize until well after the battle was over.

With Kilgore's tanks back in the fold, Sartiano now moved the troop forward to the 73 Easting, with Garwick's scouts on the left along what would become much later the seam with 3rd Armored Division, and on the right Haines' scouts, who were still trying to regain contact with Petschek's scouts on the boundary with Eagle Troop. A little to the right and behind the screen line that Haines was trying to establish sat 4th Platoon tanks in reserve, under Lieutenant Kinsley.

Meanwhile, Petschek coolly worked his way through the wall of smoke and flame that separated Eagle and Ghost troops from the Iraqi enemy to our front, engaging Iraqi armor and infantry all the way to the 73 Easting. It was here that Petschek discovered for the first time how Iraqi infantry would lie face down over their grenade launchers and machine guns, waiting for the advancing Americans to pass. Their behavior filled him with disgust. Fortunately, the Bradley gunners usually detected the fraud using their infrared sights to see the still living "hot" bodies, yelling, "They're not dead. They've got weapons!"

Petschek later estimated that his platoon fired four hundred rounds of high-explosive incendiary tracer ammunition at point-blank range into dozens and dozens of Iraqi infantrymen who had played this game. The resulting carnage was gruesome.

From the fire-support net, I learned that Sam White's battery was in place with all eight guns ready to fire, but only four guns from 6-41 Field Artillery were on hand to respond to missions. This situation was not Colonel Adair's fault.

The pointless nightlong road march to 1st Infantry Division and back to Cougar Squadron had taken its toll on Adair's artillery battalion. Adair's troops were exhausted, and their equipment was scattered all over the desert. As the night of 26 February wore on, the numbers and readiness of the artillery systems in the battalion would increase, and they would strike the enemy hard, but for most of the fight we would rely primarily on Cpt. Sam White's battery.

Fortunately, we had broken the enemy's back with Abrams tank 120-mm and Bradley 25-mm fire before a single artillery shell went down range. The question for me was, What would happen once we stopped and could no longer advance?

Whenever armored formations are static for long periods, they are at risk. That is when artillery begins to play a significant role. We were stopped. How much artillery would we need now, I wondered?

It was now getting close to 1710 hours, and we still had no positive contact between Ghost and Eagle troops. Restoring contact between Ghost and Eagle, and ensuring that Eagle Troop regained contact with Iron Troop, now three kilometers to our right rear, were critical. Worried that we still had no face-to-face contact on the ground with either Iron Troop or Ghost Troop, I called McMaster again for an update on his progress with regaining contact on the flanks.

Petschek, McMaster said, was on his way to meet Haines at a mutually agreed contact point between Ghost and Eagle troops. McMaster also told me that Gauthier was trying to make contact with Iron Troop on the radio but could not get a response.

Despite Gifford's entreaties, however, Iron Troop kept telling Eagle Troop that it was in contact and to get off its net. By 1715 hours, Lt. Tim Purdue, Hawk Company's executive officer, was providing Cougar Forward updates on Iron Troop's slow but steady movement to the 70 Easting toward the enemy defensive position through which Eagle Troop had punched right at 1618 hours.

Eventually, McMaster got on the Iron Troop command net to say, "Dan, this is H.R., we need to coordinate, over."

McMaster and Cpt. Dan Miller, the Iron Troop commander, were West Point classmates. McMaster's personal appeal worked. Gauthier's scouts regained contact with Iron Troop, and the two troops tracked each other's positions carefully for the rest of the night. Based on Iron Troop's movement, Gauthier recommended to McMaster that Eagle Troop not engage south of a 120-degree magnetic azimuth. We established this azimuth as an internal

Figure 12. Cougar Squadron on 73 Easting 1700 hrs, 26 February

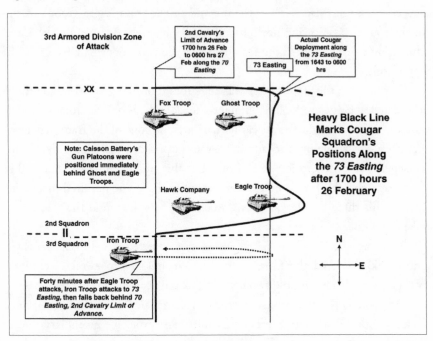

control measure until Iron Troop fell back behind the 2nd Cavalry's limit of advance, the 70 Easting, two miles behind us.

Finding Haines, however, turned out to be a tougher mission than anticipated. Petschek knew that Haines' scouts had dropped back behind the 73 Easting during Eagle's assault. He was concerned that he and the scout section that moved with him to establish contact might easily be mistaken for an enemy vehicle. As it grew darker, the intensity with which the Iraqi armor burned and exploded increased the danger of fratricide. Petschek decided to move toward the hastily agreed contact point on the seam between the two troops with a scout section of two Bradleys.

Petschek moved out cautiously. He later said that there was no point in risking a firefight with a nervous Ghost Troop gunner who might be doing exactly the same thing, looking for Eagle Troop. With the two Bradleys on his right, Petschek maneuvered around some abandoned bunkers and burning equipment that seemed to mark the perimeter of another Iraqi defensive position.

About 1,500 meters short of where Petschek expected to find the contact point, he sighted between nine and thirteen armored vehicles, including several intact T72 tanks in a circular defensive position. This discovery came as a complete surprise, because the fire and smoke from Eagle Troop's battle in the south was blowing north along the 73 Easting. As a result, the Iraqi strongpoint that straddled the seam between the two troops had been missed completely.

Fortunately, the Iraqi troops walking around on the ground beside their armored vehicles were looking straight ahead, perhaps anticipating a frontal assault, based on Eagle Troop's earlier tank attack. None of the Iraqis detected Petschek. No scout likes to admit he was surprised on the battlefield, and Petschek was no exception to the rule, but this was no time to lament the circumstances. The Iraqi soldiers were no more than nine hundred meters in front of his three Bradleys, and any second they might sound the alarm and take him under effective fire.

Cool as ice, Petschek halted his section, erected his TOW launcher, and quickly ordered the firing of two TOW missiles in rapid succession, concentrating his fire on the two nearest T72 tanks.

As soon as the two tanks exploded in flame, all three of his remaining Bradleys opened up with a mix of 25-mm high-explosive incendiary tracer rounds, rounds that glow red hot as they race to the target, and 25-mm sabot ammunition. Like its bigger brother, the 120-mm sabot round, shot from tanks, the Bradley 25-mm sabot has a depleted-uranium warhead, and it flies with amazing speed and accuracy.

The Iraqi BMPs managed to get off a few rounds, but nothing came close to hitting Eagle Troop's scouts. After three minutes of furious firing, Petschek ordered the group to cease fire, and it continued its trek to Ghost Troop.

A couple of minutes later, Petschek crossed the boundary between the two troops, found Ghost Troop's 3rd Scout Platoon, drove up, and parked beside a very surprised but grateful Lieutenant Haines. At roughly 1720 hours the two scout platoon leaders exchanged information. After a brief discussion, Haines agreed to follow Petschek back to the point in the desert where Eagle Troop's left flank would be anchored. On the way back, however, Petschek discovered that one of the Iraqi tanks had escaped detection earlier during the first battle and was now scanning the desert to its front with its main gun.

Petschek decided not to fire a TOW missile, because the warhead would be flying through Eagle Troop. Instead, he moved in close to improve penetration velocity for his shells. Closing with the enemy in a Bradley fighting vehicle is not the recommended solution when the enemy is a T72 tank, but Petschek reasoned it was unavoidable on this occasion. He poured twenty rounds of 25-mm HEAT into the side of the enemy tank until smoke poured from every opening.

Satisfied that the Iraqi defenders were finally all dead, Petschek continued his move south. However, it would be close to 1800 hours before Petschek finally regained contact with Eagle Troop.

Meanwhile, Iraqi armored units began reappearing, about 800 to 1,500 meters to Eagle Troop's right front. Like large rocks that reinforce a pier protruding into the ocean, mounds of burning Iraqi tanks and armored fighting vehicles began piling up in a "U" around the right flank held by Eagle Troop. It was unclear whether the Iraqis were deliberately throwing whatever they had against the peninsula formed by Eagle Troop's tanks and scouts along the Cougar Squadron's right flank with 3rd Squadron or were just retreating across the regiment's front until they ran into Cougar Squadron, but from 1710 hours on, Eagle Troop's convulsive tank and TOW missile fire was deafening. Bullets kicked up dirt in front of the tank, periodically pinging off Ward's hatch and the front slope, but the enemy attacks were repulsed. Nothing remained of the Iraqi forces but wreckage and bodies.

About this time, Burns pulled Cougar Forward in between Eagle 6 and my tank and began engaging Iraqi vehicles with his TOW missile launcher and 25-mm.

Normally, I would have welcomed this development, but there wasn't much room left along the front where the tanks were positioned, and the noise was deafening. McMaster called me to complain that Burns had positioned Cougar Forward dangerously close to his tank.

I agreed.

When I told Burns to back Cougar Forward off the line, he was disappointed. He made a typical Burns comment: "Shit, I'm just trying to get some scraps off the table."

It was time to pull back Cougar Forward and set up a temporary static command post twenty-five meters behind my tank. This suited John Hillen, who was now heavily engaged with Dragoon Base on the radio and could hardly hear the command nets over the firing from the tanks and Cougar Forward.

I'LL BE GODDAMNED IF I'LL FALL BACK

In the desert, nightfall normally falls like a hammer, but this time the transition from day to night did not bring real darkness.

Visibility worsened, but it never really grew dark. Iraqi T72 tanks, trucks, and other armored vehicles burned furiously from horizon to horizon. In fact, fires burned well into the night that followed, with secondary explosions splitting the air about every fifteen or twenty minutes until midnight.

With tank and TOW fire coming into their flanks and across their routes of withdrawal, the Iraqi armored formations moving to our front disintegrated and the buildup of burning and tangled wreckage around the peninsula formed by Eagle Troop grew larger and larger.

It was soon apparent to us that the mountain of wreckage provided the Iraqi troops who survived the encounter with new positions from which they could fire at us, primarily with small arms and automatic cannon.

Our inability to advance beyond the 73 Easting granted the Iraqis to our front a temporary reprieve from execution. This is where the 4.2-inch mortars came back into play. Eagle Troop mortars repeated the deadly tactic of mixing ground-burst white phosphorous ("Willie Pete") rounds with air-burst high explosive to decimate anything living that our main guns could not effectively engage. As soon as the "Willie Pete" rounds burst among the trenches and shattered armor, Iraqi troops would jump out to escape the acid-like white phosphorous while high-explosive rounds filled the air around them with shrapnel. Seconds after the mortar attack started, machine guns and 25-mm chain guns opened up, completing the slaughter.

After a short while, an occasional spray of bullets peppered the desert floor beneath our tank or a larger-caliber round would hiss by, but by and large the enemy's fire slackened to the point where I could no longer suppress my hunger.

I absolutely had to eat. It was about 1715 hours when I lifted myself out of the hatch, keeping one eye on the enemy to the front while moving to the rear deck, where I could stand and get at the bustle rack on the back side of the turret. To my great relief, despite the small-arms and RPG hits on the tank, the ammo can that contained the ingredients for my peanut butter and jelly sandwich was intact. I quickly opened the can and put together a sandwich oozing with peanut butter and jelly. Standing on the back deck of the tank, behind the turret bustle rack, I sank my teeth into one of the most delicious peanut butter and jelly sandwiches I have ever eaten.

When I finished wolfing down the sandwich, I climbed back inside the turret. Sergeant Jones had been keeping watch to the front and told me that he had "acquired" another armored vehicle in a defensive position.

With the laser range finder, Sergeant Jones determined that the target was about 1,500 meters away.

After a short discussion, Abercrombie loaded a HEAT round, and Jones sent a roaring ball of fire into the target. The fiery splash signaled that we had hit something substantial, but we were never quite sure just what it was.

Four thousand meters to my left, Lt. Keith Garwick reported to Sartiano that BMPs and tanks were concentrated to the left of his scout platoon at a range of perhaps 3,500 meters and moving in his direction. Since these Iraqi elements were really in the 3rd Armored Division's zone of attack, Sartiano's principal concern was that Garwick establish positive identification of the enemy before engaging. However, when Mecca confirmed with Ierardi that 3rd Armored Division's cavalry squadron was still at least an hour or more behind us, Garwick got permission to engage.

By 1705 hours, Ghost Troop was fighting a serious battle on the squadron's northern flank.

From where eighteen-year-old Pvt. 1st Class Jason E. Kick sat in the driver's seat of Ghost 14, a Bradley fighting vehicle in Garwick's scout platoon, the whole action looked like chaos. Speaking into the tape recorder he brought along, Kick repeated, "This is chaos here, this is total chaos."[2]

Listening to Garwick's fire commands, Kick noted, "Red 1 [Garwick], he's the platoon leader. You can hear it in his voice, he's all shook up."[3]

Kick was right, but lieutenants and captains are paid to create order out of chaos at the platoon and company levels, where chaos is the soldier's constant companion in war.

As this was his first significant engagement with an enemy who shot back, Garwick was surely shaken. But like the officers in Eagle Troop, Garwick controlled his emotions and suppressed the nagging fear of death that makes cowards of otherwise brave men. He asked Sartiano for immediate tank and artillery support.

Thanks to the combat observation lasing team (COLT)—an M981 fire-support vehicle—operating with Garwick's scout platoon, Garwick knew that the range to the Iraqi formation was about 3,600 meters. Deskevich and Mecca worked with Garwick and 2nd Lt. Greg Franks, the COLT leader, to get the artillery started.

When asked for artillery support, however, Cpt. Jack Millar, the Cougar Squadron fire-support officer, said no, on the grounds that the target area was in 3rd Armored Division's future zone of attack. The fire direction officer

(FDO) of 6-41 FA knew that 3rd Armored Division was still hours behind us, heard Millar on the fire-support net, sensed the urgency of the situation, and overruled Millar.

The FDO had tactical control of the guns, even if eight of the twelve guns were in Sam White's battery, and could do as he wished with them. Seconds later, the guns roared, and rounds were on the way. The FDO's instincts for the battle were superb.

While Garwick reported to Sartiano, Sergeant Garcia in Ghost 12, another Bradley fighting vehicle in Garwick's platoon, launched the first of eight TOW missiles into what Garcia described as a platoon of Iraqi tanks three thousand meters or more to his front. The tanks were backing out of their defensive positions before moving to attack Ghost Troop's positions along the 73 Easting when the rest of Garwick's scouts joined in and engaged them.[4]

Grasping that Garwick's situation had changed dramatically, Sartiano and Mecca moved north to join Garwick's scout platoon, "scrambling" the troop as he drove across the desert and sending Kilgore's four tanks 1,800 meters north to positions right behind Garwick's platoon. "Scrambling" reorganized Garwick's scout platoon and Kilgore's tank platoon into scout-tank teams, as they had practiced in January. Ghost Troop called these "viper teams" (1st and 2nd platoons) and "dragon teams" (3rd and 4th platoons).

Staff Sergeant Lundquist from 2nd Platoon picked up a scout section of four Bradleys from Garwick's 1st Platoon scouts, and Sergeant First Class Lawrence, Garwick's platoon sergeant, added two tanks to his four Bradleys. Once integrated with fifty or sixty meters between vehicles, the force of six Bradleys and four tanks began systematically engaging the stationary Iraqi armor.

As soon as Kilgore's tanks showed up, the tank gunners "lazed" the mix of eleven BMPs with perhaps nine tanks. The laser range finder returned a range of three thousand meters. Sartiano also placed Kinsley's four tanks in reserve behind and to the left of Haines' scouts.

Without waiting for the artillery to fall on the Iraqi troops, Kilgore's tanks went immediately into action, firing four sabot rounds into the mix of Iraqi armor. Garwick in Ghost 11 and Sergeant Robbins in 15 didn't wait either. They launched two more TOW missiles.

The veins on the Bradley gunners' hands turned blue as they tightly gripped the fire controls, guiding the warheads through the dim light into the Iraqi tanks.

Seconds later, the artillery rained down on the Iraqi armor and stopped them dead in their tracks just as the warheads on the TOW missiles detonated against the sides of two BMPs. In what would be a pattern for the rest of the night, whenever Iraqi troops came under artillery or mortar fire, they just halted.

This was the first time the scouts had seen DPICM in action, and they were amazed at the effect the bomblets were having on the Iraqi armor. Imagine a thousand exploding baseballs crashing into a metal box in which you are sitting, and you have some idea of what the scouts saw and what the Iraqi troops must have experienced.

After fifteen tense minutes, the tank and Bradley gunners finally relaxed, watching columns of flame and smoke rise up in their sights where the Iraqi tanks had deployed on line. When Garwick's scouts and Kilgore's tankers saw no evidence of further movement, no sign of life, they began cheering inside their turrets.

Hearing Mecca report destroyed enemy tanks and BMPs to "Cougar 32" (Ierardi), I decided to dismount from my tank and see what was happening inside Cougar Forward, where I knew the communications were much better. While the tank main guns and TOW missile launchers sporadically engaged enemy armor and troops to our front and right flank, I walked back to Staff Sergeant Burns' Bradley, where John Hillen was struggling to explain events over the radio to Regiment.

As I dismounted, I found McMaster waiting for me behind my tank. He was ecstatic.

Immediately, I slapped my hand into McMaster's and said, "Congratulations, Captain. Brilliant performance, you did exactly what you were supposed to do. Well done."

McMaster responded: "Wasn't it great? We smashed right through them!"

When he shook my hand, it was obvious McMaster was relieved to hear me tell him that he done the right thing. And he was justifiably delighted with the performance of his soldiers. The months of preparation, of demanding gunnery training in Germany, of endless and exhausting maneuvers in the Arabian Desert, and McMaster's own brand of inventive and aggressive leadership had paid off handsomely.

McMaster asked me what I thought was happening at Regiment and quickly followed up with the $64,000 question: "Where is Colonel Holder?"

I said, "H. R., I don't know."

McMaster kept repeating over and over, "Sir, he should be here. He should see this, don't you think so?"

Of course, McMaster was quite right, but I did not expect to see the regimental commander. Holder had to contend with the corps commander. I assumed Holder would continue to try to orchestrate operations from his command post, several kilometers to the right and rear of our position on the 73 Easting.

"H. R., I don't think Regiment has the slightest idea of what the hell we just did. But that won't matter when they find out."

"What do you mean?" asked McMaster.

"Remember what Wellington said after the battle of Waterloo?" I asked.

McMaster knew that Wellington had said a lot, so he simply nodded, not really knowing what I might quote.

I continued, "Defeat is an orphan, but victory has many fathers. H. R., you can bet there will be a lot of paternity suits on the street when this motherf—er is over."

McMaster laughed until our discussion was interrupted by a sudden outburst of tank fire from the line behind us. McMaster said he better get back to the troop. I agreed. We shook hands and parted.

When I arrived at the rear of Cougar Forward, I found that Burns had dropped the rear ramp and that the entire crew, including T. K. Wightman, Burns, and Holloway, was waiting for me. The incessant racket of tank and artillery fire did not stop them from enjoying the fresh night air.

Hillen was comfortably reclining with his legs outside of the vehicle and the rest of him inside. I could not hear the radio clearly, but I could see that John was engaged in a heated conversation with Dragoon Base. John's face was somewhat contorted as he raised his voice to make his point again and again.

"Dragoon Base, this is Cougar Forward. We are located from right to left along the 73 Easting vicinity Papa Uniform—we are at 100 percent combat power. We are in a strong position, over."

After the first half-hour of dealing with Regiment's apparent indifference to anything Hillen or Ierardi reported while bouncing all over the battlefield, Hillen turned to Wightman and said, "Why am I even bothering? We could be fighting giant squid on the moon for all the good it's doing to tell them anything."

Wightman nodded his head but kept silent.

Hillen continued to repeat the message that we had arrived without any losses along the 73 Easting after destroying an undetermined number of enemy tanks, BMPs, and infantry, finally telling Dragoon Base, "Stand by."

Because I could not quite hear the content of the discussion, the whole thing puzzled me, so I asked him what the hell was happening.

Eventually, John put down the hand mike, looked at me, and said: "Regiment wants us to fall back to the 69 Easting, at least behind the 70 Easting."

Hillen pointed out that Dragoon Base was never interested in understanding or appreciating what happened—no matter how Ierardi or he portrayed it. Like Franks, Holder and the regimental staff were blindly wedded to the January battle plan, and beyond Regiment's insistence that we drop back to a now irrelevant limit of advance, they never offered anything—counsel, fire support, orders, supplies, maneuvering of the rest of the regiment, whatever.

In the end, John said in a voice filled with disappointment, "Regiment's only response is to retreat."

All at once, every ounce of frustration and disgust I had felt for months with the chain of command's ardent opposition to a rapid, decisive attack erupted from the depths of my soul.

In nearly six months of service in Saudi Arabia and Iraq, I was genuinely angry only twice. The first time occurred during training in January. The second time happened at about 1715 hours on 26 February 1991.

I could not believe it. Fall back? Incredible, I thought. After this battle, and they tell us to fall back? I was enraged.

"Goddamn it, John. I will be goddamned if I will fall back in front of this incompetent scum. Nobody with my name has ever fallen back in front of anybody, never! Not in front of Arabs, Chinese, Afghans, Germans, Japs, or anything else, and I will be damned if I will now. What the hell is wrong with them? This is outrageous. What the hell is wrong with them? Why not attack instead? My God, what is wrong with them?"

Realizing that I was raging at John, who was now straightening himself up as if he were soon to be shot, I stopped and regained my composure.

"John," I said, "call Dragoon Base and ask them to pass the following message directly to Dragoon 6: Tell Dragoon 6 that Cougar 3 says we are in a strong position; there is no reason to fall back. Strongly recommend we stay where we are."

Hillen sent the message. As the gunfire was picking up, I went back to my tank to try to contact Regiment myself. As I walked back to the tank, Hillen turned to Burns and said, "That man can get mad as hell faster than anyone I have ever seen. But why the hell is he yelling at me? Christ, I'm not the one holding up the train."

Burns and Holloway burst out laughing. Burns said, "He's not mad at you, Lieutenant. He's just blowing off four months of frustration with the chain of command in one night. I wouldn't worry about it. When Holder hears the message, he'll let Macgregor stay here."

Overhearing the traffic between Dragoon Base and Cougar Forward, Steve Robinette walked over to the map and checked the coordinates that Hillen provided. He asked, Why not? Robinette saw no reason why Cougar Squadron should fall back. He picked up the mike and said, "Cougar Forward, Dragoon 5, tell Cougar 3 he can remain in position along the 73 Easting, over."

This news came at about 1730 hours. Robinette's call was a welcome relief to Hillen, who was tired of arguing the point.

Wiping the sweat off his brow, Hillen breathed a huge sigh, saying simply, "Dragoon 5, Cougar Forward, many thanks, roger, out!"

16, YOU'RE SKYLINED!

On the left flank where Garwick's scouts and Kilgore's tanks had just cheered the destruction of the Iraqi armor, three shells, presumably from more Iraqi tanks, struck the desert floor in front of the two Bradleys on Garwick's right just as permission came to Hillen for Cougar Squadron to remain along the 73 Easting.

Garwick's scouts reacted by reloading TOW missiles and 25-mm ammunition in anticipation of another round of action.

Noticing that one of the Bradleys, 16, which was Staff Sergeant Chaffee's track, was sitting on top of the spur that ran parallel with the 73 Easting, several people urged Chaffee to pull back, but he did not respond. For some strange reason, Chaffee and Sergeant Moller, his gunner, actually moved farther forward, probably to get a clearer shot at the enemy.

Upset with what was happening, Kilgore came on the radio, yelling the administrative call sign so there would be no doubt to whom he was speaking: "Sixteen, you're skylined, back down, over!"

Staff Sergeant Chaffee may not have heard the warning, because he was busy trying to clear his jammed 7.62 machine gun coaxial with and to the right of his 25-mm gun in the cramped Bradley turret. However, when he saw several Iraqi infantrymen running in his direction, Chaffee immediately stopped what he was doing and asked, "Moller, you got enemy troops to the front!"

Sergeant Moller could not pick them up in his sights, so he popped out of his hatch to take a look.

A split second later, an explosion shook the Bradley with the force of a sledgehammer, driving the twenty-six-ton Bradley backward for a meter. A few seconds later, a second round struck the Bradley, showering the front of the vehicle with sparks and hot metal.

Without a gun shield in front of him on top of his turret, Sergeant Moller was killed instantly.

Patrick Bledsoe, the driver of 16, looked behind him and yelled to see if anyone was alive. When he heard nothing, he jumped out of the driver's compartment and ran to the rear of the Bradley next to him. He pounded on the door. When the rear door didn't open, he went forward to the driver's hatch and pounded on it until it opened. Bledsoe pointed to 16, which was now smoking and said, "We just got hit. I think Sergeant Moller's dead."[5]

Watching the drama unfold from the commander's hatch of the COLT, Sergeant Foltz, a powerful man over six feet tall who cut a hulklike figure, got out of his track and ran toward 16 to pull out any survivors.

Kilgore provided covering fire while Foltz tried to get the survivors out of the Bradley hull before the TOW missiles inside blew up. When he could not open the rear door, Foltz jumped up on top of the vehicle and tried to open the cargo hatch. It was jammed shut.

The force of the striking round had actually jammed the cargo hatch shut, turning the damaged Bradley into a potential coffin for the survivors inside. Undeterred by the bullets whistling by his head, Foltz now picked up a tanker's bar (a solid steel rod about sixty or seventy inches long used to lift the tank's heavy track blocks) and began, in Deskevich's words, "beating the living hell out of the cargo hatch until it opened."

With the hatch open, Foltz reached inside, pulling out Chaffee and the observer in the back. Bradley 15 picked up the survivors, Spec. Terry Lorson and Staff Sergeant Chaffee, and sped them to the rear. Foltz would later receive the Silver Star for his heroic and unselfish actions under enemy fire. Chaffee and Lorson recovered from their wounds.

Dazed by the incident, Garwick announced on the troop net that Moller was dead. The net instantly went silent. Fortunately, Mecca once again dropped down to the platoon net. He broke the silence on the 1st Platoon scout net to get the report and get Garwick to repeat it without compromising security—this was a pain in the ass for Mecca. Hearing Mecca's voice on the radio, Garwick recovered quickly, telling his scouts, "Keep fighting. Don't lose focus. Keep fighting, out."

Garwick's fight coincided with continuing action in front of Eagle Troop. Iraqi armor in section and platoon size formations seemed to crash every fifteen or twenty minutes into Eagle Troop's flank. Hamilton's tanks fired repeatedly into a half-dozen Iraqi armored vehicles, which seemed to disintegrate under the impact of the tank fire. When artilleryman Lt. Danny Davis, the Eagle fire-support team leader, identified an Iraqi T72 tank from his vehicle maneuvering to Eagle Troop's front, Hamilton shot it to pieces with one sabot round before McMaster could find the tank and fire. Knowing the salvo had come from Hamilton, he called Hamilton and said, "White 1, that was spectacular."

Hamilton, yelling into the mike under his CVC helmet, replied "Roger. That is what we call the Hammy-Slammy, over."

To some, Hamilton's comment might seem out of place. But Hamilton's response was not bravado. His tank commanders were brimming with the confidence that superior training and leadership instill, and the big Canadian was having the time of his life.

As these actions wore on, they began to assume the character of a repetitious litany. It was hard to tell if these events really represented counterattacks or just retreating Iraqi forces struggling to get out of Kuwait.

Since we were roughly two miles farther east of the 70 Easting grid line, the 2nd Cavalry's established limit of advance, I assumed many of the Iraqi units were probably driving across the 2nd Cavalry Regiment's front without being engaged until, to their misfortune, they stumbled into Eagle Troop's killing machine on Cougar Squadron's right flank.

Not all of the Iraqi troops that collided with the right flank died, however. Staff Sergeant Foy, DeStefano's platoon sergeant, recognized that with the advantage of thermal sights his tanks could afford to exercise some restraint until it was clear that the Iraqi troops to their flank and front were attacking.

Most of the time, the Iraqi troops opened fire when they saw American armor, but thanks to Staff Sergeant Foy's cool head, Iraqi soldiers who wanted to surrender were allowed to do so. Because of Foy, two or three times in the course of the battle Iraqi troops walked into our lines as prisoners of war, where Eagle Troop's medics treated and evacuated the seriously wounded.

As Eagle Troop's most experienced medic, Sergeant George Piwetz was charged with the responsibility of evaluating and treating the most seriously wounded Iraqi troops. Piwetz, a tough but compassionate soldier, could see from the haggard looks on their faces that most of the Iraqi soldiers were relieved that their war was over. Of course, there were some exceptions. In one case, a wounded Iraqi soldier lying on a stretcher tried to stab Sergeant Piwetz with some loose hypodermic needles.

Piwetz unhesitatingly knocked the Iraqi unconscious with a right upper-cut, telling the now unconscious Iraqi he was a "dumb ass." Afterward, Piwetz continued treating his now cooperative Iraqi patient.

Sometime between 1720 and 1730, a disturbing message came over the Cougar Squadron command net. "Cougar 3, Sergeant Moller is dead."

The caller did not identify himself, and to this day none of us knows who sent the message, but whoever did, it was the wrong thing to say on a command net during a battle. First of all, we report by-name casualties on administrative-logistical radio nets. We do not use names on command nets, especially during fighting.

Personalizing battlefield losses is dangerous in war. Announcing the names of friends killed by the enemy always inflames the passions of soldiers already excited by combat. Soldiers quickly talk of revenge. Emotions run out of control. This condition must be avoided at all costs lest we lose men through uncontrolled actions. My response must have seemed heartless and cold to those listening, but I had to stop all further transmission of this kind:

"This is Cougar 3. Do not report our casualties on this net. Cougar 3 Out!"

Within seconds, Mecca reported over the logistics net that the Bradley designated as 16 had been destroyed with one killed and two wounded. Sartiano then broke in and added: "Continuing mission, Ghost 6 out."

"Continuing the mission," was the right statement for Sartiano to make. Indeed, what else could Sartiano say? In any case, I was reassured. No matter what happened, we had fought our way up to the 73 Easting, and we were not going to leave.

THEY JUST KEEP COMING

Watching through his thermal sights for movement in the desert to his front, Kilgore sweated heavily under his helmet. He could see more Iraqi armor moving toward the depression in the middle of 3rd Armored Division's zone of attack, about 3,500–4,000 meters away.

Kilgore lost no time in telling Garwick and Deskevich. Monitoring the report on the fire-support net, the fire direction officer at 6-41 FA made the decision to concentrate the fire of sixteen guns, including Caisson's eight guns, against this new target set. Ghost Troop now had all the available artillery working for it, and the fire-support officers, platoon leaders, and Mecca were hustling like mad to make full use of it.

Inside Captain White's fire direction center, with the hatches shut to maintain light discipline (that is, to prevent light from escaping and alerting the enemy to the fire-direction center's location), the radios blaring, and the computers running, five soldiers coping with the requests for fire were stripped down to their boots and underwear, drenched in sweat.

Caisson's guns had fired nonstop since 1700 hours, and the heat inside the M577 was unbearable, but this was what artillerymen craved—an opportunity to shoot relentlessly through the night.

This new group of attacking Iraqi troops made excellent targets. Just like their predecessors earlier in the evening, they came to a halt under the hail of artillery fire. It wasn't long before Garwick and Kilgore discovered they had a new set of stationary Iraqi targets for their gunners. Nine more TOW missiles were launched into the collection of Iraqi vehicles. Thirty seconds later, Garwick's gunners could see plumes of smoke rising from the burned-out hulks that a few minutes ago had been tanks and BMPs. This time, thirty Iraqi soldiers struggled out from the carnage to surrender.

Amazingly, despite the torrential artillery and TOW missile attacks, more Iraqi tanks, BMPs, and trucks continued to move into the depression. Garwick knew he had fired all of the TOW missiles on board his vehicle. Hearing Garwick's report that this new enemy concentration was potentially larger and moving much faster than the last group, Captain Millar, who had been listening to Deskevich describe the situation on the fire-support net, turned to Cpt. John Rogler, the squadron's air liaison officer, and asked him if he could do anything about the developing threat on Cougar Squadron's northern flank.

Rogler knew A-10 Thunderbolts were operating over 3rd Squadron, so he called Cpt. Greg Andreachi, the air liaison officer with 3rd Squadron, and asked him for assistance.

Fortunately, there were A-10s with fuel and bombs but no targets to strike. Andreachi said, "Sure, I'll send you two A-10s right away."

Rogler went to work immediately to establish the required airspace-coordination measures. This was no small matter for Rogler. Though there was still light on the battlefield, it was diminishing; that and the proximity of the enemy to Ghost Troop's scouts worried the hell out of him. We had come through a series of confusing engagements without shooting ourselves, and fratricide was the last thing he wanted now.

To make use of the airpower, Mecca and Eagle Troop's executive officer, Gifford, had to work feverishly to confirm the front trace for both troops. What was thought to be a blessing became a curse. Everyone in the chain of command in the two cavalry troops turned their attention to the air and artillery strikes while scouts and tanks were still in direct-fire contact with the enemy. Eventually, though, the scout platoon leaders in both troops sorted out the details with their respective fire-support team leaders to organize the A-10 strike while the troop executive officers worked with the scout platoon sergeants to get the details straight for the artillery strike that would follow the air strike.

Finally, the control measures were established, and Rogler made contact with the two A-10s over the radio. After briefing the A-10 pilots on their mission, he directed them to come up on the fire-support net with Deskevich, inside his M113 fire support vehicle. To mark the frontline trace for the incoming pilots, the artilleryman Deskevich placed a strobe light on top of his fire-support vehicle, a tracked armored vehicle.

The two Louisiana Air National Guard pilots with call signs "Cajun 33" and "Cajun 34" made contact with Deskevich and confirmed they were able to see the strobe light and the scouts now engaging the enemy with TOW missiles. Rogler was reassured enough to wipe the beads of sweat off of his forehead.

Rogler now spoke directly with the pilots: "Cajun 33, call in with direction, expect clearance on final, call friendlies and target in sight."

The pilots shot back with, "Roger, Cajun 33 and Cajun 34, thirty seconds out."

Rogler said later, these seconds were like minutes. He was deeply worried. From where he stood inside the Cougar Squadron TOC, it seemed dark as hell outside. It was nerve wracking to do this stuff in the daylight; in the darkness, it was a nightmare. Then, at about 1835, the A-10s popped up on the radio once more.

"This is Cajun 33, in from the west, friendlies in sight, targets in sight."

"This is Cajun 34, in from the west, friendlies in sight, targets in sight."

Rogler took a deep breath and answered, "Roger, Cajun 33, Cajun 34, you are cleared hot!"

On their first pass, the A-10s dropped five Mark 82 five-hundred-pound bombs, which burst over the heads of the Iraqi armor. Chain-smoking nonstop throughout the action, Rogler listened for the report over the radio. For an Air Force officer directing air strikes, the fear that something, anything, could go wrong, that Americans, not the enemy, could be killed, creates a feeling of broken glass in the stomach. Predictably, Rogler kept saying over and over under his breath, "Oh my God, I hope to hell we did not hit any friendlies."

Rogler should have relaxed. Everyone in the air and on the ground had performed their assigned tasks well. When Deskevich excitedly announced over the troop command net that A-10s were inbound, Ghost Troop seemed to execute a well-rehearsed "heads up," looking for the A-10 show. But the collective expectation of a grand and horrible scene of destruction was not fulfilled. The air strike was deeper in the dark battle space than could be seen by the troops in the flickering light of burning Iraqi armor in the distance.

Whether the bombs actually struck anything was never determined, but the combination of their bombing with their subsequent strafing with 30-mm GRU8 cannons definitely halted the Iraqi advance.

Meanwhile, as Deskevich was still engaged with the A-10 pilots from Louisiana, Mecca relayed Garwick's request to "repeat" more than five times, while scouts pounded the halted Iraqi armor with TOW missiles and 25-mm high-explosive ammunition. With each salvo, thirty-two of the 155-mm DPICM rounds, together with dozens of mortar rounds from Sergeant First Class Newman's mortar section, fell on top of the Iraqi formations.

Starting with a spectacular airburst, the exploding artillery bomblets created incredible scenes of destruction in the troop scouts' thermal sights. In fact, scouts said that the bomblets seemed to explode twice, striking in and around the enemy's vehicles, apparently annihilating everything in their path.

Mecca recalled having seen the so-called million-dollar minute of artillery fire during ROTC summer camp at Fort Bragg, North Carolina. But in comparison with the display of artillery killing power in the Iraqi desert, the million-dollar minute looked like a bunch of backyard bottle rockets.

The action in front of Garwick's scouts was diminishing. Iraqi vehicular movement stopped. Whatever remained intact of the original Iraqi defense hunkered down northeast of the depression astride 3rd Armored Division's zone and our own zone of attack.

By 1915 hours, Ghost Troop's scout-tank teams had repelled several Iraqi counterattacks, and Cougar Squadron's focus had shifted to the left flank, where the 4th Squadron of the 7th Cavalry, "Garry Owen," was expected soon.

NINE

My God, It Looks Like Armageddon!

As long as one tank is able to move it must go forward. . . . This is our
big chance. What we have worked for. . . . Make it worthwhile.

COL. GEORGE S. PATTON JR., INSTRUCTIONS TO THE AMERICAN TANK TROOPS,

11 SEPTEMBER 1918

1950 HOURS, 26 FEBRUARY 1991, ALONG THE 73 EASTING WITH GHOST TROOP

To this point in the battle, the 3rd Platoon scouts on Ghost Troop's right flank
had not been engaged as heavily as 1st Platoon's scouts.

This is not to say that Haines' scouts were on holiday. On the contrary,
there was plenty of anxiety to go around, as remnants of Iraqi elements that
managed to survive their encounters with Eagle Troop periodically crawled
across the front of Haines' scout platoon. But attempts to hit any of these Iraqi
forces were usually futile. They were too far away.

Staff Sergeant Michalec watched from his position on the right flank
near Eagle Troop as one of his TOW missiles struck the ground just short of
the retreating Iraqis armor. The Iraqi vehicles and troops were more than four
thousand meters away. Only artillery could reach them—that is, until now.

Specialist Kelly, who had only recently joined Cougar Squadron from
the 194th Armored Brigade, was the first to see them. Kelly was the driver
for Lieutenant Deskevich's fire-support team vehicle. He had positioned
Deskevich just behind the Haines' 3rd Platoon scouts on the southern flank, a
position from which Deskevich's team had sent a steady stream of fire missions
throughout the evening to the howitzer battery.

But these earlier fire missions had been focused on enemy targets between the 75 Easting and 78 Easting in support of Garwick and the COLT. The Iraqi vehicles and troops to the front and right were definitely something new.

Staff Sergeant Lashley, the fire-support track commander, said he couldn't identify anything at all, but Kelly stuck to his story. He kept insisting there was something there. Finally, seven vaguely defined silhouettes, spitting flame, appeared suddenly, as if they had sprung from a tunnel beneath the desert. Almost immediately, Iraqi green tracers shot past the fire-support track (American tracers are red). The Iraqis were firing furiously, but their fire was inaccurate; the Iraqi gunners were too reliant on the artificial light created by burning wreckage that illuminated the battlefield to see the Americans clearly. But this was not immediately obvious to the Haines' scouts.

Ghost Troop scouts, however, reacted swiftly to the tracers and main-gun rounds fired in their direction. Haines strained to see through his thermal sights. His eyes were tired, and when he realized that three of the attacking vehicles were tanks, he was scared. For the first time on the 26th of February, Iraqi tanks and BMPs were driving straight at him.

Haines yelled, "Engage, engage, engage, Blue 1, out!"

Haines' Bradley was the first in the platoon to engage, soon followed by the rest of his scouts. When Haines screamed the report of "Tanks front, out!" on the Ghost Troop net, he made Sartiano and Mecca jumpy as hell.

Mecca, very confident and cool to this point, was now genuinely worried about whether Haines could handle the new contact.

Haines told his gunner to adjust the 25-mm to a high rate of fire and fire at will. While Haines fired 25-mm, Sergeant Michalec's gunner, Sergeant Strong, launched a TOW missile. The pattern of alternating TOW missiles and 25-mm fire continued across the six Bradleys in the platoon, but the ground was not level, and the wire-guided TOW missiles had to be literally flown over the rises in the desert terrain by the gunners.

One Iraqi tank was hit right away, reduced its speed, and seemed to cough up black smoke, but the rest of the armored vehicles kept coming.

Sergeant First Class Newman's mortar section, seeing the action from its position roughly a hundred meters behind the fire-support track, began engaging with .50-caliber machine guns in direction of the green tracers while simultaneously direct laying the gun tubes toward where the tracer rounds originated.

Before the evening was over, Newman's mortar section would fire 248 rounds, so many that the mortar tubes would begin to glow from the heat. Ghost Troop mortars had already burned up nearly two hundred rounds in support of the rest of the troop. Now they would fire forty-eight more of their remaining rounds at this new Iraqi threat. Wanting to use the artillery resources at hand as well, Deskevich asked his crew, "Jesus Christ, somebody is shooting at us. Give me a direction and a distance."

"Sir, I put it at five hundred meters, direction 1820 to the southeast," yelled Sergeant Lashley, the fire-support vehicle commander, Deskevich wrote down the information, estimated a center-of-mass map grid coordinate for the attacking Iraqi elements, and told Specialist Harvey: "Send it."

"I've got it," said Harvey, calling on the fire-support net: "Immediate Suppression: Cougar 13, Ghost 13, immediate suppression, over!"

Turning back to Deskevich, he said, "Cougar 13 wants to know if you are sure they are enemy?"

"They're f—king shooting at us, I don't care," said Deskevich.

Deskevich's call requesting immediate suppression silenced everyone on the fire-support net. Cpt. Sam White heard the call and didn't wait for the fire direction officer to respond. He knew Deskevich well enough to know when Joe was serious. White picked up the call for fire and sent the data straight to his guns. Seconds later, Caisson erupted with fire in the direction of the Iraqi troops.

Down on the gun line in Caisson, the action was ferocious. Sergeant First Class Joe Daniels later described what he saw when his column of heavy expanded-mobility tactical trucks, or HEMTTs, pulled up and parked next to the guns to off-load more 155-mm artillery rounds: "It was incredible. The guns had been firing so long without a break that carbon was building up in the tubes. When one of them fired—no kidding—it was like watching a World War II film clip of a sixteen-inch gun firing off a battleship. There were flames 20 feet long shooting out of those howitzers."[1]

In Deskevich's words, the spectacular display of flame and shot added a sense of vengeance to the battle. The display seemed fitting after Sergeant Moller's death a couple of hours earlier.

As a scout section drove by to take position on flat ground behind Deskevich's fire-support vehicle, Sergeant Lashley told Deskevich, "Sir, we need to fire smoke grenades and disengage."

Deskevich would have none of it. He knew that in the poorly illuminated night, smoke would simply identify where the fire-support vehicle was. "No! Stop that crap now. The Iraqis do not know where we are in the dark, so don't mark our position."

"Ok, sir," snapped Lashley, "Then, we'll move."

"No f—cking way!" yelled Deskevich, "We are not broadsiding ourselves. We can't pivot steer out of here in this thing. Stay where you are."

"Then it's on you if we get killed," yelled Sergeant Lashley.

"Fine," replied Deskevich. "We'll justify it to God if we get there." Hearing on the fire-support net "Splash out, splash over," signaling steel on Ghost 13's target, Deskevich asked where the hell Kinsley's platoon was, calling directly to Kinsley, "Green 1, Ghost 13, do you see what is shooting at us?"

After a couple of calls from Deskevich, Kinsley answered, "Ghost 13, negative, over."

"Why not?" asked Deskevich "Can you shoot in my direction?"

"Negative Ghost 12, the firing pin in my tank is broken, over," answered Kinsley.

"Roger, what about the other two?" asked Deskevich.

"Can't identify the targets," answered Kinsley in a voice that was barely audible. "They have electrical problems too, over."

That's bullshit, thought Deskevich. How can those tanks be down now? What do you mean, they can't see? They haven't fired a single main-gun round.

Fortunately, the artillery falling on the advancing Iraqis made the matter academic. Once again, as soon as the artillery poured in around them, the Iraqis stopped, making themselves easy targets.

Hearing Deskevich's calls for assistance, Sartiano turned the *Godfather* south and sped toward Haines' screen line. On arrival he discovered that Haines' platoon had pulled just behind the small rise that ran parallel with the 73 Easting and was engaging the halted Iraqi tanks and armored vehicles to his front.

Sartiano pulled up on the Iraqis' flank and opened fire with his main gun. Sartiano's gunner was by now accustomed to Sartiano's battlefield opportunism. He carefully aimed, without haste, and fired.

Sartiano, unimpressed with the Iraqi tanks, called Mecca on the radio saying, "Hey XO [executive officer], come up on line and start shooting."

Mecca, who was already on his way drove up, and halted fifty meters to Sartiano's right. Before the second main-gun round went off, another danger-close mission—meaning there were friendlies close to the target—of forty-eight rounds of DPICM crashed down on the Iraqis while Mecca opened up with twenty rounds of 25-mm sabot ammunition. Mecca now called Kinsley on the troop command net and told him, "I'm firing to your left and marking the enemy with 25-mm for your platoon to engage."

Announcing, "Gunner, sabot BMP," to his gunner, Sergeant Hunnicut, Mecca engaged a BMP that pulled up behind the four Iraqi T72 tanks. Mecca, not expecting to see much effect from his 25-mm, was surprised to see a direct hit achieve complete destruction of the BMP. Upon seeing the explosion, Mecca took aim at another—destroying that BMP too.

At this point, Sergeant Hunnicut was flying high. He asked Mecca on the intercom, "Hey sir, you want to try a tank?"

Mecca replied, "What the hell, give it a shot!"

Sergeant Hunnicut fired nine rounds of 25-mm sabot ammunition into the rear panel of the last of the four T72 tanks, engulfing it in flames. Mecca and Sartiano continued to engage and destroy the four T72 tanks and BMPs. Within minutes, all the Iraqi vehicles were destroyed and all of the Iraqi troops were dead. Privately, many of the soldiers in Ghost Troop were happy they did not have to take prisoners. The memory of Sergeant Moller's death was still fresh in their minds.

For good measure, one of the Bradleys in Haines' platoon decided to launch a final TOW missile in the direction of a hot spot that looked like a tank *out* beyond 3,500 meters, but the weapon blew up just after leaving the tube. Fortunately, no one was hurt, but this was one of several defective TOW missiles that launched and then detonated within a few meters of the Bradley. We later wondered how many of the missiles in Cougar Squadron's first basic load of TOW missiles were also defective.

By 2030 hours Ghost Troop's third major action was over, and the condition of Iraqi troops to our front was dismal. Scattered here and there among the wreckage, many of the Iraqi troops who were still alive fired pointlessly in our direction. At times, the Iraqis would stick their heads up and plink away at us from the distance. Occasionally, section-sized elements would charge forward, only to be cut to pieces in seconds. Iraqi resistance at this point was worse than futile, It was suicidal. But many of the Iraqi soldiers seemed to fight with the courage of despair.

Staff Sergeant Foy, who had played a leading role in the tank assault, spotted a truck full of Iraqi troops moving from right to left across the front of his platoon, on Eagle Troop's right flank.

Before anyone could engage, Foy said, "Hold your fire. Let's see if these guys really want to fight."

Thanks to Foy, several dozen Iraqi Arabs missed the opportunity to see paradise early. Foy's instincts were right. This bunch was just trying to get out of the beaten zone. When Foy fired a few 7.62-mm rounds over their heads, they quickly surrendered.

THE ENEMY IS BROKEN

Sitting a couple of hundred yards away as I participated in the adjustment of white-phosphorous rounds from Eagle Troop's mortars onto the heads of the Iraqi soldiers concealed in the wreckage to my front, I suddenly paused and asked myself, "What the hell am I doing?"

The battle was over. These men no longer needed to die. Perhaps the Iraqi soldiers were still firing at us because we were firing at them. None of the surviving Republican Guards presented a serious threat any more. In fact, it was worse. Whatever else these Iraqi soldiers were, they were still human beings.

Out of curiosity, I dropped down to the Eagle Troop net and listened to tank commanders speculating on which tank or Bradley would succeed in dropping mortar rounds on the few Iraqis who remained alive. This change in atmospherics disturbed me.

There was no glory or glamour in this enterprise. The fiery desert to our front had become a valley of death, a place of ruthless extermination. I was no longer orchestrating a battle. I was now just the principal executioner.

Reasons of statecraft and national interest had brought me, along with thousands of other American soldiers, to Iraq, but I had not come to Iraq to spread hatred and cruelty or to wage a ruthless war of extermination, a *guerre à mort*. The killing had to stop and stop now, I told myself. I called McMaster on the Cougar Squadron command net: "Eagle 6, this is Cougar 3, meet me behind my tank ASAP, over."

McMaster acknowledged, "Eagle 6, roger out," and dismounted from *Mad Max*.

I pushed the switch to intercom and told the crew—Ward, Jones, and Abercrombie—"Listen guys, I am getting out. Until further notice, we've got to cease-fire, understand?"

"Roger that, sir."

Then, Ward asked, "Sir, do you mind if I get out with you?"

"No problem, but one of you three needs to stay behind the gun until this thing is over. I am going to call a cease-fire and see if these people will surrender. I think we've killed enough for one day."

With that comment, I took off my CVC helmet, grabbed my Kevlar one, and climbed down from the tank. McMaster was already behind the tank waiting for me. Ebullient and excited, McMaster reached out and slapped his hand into mine a second time saying, "Goddamn, this is great, isn't it?"

I nodded in agreement but came right to the point.

"H.R., I want a cease-fire so I can see if the few who are left alive will surrender."

My words struck him like a right punch to the jaw. McMaster was clearly surprised.

"Sir, already? I mean we're kicking their ass. Why stop now?"

"H.R., the enemy is broken. They may be the Republican Guard, but they do not all deserve to die. Please, get on the net and tell your troops to cease fire immediately. Understood?"

There was a hint of agitation in McMaster's voice, so I added, "H.R., I don't have time to discuss this. I am bringing up the PSYOPS team, broadcast a surrender appeal, and see what happens."

McMaster and his soldiers had done so much to win this battle that they were still caught up in the excitement of combat. But since we could not advance any farther, it made sense to me to try and stop the killing. McMaster's face indicated a certain amount of disappointment that the battle was over, but he understood.

"Got it, sir," he said, "I will get my guys on the radio right away."

With that, McMaster scurried off toward his tank, and I returned to Cougar Forward to make the call to the PSYOPS team myself.

As I walked back to Cougar Forward, Lt. Danny Davis, Eagle Troop fire-support team leader, walked up to me. Danny knew that I was frustrated at our inability to advance and finish off the remaining enemy. He approached me with a plan for an artillery strike that would terminate the action once and for all. Explaining that enough guns were in place to put five hundred rounds plus rockets into the main concentration of enemy troops to our front, Danny Davis asked for permission to prepare the mission.[2]

I paused for a second, then, said, "Danny, go ahead." But I also insisted that I wanted him to tell me when the guns would be ready to fire before anything happened. He assured me he would do so and returned to his track, where he and McMaster jointly planned and organized the strike.

I walked back from the tank line to talk with Hillen to catch up on whatever traffic was coming in from Dragoon Base, because I could no longer hear the traffic from Regiment. Then we heard Ghost Troop report it was "black on TOWs" through the administrative logistic radio net to Dragoon Base, the regiment. This report meant that Ghost Troop's scouts had fired all of their TOW missiles. This was, of course, utter nonsense. As soon as I heard the report, I knew it was nonsense.

"John, that's bullshit, and you know it." John agreed. I said, "Get Mecca up on the f—cking net and tell him to send us the true picture, ASAP."

Quite suddenly, Larson's tank reappeared, driving out of the darkness behind us, parking near Cougar Forward. Larson dismounted from his tank and hurried over to where Hillen and I were talking. He seemed genuinely happy to see me. Dispensing with the usual greeting, he immediately mentioned the Ghost Troop report concerning TOW missiles, asking: "Doug, did you report that Ghost is 'black on TOWs' to Regiment?"

I quickly said, "No, sir, I did not. I think the report is nonsense. Ghost is probably overreporting the situation on the ground. They need to cross-level between vehicles." "Cross-leveling" involves redistributing TOW missiles between scout sections inside the troop.

Larson ignored my response. He was clearly irritated that I had not sent the message up to Dragoon Base.

"Doug, I think we should report that Ghost is black on TOWs to Regiment. The regiment does not understand what we are doing here, because you are not reporting enough."

Larson was not entirely wrong. I had told Tony to be careful what he relayed to Regiment from Cougar Forward and from me. But I was concerned as much about accuracy as exaggeration. Both Ierardi and Hillen understood my concern very well.

As Holder was fond of saying, "The first report is always wrong." I was quite convinced that Holder's adage applied to Ghost Troop's report of "black on TOWs."

"Sir, John is reporting routinely what we know to be true. Under the circumstances, I strongly recommend we wait for verification from John Mecca before sending anything up to Dragoon Base."

My response did not placate Larson. Larson again insisted that we report the information to Regiment.

Seconds later Mecca came up on the Cougar Squadron command net and corrected the earlier report. Ghost was not black on TOWs. During the months of training prior to G-day, the troop executive officers and Hillen had established a "private" radio net for frank lieutenant-to-lieutenant conversation. It was originally Lt. Jack Waldron's idea. Anyway, the lieutenants used the radio frequency normally designated for use by the "F Troop mess team." Since there was no such mess team, the lieutenants used it as their own forum to keep their bosses out of a trouble.

The code phrase "Meet me on the side" was used by the lieutenants to indicate they needed to talk on the secret net about some serious—and at times, not so serious—issue. The conversations were often heated, but mostly they were just frank prodding to get things done. Mecca lost no time in telling Hillen that Garwick's report was wrong.

In the excitement of battle, Garwick reported that he had fired all of the TOW missiles on his Bradley. Mecca now reported that Ghost Troop was cross-leveling its TOW missiles. Larson was silent when Hillen gave him the news. In the meantime, I told Hillen to revise the earlier report and inform Dragoon Base. Hillen called Dragoon Base and explained what had happened, but the report was never changed at Regiment. The exaggeration stuck.

While we waited for the PSYOPS team to arrive, the Iraqis in front of Ghost Troop briefly renewed their assault. In less time than it takes to read these lines, the fight with the last counterattacking Iraqi troops ended with an exploding TOW missile. Sergeant First Class Lawrence, Garwick's very able and competent platoon sergeant, launched one more TOW at an Iraqi armored vehicle he saw in the thermals about 3,500 meters to the front. When the missile left the tube, however, it exploded almost immediately, engulfing the whole Bradley in flame.

Alarmed by the sight of the Bradley's turret in flame and smoke, Sartiano called Lawrence to see if anyone was hurt,

"Negative," said Lawrence. "It will take more than a little explosion to keep me out of the fight."

Sartiano was relieved, but he was not happy. He wanted to deliver a killing blow against the Iraqi armored elements three to five kilometers away, lying beyond the 73 Easting in 3rd Armored Division's zone of attack.

Deskevich, working with Mecca and the Ghost Platoon leaders, directed artillery strikes throughout the evening against these columns of Iraqi troops. Once again, Iraqi troops who fell back in disorder hid inside the bowl-like depression about a thousand meters to Ghost Troop's left front.

Plunging fire from Ghost mortars into the depression pinned down some of the survivors, but the depression offered a temporary sanctuary from Ghost Troop's devastating direct fire. Mecca also complained that Iraqi artillery rounds continued to periodically fall behind Ghost's line of contact in and around the Ghost Troop supply trains, disrupting Sergeant First Class Davis' resupply operation. The whole thing bothered Sartiano, who became more determined than ever to root out the remaining Iraqi troops to his front, once and for all.

"Cougar 3, Ghost 6 over,"

"Ghost 6, send it."

"Cougar 3, request permission to move to positions one thousand meters farther east, break. From there I can wipe out the enemy and end this, over."

Now, there was a thought. Why not advance to complete the enemy's destruction? What a wonderful idea, I thought, but our opportunity had passed.

"Negative, Ghost 6. Sorry, can't do it. Spearhead is on its way, our air is forward of the 73 Easting right now, break, can't risk it, over." A short pause followed until Sartiano finally spoke.

"Roger. Understand, Ghost 6, out."

Sartiano's instincts were right. We should never have stopped, but there was nothing any of us could do about it. I had to turn my attention back to the PSYOPS team.

About ten minutes after I told Cougar 32 to send forward the PYSOPS team to my location, two Humvees rolled up and parked next to where I was standing, just to the right of my tank. The first to step forward was the team leader, a reservist who normally taught high school English. I said "Welcome" and shook his hand. He suggested that I speak directly to the interpreter who would actually broadcast the surrender appeal in Arabic. With that, the Kuwaiti interpreter, a student at George Washington University, in Washington, D.C., stepped forward to receive instructions.

I told him, "Call them on the public address system and give them a couple of minutes to surrender. Tell them if they do not surrender, the divisions that are now closing fast behind us will soon be here and they will destroy them. OK?"

"Sir, I recommend that we give them no more than sixty seconds."

"Really? Do you think that is enough time?" I asked.

"Sir, based on our experience, I guarantee it is. Believe me, if they do not come out after sixty seconds, they aren't coming out at all."

"Very well, then. Make it sixty seconds. Let's do it."

As the Kuwaiti interpreter predicted, it did not take long for dozens and dozens of Iraqi soldiers to fumble over the trenches and wreckage, move forward, and surrender. Within seconds I was astonished by the number of little white flags that suddenly popped out of the wreckage to our front. Some men staggered, some walked, and a few were carried, but they all displayed anything white they could get their hands on.

Within a couple of minutes at least twenty pale and bloody Iraqi soldiers in dirty green uniforms cluttered the ground around my tank. Lieutenant Gio Kotori's medical platoon, which had practiced so long and hard to keep us alive if we were wounded, now went to work saving Arab lives. Some of the wounds were quite gruesome and required immediate medical attention.

Staff Sergeant Burns took charge of securing the prisoners, in his usual humorous way. To his everlasting credit, Sergeant Burns was anything but harsh. Burns was firm, yes, but not severe. He made a point of smiling, reassuring the tired and the wounded that they had nothing to fear. After searching through pockets, he carefully returned all of the Iraqi soldiers' personal items, such as the pictures of girlfriends and family.

What I saw next shocked me. If anyone wanted proof that Gen. William T. Sherman was right when he insisted "war is hell," the proof was here in abundance. As I walked around inspecting the motley gang of Iraqi wounded, I noticed quite by accident a gash in one Iraqi soldier's arm. A small speck of white phosphorous from a 4.2-inch mortar had eaten like acid right through the man's arm. Small wonder the Iraqis popped out of the bunkers and trenches when these "Willie Pete" rounds were dropped on their heads.

How long the man with the wound in his forearm had suffered I do not know, but the look on his face was beyond pain. He sat motionless in front of me, saying nothing, staring into the distance while his comrades lying next to him clutched white bandages to wounds in their heads and torsos. It was the first time my nostrils had been filled with the putrid smell of burnt human flesh. But these surviving Iraqi soldiers were the lucky ones. Far more of them were dead. We will never know how many we killed.

Miraculously, more and more Iraqi soldiers surrendered and walked into our lines. Meanwhile, the eyes of the recently captured Iraqi Republican Guard officer darted quickly between Sergeant Ward and me. The Iraqi officer, who survived the battle, turned out later to have been the Republican Guard brigade commander. He told me afterward that during the war with Iran, Iranian tank attacks had been followed by waves of dismounted Iranian infantry, reminiscent of the Red Army's tactics during World War II. Apparently, it had not occurred to the Iraqis that our tanks would have instead armored fighting vehicles with 25-mm automatic cannons and 7.62-mm machine guns just behind them, carrying scouts who could dismount under armor protection if needed.

Nearly fifteen minutes had elapsed since we had begun accepting the surrender of Iraqi troops. No more white flags were visible anywhere. The fight appeared to be over. I decided to walk over to the Iraqi commander and ask him if he thought any more of his soldiers might still be out there.

To my horror, he said: "Yes. There might be some badly wounded men . . . men too badly wounded to walk."

I was furious. I immediately walked back to Cougar Forward to ask Lieutenant Colonel Larson if I should not go forward to see if there were any more survivors. I said, "Sir, perhaps I should take a detail and see if any wounded men out there are still alive."

Larson was strongly opposed. He was adamant that I stay where I was.

His high-pitched voice rang in my ears, "Doug, absolutely not. John [Hillen] says Apache attack helicopters are flying forward of us. There is no way to turn them off. You don't need to become a friendly-fire victim."

Larson was right, and I knew it. But the whole affair made me angry with the Iraqi brigade commander. Why had he waited to mention that some of his wounded soldiers might have been left behind on the battlefield? This lack of regard for his own troops reflected a casual attitude toward human life that was quite common among the Arabs, as we would confirm weeks later in the Euphrates River valley near An Nasiriyah, but I did not like it.

"Sir, I know you are right. I am just angry that there is nothing I can do about it," I said to Larson. Thinking about it for a second, I followed up with, "Anyway, if there is anyone still alive out there, they won't be alive much longer." I then told Larson about the planned artillery strike to our front.

Davis now walked up behind me to tell me that all was ready for the artillery strike. So I said, "Let it rip."

It wasn't long before we heard the guns fire and Davis' artillery strike begin. This was the first time in most of our lives that we had seen concentrated artillery fire, fire that began falling no more than a thousand meters away from us. Just as it had impressed Mecca earlier in the evening, the violence of the falling artillery now shocked me. The rounds fell in sheets like rain and seemed to walk deliberately across the desert.

Danny Davis stood next to me during the artillery strike. As Davis and I gasped, startled by the storm of destruction to our front, I turned to Davis and said: "My God, it looks like Armageddon." Davis agreed. The name stuck, and forever after we referred to this artillery barrage as "the Armageddon strike."

When it ended—with the firing of the last of 1,100 155-mm artillery rounds in the space of perhaps three hours—Lieutenant Colonel Larson engaged me on an entirely different matter.

Larson surprised me with the revelation that he wanted to relieve Ghost Troop, move it into reserve, and replace it with Hawk, Cougar Squadron's tank company.

Larson's idea really worried me, but I did not interrupt him as he explained his rationale for his course of action.

"Doug," Larson continued, "Fox led all the way up here. Eagle and Ghost have had their opportunities to do stuff. The tank company really hasn't had a chance to do anything."

To me, the notion that we were running a kind of military talent spot in the desert was disturbing. I did not give a damn how many rounds the tank company fired in anger. We might fight again tomorrow or the next day, in which case the tank company, if left in reserve, would be fresh and ready to go. The whole matter irritated the hell out of me, but I suppressed the urge to be sarcastic.

"Sir," I stopped to clear my throat, "Hawk's job is to act as Cougar Squadron's reserve, and they've done that very well. We can commit them if we need them, but right now we don't need to commit them. In addition, I recommend not moving Ghost Troop back and Hawk Company forward while Ghost Troop still has sporadic enemy contact, regardless of how weak or intermittent. It's just too dangerous."

"Doug, Ghost Troop is probably tired, and Hawk really needs to get into the fight," Larson insisted plaintively.

"Sir, the troops are undoubtedly tired, but not that tired. It is dark, and there are still Iraqi troops wandering around the battlefield. The tank company will have itchy trigger fingers. Frankly, executing a relief in place at night after significant enemy contact is not a good idea. Please consider conducting the relief at first light when there is less likelihood of confusion."

Hillen watched with more than a little interest because we were now being told to prepare for a passage of lines forward on the left flank by 3rd Armored Division and right through Cougar Squadron by the 1st Infantry Division. Adding complexity to an already increasingly complicated situation made no sense to us, but none of my entreaties not to replace Ghost with Hawk before first light changed Larson's mind.

"Doug, I want to conduct the relief of Ghost Troop with Hawk."

Larson's mind was made up, and there was little I could do to change it.

Of course, I felt terrible, but any idea on my part of raising this matter on the evening of 26 February was pointless. Since arriving in Saudi Arabia, Larson had deferred to my judgment and consistently supported my directives to Cougar Squadron from the time we crossed into Iraq. What else could I say other than "Yes, sir?" Perhaps, I thought, we can make it work. After all, the contact on the left had diminished dramatically. The reports from Sartiano and Mecca did not indicate a serious problem. I was preparing the PSYOPS team to go to Ghost Troop's zone of attack and broadcast surrender appeals.

"Sir, it will be done," I responded. "Hillen will inform Ghost and Hawk on the command net, so that everyone knows what's happening. The two executive officers, John Mecca and Tim Purdue, will work out the details of Hawk's movement forward. However, can we do it after 2100 hours?"

Larson was pleased at last, enthusiastically responding with; "Yes. Yes, that's what I want to do. I am going over to Ghost Troop right now to talk to Joe about the relief in place and make sure it goes the way it should."

"Sir, very well," I said. "Then, I will remain here until the situation changes or you direct otherwise."

"Good, Doug, you stay here with Eagle Troop, and I will go to Ghost Troop." With that statement, Larson adjusted his gear and moved out.

I stood at attention, saluted, and watched as Larson drove off in his tank to personally supervise the relief of Ghost troop by the tank company.

As his tank disappeared into the darkness, Larson could be heard on the Cougar Squadron command radio net telling Ghost 6 nervously, "This is Cougar 6 moving toward your location. Do not shoot. I am in the tank moving across your front to your location, do not shoot, acknowledge over."

Larson's plea on the squadron command net precipitated some laughter and snide remarks on the Ghost Troop command net. Sartiano intervened to silence it.

By this time, Caisson, our howitzer battery was firing rocket-assisted propellant (RAP) rounds against targets beyond the 80 Easting, and the 210 Artillery Brigade was now striking targets for Davis in Eagle Troop.

Other than the guns behind us, only the occasional burst of machine-gun fire was heard in our immediate vicinity. Looking up briefly, I noticed the night sky was now completely clear and filling up with stars. I took in a deep breath and, for a second, relaxed.

"Thank God," I said to myself. "Thank God."

The next item on the agenda was the proposed passage of lines. I told Hillen to get hold of Tom Sprowls and with Captain Clark, the engineer company commander, and ask both of them to report to me as soon as possible. Fox Troop would handle the passage of lines for the squadron, and Captain Clark would support him by helping to mark the passage lanes. So that I could stay forward on the firing line in the event that the enemy renewed contact with us, I called Tony Ierardi and told him that once I personally briefed the Fox Troop and engineer company commanders on the mission and its specialized requirements, he would have to coordinate directly with the brigade S-3s from the 1st Infantry Division and the 3rd Armored Division as necessary.

This was one of those moments when I said a short prayer of thanks for Tony Ierardi. I knew that Tony was the man running the squadron TOC. Fortunately for Cougar Squadron and me, Tony had the energy and presence of mind to do the job. Tony would talk to 3rd Armored Division and 1st Infantry Division throughout the night until their units had moved forward on our flank or through us on their way into the battle.

While I waited for Sprowls and Clark to arrive, McMaster walked over to the command Bradley, where he found me talking to Hillen. McMaster slapped his hand into mine and said, "Sid Vicious, how's it going?"

"Not bad, H. R., not bad at all. What's happening in Eagle Troop? Find anything new out from our Iraqi prisoners?"

"Yes. The Iraqi brigade commander, who holds the rank of major, claims he is a graduate of the Infantry Officers' Advanced Course at Fort Benning, Georgia. The man's English is really good."

"Well, Fort Benning explains a lot," quipped Hillen, "No wonder these Arabs are so f——cked up." Hillen's levity was welcome, but I really wanted to know what else Major Mohammed Whateverhisnamewas had said.

McMaster continued, "He keeps insisting that the Iraqi army is actually much better than it seems."

Hillen couldn't resist the opportunity and smarted off with, "That wouldn't take much effort."

"No, really," explained McMaster, "He says that Saddam Hussein removed all of the competent generals and replaced them with 'yes men' who would follow orders regardless of how stupid they were. He says he served for eight years in the war with Iran and that they have better generals than the people Saddam put into command."

As always, McMaster did not miss the opportunity to rib me for what he called my explosive drive through the minefield. He remarked, "Only a thick-headed infantryman would drive straight into a minefield."

"It was not Ward's fault, H. R." I said. "We were moving very fast down the middle of the formation trying to maintain some form of contact with Ghost and you at the time. Had I been driving, I would have probably done the same thing. While Eagle's tanks may have seen it, I did not. It was my fault, not Ward's."

McMaster was too busy laughing to listen to my defense of Ward's driving skills. Fortunately, Ward was not around to hear McMaster's comment; he was guarding prisoners. Ward is a good professional soldier and would have taken it very, very hard.

Sometime after the artillery's "Armageddon" strike and my conversation with Lieutenant Colonel Larson, the Iraqi brigade commander approached me with a proposal I will never forget.

"Why are you stopping?" asked the Republican Guard officer, who was now near the back of my Bradley fighting vehicle as a prisoner of war in the hands of the 2nd Armored Cavalry. "Why do you not go to Baghdad now? You have the power. Your army rules the heavens and the earth. Do you think we love Saddam?"

Was my grasp on reality slipping? It was the second time in the course of the battle that someone had asked me to continue the advance, to press the attack.

First it had been Joe Sartiano urging me forward, now it was a captured Iraqi officer of the Republican Guard, a man in his mid-forties with eight years' experience of fighting in Iraq's war with Iran.

"Saddam killed our best generals. He kills everyone." In a voice filled with more anguish and frustration than fear, my prisoner looked me straight in the eye and said in heavily accented English, "Major, you must go to Baghdad and end this. You must save Iraq."

"Save Iraq?" I wondered. What an amazing thing for a prisoner of war to say to his captor about his own government. Of course, our argument was with the leadership of Iraq, not its people. We treated the Iraqi prisoners we took with dignity and humanity. In turn, they responded positively to us. And the Iraqi commander had a point. Why commit this enormous force to battle and then just stop?

But I knew there was no appetite at Regiment or Corps to do any such thing. From the time we had crossed into Iraq, the chain of command had seen only danger, never opportunity. Sadly, Regiment and Corps were content to keep their distance and run the Iraqis out of Kuwait. The grossly inflated picture of Iraqi military power had been undiminished by the reports of weak resistance we sent up the chain.

The original war plan, however irrelevant, would be followed. There would be no appreciation of the strategic importance of what the Iraqi brigade commander was saying. It did not take much imagination to figure out why the colonels and generals were not interested in anything we "at the point of the spear" might suggest. They were too busy gazing at campaign maps spread on the walls of distant command centers in Iraq and Saudi Arabia, as though if they looked hard enough they might find easy options instead of hard, critical decisions to make.

Still, I was not inclined to explain the U.S. Army's internal problems to my enemy. Stymied by the boldness of his question, I said the only thing to the Republican Guard officer I could think of: "We are ordered to halt. I have orders. I cannot advance. That's the way it is."

More bewildered than anything else by my response, the Iraqi officer slowly turned around and walked at a deliberate pace back to a group of Iraqi prisoners huddled nearby. What he really thought, I will never know. I only knew what *I* thought. I agreed with him. It made no sense to stop, at least not until we were certain that we had destroyed the Republican Guard.

Soon after my encounter with the Iraqi commander, I found out that T. J. Linzy was leading 3rd Armored Division's cavalry scouts forward into their zone of attack along Ghost's flank. As Linzy brought them forward, Garwick coordinated with them on their command net, warning them not to crest the rise to their front.

"There are still enemy vehicles in the depression on the other side," Garwick said. "We drove them back, but there are still some live ones in there, over."

CEASE FIRE, CEASE FIRE!

Coordination between Ghost Troop and Hawk was well under way when Lt. John Stephenson, Hawk Company's fire-support team leader, drove up in a Humvee behind Deskevich's fire-support vehicle, a modified M113 track.

Stephenson got out of the Humvee and banged on the armored fire-support vehicle's rear door. Inside, Deskevich's crew was still jumpy, and someone suggested that it might well be an Iraqi soldier who had somehow managed to walk through the screen line in the dark. When Stephenson blurted out his name and knocked again, everyone inside the fire-support vehicle breathed a sigh of relief. The door opened.

Stephenson knew that an American Multiple Launch Rocket System (MLRS) artillery battery supporting the 2nd Cavalry (C Battery, 1-27 Field Artillery, a 227-mm rocket battery), was now firing at deep targets beyond the 78 Easting. What Stephenson did not know was that Deskevich had opposed Captain Millar's plan to position the MLRS battery just behind Ghost Troop.

Deskevich had said no because he felt that moving the MLRS forward would place the rockets too close to friendly troops. Grudgingly, Millar accepted Deskevich's argument and held the MLRS in a position farther to the rear from which it continued to fire at deep targets for the rest of the evening. These strikes definitely had an impact on the Republican Guard storage areas to our front, creating major explosions and fires until well after midnight.

Because the left flank was still exposed to periodic fire from Iraqi units milling around on the edge of 3rd Armored Division's zone, Sartiano told Garwick to hold his position and tasked Haines with the mission to go back, pick up Hawk Company's fourteen tanks, and lead them forward. Things seemed to go relatively smoothly until Hawk's lead tanks reached the forward edge of the battle area.

Due to the extreme heat generated by TOW missiles that had exploded inside Ghost 16 after it was hit, the Bradley's turret had melted into the chassis, creating the illusion from only twenty-five meters away that it was an MTLB or BMP. Even in the thermal sights of one of Hawk's tanks, the Ghost Bradley, glowing brightly, looked exactly like a sleek, low-profile MTLB.

Inside Hawk Company, there was no doubt in anyone's mind that the bright-red armored vehicle was Iraqi, seeking to infiltrate Ghost Troop's collapsing screen line. In short order, the fire commands went out: "BMP, direct front! Up! Identified! Fire! On the Way!" . . . *boom!* A sabot round punched through the glowing remains of Ghost 16 before anyone could prevent it.

From where I stood next to Cougar Forward, I could hear Sartiano yell, "Cease fire, cease fire, you just engaged one of my Bradleys!" Larson chimed in with, "Cease fire, cease fire, cease fire!"

John Hillen and I said nothing. We didn't need to.

What we feared would happen had happened. When Hillen established that Hawk Company had fired a sabot round into Ghost 16, Sergeant Moller's now abandoned Bradley, I was saddened but relieved to know that no one had been killed.

Walking from vehicle to vehicle, Mecca got control of the situation and hurried Ghost Troop to the rear, where fuel and water were waiting. For Mecca, however, the fight was not yet over. The Ghost Troop first sergeant and Cougar Squadron's command sergeant major were waiting for him when he brought Ghost Troop back from the firing line.

"Why did you leave Sergeant Moller's body up there, lieutenant? You never leave a man behind like that. What the hell were you thinking, Lieutenant?" yelled the sergeant major in his squeaky voice and heavy southern accent. Mecca was tired but still tried to be polite.

"Sergeant Major, it was too dangerous to bring up the M88 and the ambulance. There was too much shooting, and the TOW missiles on board the Bradley were exploding inside the vehicle."

Sergeant First Class Lawrence's Bradley had gotten the wounded out, and, in truth, there was very little of Sergeant Moller to retrieve after the devastating explosion and fire that had killed him. But Mecca didn't want to go into details. Unfortunately, neither the first sergeant nor the command sergeant major would let up.

Finally, Mecca could stand it no more. He said, "Sergeant Moller's body was in pieces. Do you want me to draw you a picture? Now that's f—cking it. You have no right to question my decision in the middle of combat."

The two noncommissioned officers withdrew, finally realizing that they had pushed too far and that Mecca was exhausted.

Not long after the altercation with the first sergeant and the command sergeant major, Mecca and Deskevich ran into the reconnaissance platoon leader from the Centurions—2nd Battalion, 66th Armored Regiment, in the 3rd Armored Division. The 2-66 lieutenant reported that 4-7 Cavalry (that is, 4th Squadron, 7th Cavalry Regiment had lost six Bradleys in the area where Ghost had repelled several counterattacks.

Mecca was sad and angry. He knew that Garwick had warned 4-7 Cavalry as it moved forward into the zone on Ghost's flank, but most of all he regretted the fact that the 73 Easting limit of advance prevented Ghost Troop from attacking into the area and cleaning it out. Mecca had a point, but he had no idea just how complex our small part of the battlefield had become.

Around 2100, I received word from Tony Ierardi that despite his lengthy coordination meetings with the brigade of the 1st Infantry Division that was planning to pass through our lines, the 1st Infantry Division leadership had decided to simply drive through us wherever they liked. In other words, the extensive work by Sprowls and Clarke to mark lanes, position vehicles, and assign Fox Troop scouts to provide guides and liaison would be ignored. I temporarily suspended my disbelief and called Colonel Robinette.

U.S. Army manuals are filled with elaborate schemes to conduct the passage of attacking combat troops forward through defending units, but I had never been comfortable with the idea, for reasons rooted in personal experience. Werner Binder, the former Wehrmacht officer who was my intellectual godfather, had related to me more than once how the German army on the Eastern Front abandoned the idea of moving fresh combat troops forward through defending troops in contact. Instead, the German command would establish a time at which all its troops in defensive positions would be withdrawn into the flanks of defending units and then fresh, attacking troops from the rear moved forward through the now-empty sector.

The attacking troops were told that once they crossed the so-called line of departure, drawn just behind the old defensive positions, they could engage anything they found to their front. Ninety-nine percent of the time, the Germans found that if their troops on the line of contact maintained good light and noise discipline, the Russians could not react fast enough to exploit the German withdrawal. This approach dramatically reduced incidents of fratricide and allowed the attacking troops to focus on their offensive mission without fear of accidentally killing or injuring their countrymen.

We knew of the fratricide that had already occurred in the 1st Infantry Division. In addition, when Colonel Adair returned to Cougar Squadron after several hours with the 1st Infantry Division on the night of 25–26 February, he related to me how a battalion task force had described his own artillery battalion on the radio as "slow, lumbering enemy tanks" and requested permission to engage. Fortunately, Adair overheard the transmission, reminded the 1st Infantry Division of his presence in their formation, and averted a disaster. None of this buttressed my confidence in the 1st Infantry Division's ability to distinguish us from the enemy in the middle of the night.

Talking to Robinette, I made no secret of my concerns, concerns he readily shared. After a short discussion, I told him that I would use all of the glow sticks and lights in the Cougar Squadron battle group to decorate the rear of our armored fighting vehicles. I realized this was unorthodox on any normal battlefield, but I was unwilling to take any chances.

I said, "Dragoon 5, this is Cougar 3, just so you know, the Big Red One will think it is Christmas in the desert before I am through, over."

Robinette unhesitatingly approved my plan. From the rear, the sight must have been something to behold: hundreds of armored vehicles and trucks illuminated in outline by lights glowing green, orange, and yellow.

At about 2315 hours, we received new orders: "Republican Guard Corps fighting at greatly reduced strength and appear to be moving north. Second Armored Cavalry Regiment occupies Assembly Area Spur as corps reserve at 270630 February [meaning 0630 hours on the 27th]; 210 Field Artillery Brigade reinforces 1st Infantry Division."

For the moment, the 2nd Cavalry would turn the war over to the rest of the VII Corps. Given what the soldiers of Cougar Squadron had just done, I didn't mind too much. I decided to lie down on top of the tank turret and get some rest.

In what had become his nightly ritual, Hillen pulled out his *Sports Illustrated* swimsuit calendar, writing in the block marked 26 February: "We moved 35–40 km east in the late morning/afternoon. Fought the battle. 1st Armored Division, 3rd Armored Division, and 1st Infantry Division passed through our lines that night."

Thirty minutes later, I was dozing when Hillen shook me to tell me that the 1st Infantry Division was moving primarily through 3rd Squadron's zone after all and that 3rd Armored Division was moving in great strength through its attack zone on our northern flank.

"With everybody else getting into the fight," noted Hillen with some degree of relief, "all we have to do is wait for morning."

Cougar Squadron's roller-coaster ride across Iraq's southern desert to the 73 Easting was over.

Perhaps, I thought, we will get back into the fight later. Maybe we will swing north toward Basra. After all, someone has to go to Baghdad and end this thing once and for all, right? But I was too tired to speculate.

Now, as I stretched out on top of the tank turret, only the occasional groan of distant artillery and tank fire broke the quiet that enveloped us. Thanks to the fires burning to our front, the night never seemed to grow completely dark.

I fell asleep.

MORNING, 27 FEBRUARY 1991, ALONG THE 73 EASTING

Sunrise was hardly noticeable. The morning skies were so heavily overcast that it took time to sense the increase in illumination. Thankfully, there was no more black rain.

Around us stood the ruins of an army: abandoned bunkers, smashed armor, discarded weapons, and desert sand stained red with the blood of our enemies and of one of our own—Sergeant Andy Moller. I am not sure any of us grasped what had happened the night before. There wasn't much time to figure it all out.

As soon as we had enough light to see, we began checking our engines and tracks. Rod Abercrombie called me over to the side of the tank to see where we had struck the mine during the attack to the 73 Easting. Most of the metal that constituted two ninety-pound track blocks was completely demolished, but miraculously, the metal end-connectors on the inside of the two blocks held what remained of the tank's track together. Rod and I were amazed. This small miracle had kept us rolling straight through the minefield. This time we both gave thanks to Detroit and Tank Automotive Command. They had screwed up the engine by installing a gas-guzzling turbine when we should have chosen a good diesel piston engine, but they had definitely got the rest of the tank right.

Not until first light did the last shot ring out. McMaster called me on the radio insisting that an Iraqi T72 tank about five hundred meters to our front had somehow acquired a new crew of Iraqi soldiers during the night. Eagle scouts confirmed that the gun was traversing. McMaster wanted to engage before the enemy tank got a round off. Knowing that troops from the 3rd Armored Division and the 1st Infantry Division were, though well forward, still in front of our positions, I gave permission to McMaster to engage the tank but instructed him to use a HEAT round, which would detonate on contact. A hypersonic sabot round would go right through the T72 tank and potentially end up striking an American element in front of us.

McMaster acknowledged my transmitted order, and about ten seconds later, with an ear-splitting sound, a 120-mm tank gun sent a HEAT round straight into the Iraqi tank, which instantly belched smoke and flame as its turret sank into the chassis beneath it. After McMaster's rather one-sided engagement with the last remnant of Iraqi resistance, I noticed 7.62-mm rounds occasionally striking the sand near in and around our tanks.

The fire was not aimed so I assumed that the bullets came from some distant 3rd Armored Division element to our flank and would soon stop. I walked over to Cougar Forward, where Hillen was calling the 3rd Brigade of the 1st Armored Division to remind it we were friendly and still along the 73 Easting.

Our call was answered and our presence acknowledged, so I walked back to my tank, where I shaved and enjoyed a cup of coffee. T. K. Wightman and I were chatting about the previous day's battle when T. K., gazing over my shoulder, alerted me to one of the most frightening sights I ever beheld in any desert: McMaster in the nude. McMaster was standing naked on the back deck of his tank, trying to wash off the black stain from the charcoal lining in his chemical suit. He put on quite a show for the Iraqi prisoners, who were apparently unused to such public nudity.

The stray machine-gun bullets, however, did not let up, and more rounds struck the desert around us. When the bullets reached the EPW area where

Burns and Hillen were standing, it was time to move. Burns and Hillen did a hundred-meter sprint back to Cougar Forward, with the Iraqi EPWs in hot pursuit. Burns jumped into Cougar Forward through driver's hatch, landing on Spec. Hank Wells, nearly breaking his ribs, while Hillen dove through the rear hatch—followed by two Iraqi EPWs!

Our efforts to sort out things with the 3rd Armored Division on the radio were not working, so I decided it was time to pull the plug. I had no objection to being shot at by the enemy, but I saw no point in getting shot by American soldiers. I stuck my head into Cougar Forward and told Hillen to get on the command net and direct the squadron to withdraw two thousand meters farther west. I figured that would keep us from sustaining any casualties from what I was sure were unintentional rounds from American units on the left flank.

Moving that instant was not so easy, however. We had several hundred prisoners, and there was no time to bring up trucks if we were going to avoid the friendly fire. Burns dismounted and began rounding up Iraqi prisoners and placing them in the custody of Eagle Troop scouts. Ultimately, Cougar Forward and the Eagle scouts piled as many Iraqi prisoners as possible on top of our Bradley fighting vehicles.

Once we were loaded, we cleared out quickly. Whoever among the prisoners could not ride ran alongside one of the Brads, seeking cover from the occasional bullet that whistled by. The whole scene looked a little ridiculous, with dozens of scared Iraqi soldiers hanging on to the armored vehicles for dear life. A few Iraqi prisoners were allowed to ride inside of Eagle Troop's vehicles, though under continuous guard. One of the few Iraqi soldiers allowed to ride inside of Cougar Forward was the brigade commander who had been captured the night before.

Major Mohammed, as Hillen and Burns called him, noticed the photograph of Rommel inside the Bradley asked, "Why do you have a picture of one of your enemies?" The response this question elicited surprised even me when I learned of it.

"Shut the f—k up, motherf—ker," snapped Burns. "If you had read about Rommel, your ass wouldn't be riding in my Bradley."

Holloway was a little shocked by the master gunner's aggressive response and moved quickly to defuse the situation. Holloway cracked a broad smile and laughingly said, "Chill, man, don't be so intense. The guy was just asking."

Realizing Holloway had a point, Burns smiled, turned around, raised his seat, and looked out of the turret. For Burns, however, the war was far from over.

After moving a short distance, we stopped, and Hillen jumped up on to the tank to tell me that the president was going to order a general cease-fire, mentioned the night before on the regimental command net. It would become effective at 0800 hours on February 28. For the soldiers, the announcement of a cease-fire was greeted with considerable relief. It was easy to see why. Though the Iraqi enemy had turned out to be as incapable as we had anticipated, the effect of having lived and fought under direct fire for several hours the day before could easily be read on their dirty, exhausted faces.

However, news of the pending cease-fire confused me. The 1st Armored Division, the 1st Infantry Division, and the 3rd Armored Division were only now beginning to engage whatever was left of the enemy. How could it all be over so soon? Surely, what we had seen along the 73 Easting was not all the enemy had to offer. It was hard to believe that the fighting would actually end within the space of twenty-four hours. Where was the enemy now? Until our fight along the 73 Easting the war had seemed almost civilized, but since then more fighting seemed necessary, if not unavoidable.

To me, it seemed that we had not done enough to justify a cease-fire. Apparently, in his bunker on the outskirts of Riyadh, General Schwarzkopf did not share this view. He later said, "My gut reaction was that a quick cease-fire would save lives. If we continued to attack through Thursday, more of our troops would get killed, probably not many, but some. What was more, we'd accomplished our mission: I'd just finished telling the American people that there wasn't enough left of Iraq's army for it to be a regional military threat. . . . Why not end it? Why get somebody else killed tomorrow? That made up my mind."[3]

In Ghost Troop, news of the cease-fire evoked a mixed response of relief and depression. Joe Sartiano decided to bring the troop together for a memorial service for Sergeant Moller as soon as possible. Many of Ghost Troop's soldiers were too dazed to completely comprehend what had happened to him. A few who had been close to Andy were nearly inconsolable, but most of the soldiers, sergeants, and lieutenants would deal with the experience later, quietly, in their own ways.

Joe's handling of the affair was touching and tasteful. His short remarks to the soldiers of Ghost Troop reminded everyone of the simple truth that in war there is no victory without sacrifice. As Joe put it, Andy had paid for our victory with everything he had.

A couple of hours later, close to tears, Major Ruiz told me there had not been much left of Sergeant Moller to recover. The secondary explosions from the TOW missiles inside the Bradley had caused a severe fire, burning everything inside beyond recognition. When Hawk Company's sabot round was fired into the dead hulk, the vehicle and its contents had been totally destroyed.

When John Hillen and I finished planning the move to Assembly Area Mexico, I walked a short distance away from the command post and looked out over the desert. Why, I wondered had we lost Moller?

Sergeant Andy Moller's move into the gunner's seat on his Bradley, Ghost 16, had been my call before we left Germany. I'd done it reluctantly, and now I wondered whether I should have, but I could not change the outcome. With life still streaming toward him, Moller had given up everything. Andy had looked like the all-American kid, the kind of young man any father would be proud to call "son." Perhaps, that was the reason why Sergeant Andy Moller was taken from us. I don't know, but I would think about this particular "what if" for many, many years.

As I turned to walk back toward my tank, my right boot caught on something. Looking down at the desert floor to see what it was, I saw that I had stumbled over what was left of an Iraqi soldier. He'd obviously been shot to pieces by something much larger than a machine gun, maybe a 25-mm high-explosive shell. With half the torso gone, the remains hardly looked human. In fact, but for his torn jacket, helmet, and weapon over the charred remains of his upper body, I would not have noticed him at all. As many of our soldiers put it at the time, the remains of Iraqi soldiers strewn across the desert were just "road kill."

It was indeed strange to me at the time how just a few days of close combat could modify my attitude toward death. Killing human beings should not be this easy, I thought. War should exact a greater emotional toll from the victor. In a brief moment of reflection I wondered whether this Iraqi soldier also had a family waiting somewhere on the other side of the Euphrates for word of his fate.

Then I stopped thinking and walked on.

It was unhealthy for a professional combat soldier to think about such things while a war was still in progress. It was time to mount up and move out to our new assembly area. As Goethe warned two centuries earlier, "The man of action has no conscience."

As our instructors in the Winter Ranger Course had been in the habit of telling us miserable Ranger students in December 1976, "You got a break when you got here. You get a break when you leave."

As I climbed up the front slope of my tank, the last warmth of the sun was cut off by the low gray clouds that veiled the horizon. For a change, at least, there was no wind. Still, the soft air that hung over the blood-stained desert seemed cold to me.

I shivered.

TEN

Squandering Victory

> At Antietam he [Gen. George McClellan] attacked what he thought was a partial enemy army, stunned it with heavy blows, and then at the decisive moment, held out his reserve. Lee retired to Virginia and McClellan proclaimed to the government that he had won a complete victory. Not unreasonably Lincoln thought this meant that he had smashed up the Confederates and was now about to destroy them. All that McClellan meant was that the enemy had left his front.
>
> T. HARRY WILLIAMS, *MCCLELLAN, SHERMAN AND GRANT*

Just as the German army should have destroyed the British army on the beaches of Dunkirk and secured strategic victory for Germany in 1940, Lieutenant General Franks' VII Corps should have destroyed or captured the Republican Guard south of the Euphrates River. Its failure to complete its assigned mission was one of many failures that led inexorably to Operation Iraqi Freedom in 2003 and the disastrous occupation that followed.

Saddam Hussein's regime was rescued from destruction not by the heroic efforts of Iraq's Republican Guard but by the uninspired and timid leadership of American generals who if they had some knowledge of war, lacked the temperament for it. Too many were bureaucrats in uniform, men with personalities that always saw danger, never possibilities. None of them were really players in a coherent, coordinated operational plan.[1]

Seldom in the history of warfare has a campaign won so easily and decisively at the lowest level been fought with more apprehension, skepticism, and caution at the top than Operation Desert Storm.[2] Until President George

H. W. Bush presented General Schwarzkopf and General Powell with a fait accompli—by providing them all of the forces they wanted and still more— they remained steadfastly opposed to the idea of a ground offensive to drive the Iraqi army out of Kuwait. The arrival of the VII Corps from Germany changed all that. The excuse that there was not enough "mass" on the ground to cope with Iraq's hollow army became untenable, and the generals had to fight.

Unfortunately, despite the overwhelming force President Bush provided, the mission of VII Corps—the destruction of the Republican Guard Corps— was not accomplished. Filled from the outset with apprehension based on predictions of heavy casualties—apprehension that spread down to the battalion level—pointing again and again to the Iraqis' presumed capabilities and the danger of open flanks, General Franks, the VII Corps commander, and his subordinate commanders moved with an extreme caution that guaranteed the escape of between fifty and eight thousand of Iraq's Republican Guard troops, seven hundred tanks and other armored fighting vehicles, and a fleet of helicopters.[3]

In fact, by the time 500,000 American and allied combat troops attacked on 23 February, of almost 400,000 Iraqi troops that had been deployed in and around Kuwait in early January, no more than 200,000 were left to oppose attacking coalition forces. Of these, 87,000 were taken prisoner, and an estimated 25,000 were killed.[4] Thanks to VII Corps' tactic of creeping up slowly on the Iraqis while pouring fire into them, the rest of the Iraqi troops were given plenty of time to run away, and the generals were able to avoid the battles they never wanted to fight in the first place.

While the generals and politicians celebrated their unanticipated, easy victory over the weak and incompetent Iraqi army, the notion of waiting to see if Saddam Hussein was in fact overthrown by internal revolts before withdrawing our ground forces did not seem to occur to anyone in authority. The possibility was ignored that we might employ our ground force to political advantage in the same way the Germans did in 1917 during peace negotiations with the Bolsheviks at Brest-Litovsk—sending 400,000 soldiers toward Moscow until the Bolsheviks capitulated and signed away two-thirds of European Russia. In 1991, as far as the generals were concerned, it was time to "get the hell out of Iraq" and declare victory, regardless of what happened north of the Euphrates.

Of course, pushing the Iraqi army out of Kuwait was never enough to satisfy America's strategic interests in the Gulf, any more than expelling the British army from the continent was enough for the Germans in June 1940. Removal of Saddam Hussein and his corrupt regime from power in Baghdad, not the occupation of Iraq, was the real, unspoken purpose of the campaign. The postwar argument that the United Nations resolution empowered America and its allies to evict Iraq's forces from Kuwait and nothing else misses this point.

General Norman Schwarzkopf, the CENTCOM commander in chief, definitely understood the importance to the attainment of this vital strategic interest of destroying Iraq's Republican Guard Corps. Without the Republican Guard to protect him and impose his tyranny on the people of Iraq, Schwarzkopf knew, Saddam Hussein and his regime would be vulnerable to attack and destruction from his numerous enemies inside Iraq's borders.

Schwarzkopf struggled with the Air Force commanders who wanted to destroy infrastructure in Baghdad when Schwarzkopf wanted to pulverize the Republican Guard Corps.[5] It is also the reason why Schwarzkopf assigned the mission of finding and destroying the Republican Guard to VII Corps, a force containing more than 1,100 tanks and 2,000 other armored fighting vehicles.

In Cougar Squadron, we understood the mission. We also believed Gen. Colin Powell when he told the press: "It's simple. We're going to surround them, cut them off, and kill them." What puzzled us at the time was Powell's recommendation to the president that he halt combat operations when, in our view, they had only just begun.[6]

The notion of halting, delaying or avoiding contact with the very enemy we had been sent thousands of miles to destroy, made no sense. Why deploy to fight at all if, once committed, there is no intention to close with and destroy the enemy?

Thinking that any enemy, even a weak enemy, can be trifled with and not dispatched immediately with a killing blow to the "jugular" is smug and very, very dangerous. Such an attitude offers any enemy, even a force like the Iraqi army, the chance to recover and strike back.

To the officers in Cougar Squadron, it made perfect sense to rapidly close with and destroy the Republican Guard, exactly as General Schwarzkopf demanded. But orders from Franks and Holder early on 26 February to primarily employ long-range artillery to hit the enemy before we had even made direct-fire contact thwarted Schwarzkopf's stated intent. Understanding why exclusive reliance on long-range fire does not work is important, because this kind of failure was to recur in the mountains of Tora Bora in Afghanistan, where there were no U.S. ground troops to trap and destroy the Al Qaeda leadership.[7]

It is impossible to fix a mobile enemy with artillery and air strikes alone. The whole point of having an armored reconnaissance force—to have an element strong and mobile enough to engage the enemy with direct fire and report back true findings to the senior commander, findings the commander can exploit—was missed in 1991. There was simply no appreciation at the regimental or corps levels of the ability of the armored force in VII Corps to smash through Iraqi armor without concentrating all of its strength in a deliberate, methodical attack. As a result, the chain of command forfeited its enormous advantage in armored superiority, which had been repeatedly demonstrated in the advance to the 73 Easting.

Reports to the regimental and VII Corps leadership that Cougar Squadron had swept the enemy aside in every action from the time it crossed the Saudi border into Iraq made no difference. Though Colonel Holder was undoubtedly under pressure from the risk-averse Franks to exercise great caution, his knowledge of military history should have taught him that simply finding the enemy did not equate to mission accomplishment for the 2nd Cavalry. Avoiding direct-fire contact through the use of surveillance radar (JSTARS) in very bad weather while "pushing the enemy" away could not, and did not, fix the Republican Guard Corps in place for destruction.

Colonel Holder's use of the words "body count" on 26 February made no sense in the context of Cougar Squadron's attack to the 73 Easting.[8] The evocation of the Vietnam-era nightmare suggested a complete failure to perceive the true nature of the Gulf War, the criticality of accomplishing the military mission of finding and fixing the Republican Guard, let alone the political dimension of the objective. In the end, far from fixing the Republican Guard, we simply ushered what was left of it out of Kuwait and southern Iraq.

General Franks insisted on massing the divisions of VII Corps in the "tight fist" he imagined was still required on 27 February, when the bulk of the Republican Guard and much of the Iraqi army were already well on their way out of the battle zone. Regardless of what we in Cougar Squadron reported or did on 26 February, neither Holder nor Franks seemed to grasp the criticality of pursuing the broken enemy. They failed fundamentally to understand what was happening in front of them on the battlefield. On the strategic level, General Schwarzkopf seems to have taken far too long to discover that his timetable for action on both flanks, Army and Marine, had been overtaken by events on the battlefield.

General Schwarzkopf tried to make his intentions clear to General Franks on the evening of 25 February 1991, explaining that the Iraqi military command was evacuating Kuwait and moving steadily north to safety. However, whenever General Franks was asked how soon VII Corps could attack, his answer was always "not now." The requests of his subordinates to halt in the face of the enemy do not excuse Franks' behavior. Sustaining momentum in the attack should have been nonnegotiable as long as we dominated the enemy.

Soon after the war ended, John Hillen wrote: "The commander's [General Franks'] focus was on logistics and the rear, rather than on the enemy and forward. The commander wanted to arrive at his objective with everything he started out with, despite the fact that he was surrendering the tactical advantage to the enemy every time he halted."[9]

Hillen's formulation was accurate. The slow and inadequate pace of combat operations across southern Iraq was totally incongruent with the VII Corps generals' postwar pretensions to dynamic and aggressive battlefield leadership.

Effective combat leadership in modern, mobile warfare must be from the front and not from the rear, but that was generally not the case in VII Corps.[10] With few exceptions, most of the senior leadership was far from the point of contact with the Iraqi enemy, with the result that too many senior commanders exaggerated the enemy's strengths and capabilities. In the minds of the generals and colonels in command, unable in their headquarters behind the attacking forces to see the developing battle as it really was, either its course or its outcome, that preconception did not change. Ultimately, Franks' fears distorted his perception of the Iraqi enemy to such a extent that he saw and acted on what he wanted to see, not on the Iraqi enemy who was really there.

Right up until combat operations ended, Franks and his subordinate commanders believed that a deliberate methodical attack, with carefully planned and orchestrated actions at every level, was still required. They refused to entertain the idea of hunting down and destroying the fleeing enemy. One of the reasons given by General Franks for his reluctance to attack was the inaccuracy of intelligence he received from higher headquarters.

But intelligence is much more than "happy snap" overhead imagery, streaming video, or cartographic products. These products are not truly intelligence products until a host of "value-added" processes occur, the most important of which occurs in the mind of the commander. Moreover, no amount of intelligence is helpful when generals select from the vast quantities of information only the things they want to believe—in this case material that reinforced an inflated view of the enemy. The Israelis, who knew the Arab armies well, had provided accurate analyses of what the U.S. Army was likely to encounter. Many of America's other friends and allies offered equally balanced and accurate appraisals. The simple truth is that the VII Corps commander and his subordinates did not listen. The question is: Why?

Years of sterile Cold War simulated exercises, focused on battles of attrition against superior numbers of Soviet weapons and soldiers, had produced a mentality at the general-officer level unsuited to the fluidity and chaos of real war waged by real, thinking humans. The deeply ingrained habit of planning to mass American troops and firepower in defensive positions against superior attacking Soviet forces inclined the American military leadership to see an illusion, not the reality, of Iraqi Arab military strength. This was obviously the case during Desert Storm, when neither the demonstrated ability of American airpower to paralyze masses of Iraqi ground forces during the battle of Khafji nor the Iraqis' repeated failure to effectively resist advancing American combat troops during the initial advance into Iraq persuaded Franks to abandon his obsession with a timetable and a plan that were irrelevant.

In Cougar Squadron's advance to the 73 Easting, repeated halts imposed from above meant that the 2nd Cavalry took four days—ninety-six hours—to move two hundred kilometers, or 120 miles, across a flat open desert, a distance the 2nd Cavalry could have easily covered in less than a day. The advance equated to a speed of advance of 1.25 miles an hour, or about half a leisurely walking pace. Arguments that the VII Corps could not have conducted its operation any differently do not stand up to close scrutiny.

In the U.S. Civil War, Maj. Gen. Thomas Jonathan "Stonewall" Jackson's brigades often marched fifty miles in two days *on foot* and then fought a battle.

And Jackson's men marched over difficult, often mountainous terrain. In World War II, some of the German army's spearhead units advanced fifty miles in two hours during the initial advance into Belgium on 10 and 11 May 1940. Lieutenant Colonel Creighton Abrams led his tank battalion even farther and faster through defending German troops in tough terrain during the Ardennes winter battles to break the siege of Bastogne.

The difference between what was achieved by Jackson, the Germans, and Abrams and what VII Corps did not achieve can be summed up in two words: courage and leadership.[11]

The 1,100 American soldiers of Cougar Squadron seized the day on 26 February with great courage and audacity. But Cougar Squadron's stunning success in obliterating the mix of Republican Guard and Iraqi army formations that constituted the Iraqi rear guard availed advancing American forces of nothing. The Iraqi goal of delaying the enemy with a rear-guard action so the main body could escape was attained. It was achieved not because the Iraqi rear guard warded off the Cougar Squadron but because VII Corps chose not to pursue the main body.

Because the Republican Guard Corps was allowed to escape, Saddam Hussein was able to stay in power. Because he stayed in power and, predictably, refused to honor his commitments, a combination of Saddam's brutality and his abuse of the Oil for Food program killed thousands of Iraqis every year for a decade and led, inevitably, to Iraq's second major confrontation with the United States and extended the slaughter.

In writing his narrative of the battle of Gettysburg, Brevet Maj. Gen. Abner Doubleday, 1st Corps commander at the time, charged that Gen. George Gordon Meade, commander of the Union force, the Army of the Potomac, was overcome by the great responsibilities of his command and simply clung defensively to the ridge at Gettysburg.

Even when the Confederate army was shattered and in full retreat, Meade resisted pressure to pursue the defeated enemy. Meade was afraid to attack a shattered Confederate army with his numerically superior force.

Lincoln's pleas for a rapid pursuit of Lee's retreating army fell on deaf ears. Meade's fear not only distorted his picture of the true situation but rescued the South from a crushing defeat. Meade's orders on the third day confined his army to driving the rebels away from their defensive positions and avoided a general engagement with the retreating Confederates. Meade's orders were issued at a point when it would have been easy to destroy the Army of Northern Virginia and end the Civil War.

Ultimately, Meade delayed moving until the Army of Northern Virginia was well out of danger. According to Major General Doubleday, a Confederate officer later told him that the Union forces had occupied Gettysburg so long and had been so long "in coming forward after the repulse of the enemy that it was generally thought they [the Union army] had retreated."[12]

Doubleday's disappointment is clear from a paragraph in his book, a statement that could have been written about the Gulf War in 1991:

After the battle, Meade had not the slightest desire to recommence the struggle. It is a military maxim that to a flying enemy must be given a wall of steel or a bridge of gold. In the present instance it was unmistakably the bridge of gold that was presented. It was hard to convince him that Lee was actually gone, and, at first, he thought it might be a device to draw the Union Army from its strong position on the heights.[13]

General Franks' reluctance to advance provided the Republican Guard Corps with a "bridge of gold" when we could have easily presented a "wall of steel." If only the Army's senior leadership had developed a feel for the battlefield and moved beyond electronically collected information; if only they had gone forward, even for an hour, to personally assess the quality of the enemy and the strength of their own forces.

THE ILLUSION OF VICTORY

The myth-making power of the American media presented Desert Storm to the American people as a triumphant success, an illusion fortified by the generals, who concealed the deficiency of the resistance by the Iraqi armed forces. Whether we had actually destroyed the Republican Guard and left Saddam Hussein's regime in Baghdad vulnerable to internal overthrow was ignored. Instead the story that the VII Corps had accomplished its mission, that everything the Army's generals had done had been right and proper in every detail, rapidly transformed the Desert Storm–era Army into a kind of permanent monument that all of us in Army uniform had to worship in perpetuity.

Eager to capitalize on the apparent victory in any way they could, politicians of all persuasions were quite willing to maintain the fiction that the

U.S. armed forces had inflicted a catastrophic tactical defeat on the fifth largest army in the world. American technological superiority received much of the credit for this achievement, but this was again more spin than reality. The defeat of the few Iraqi ground forces remaining in Kuwait when the ground war began was achieved at comparatively little cost; only 387 Americans lost their lives during the four-day campaign. But many thousands of veterans continue to suffer the malady called "Desert Storm syndrome."

War is always a struggle between opposing intellects, or wills, and the will to secure America's long-term strategic interest was lacking. Without directly threatening to extend the war to Baghdad by moving ground troops in that direction until American security demands were met, the generals and their political masters sacrificed the opportunity to leverage American military power for significant political gain.

As events unfolded, a strange moral and political blindness clouded the vision of America's senior political and military leaders. General Schwarzkopf himself concealed the truth of the VII Corps' failure to fulfill its mission of destroying the Republican Guard. At the postwar press conference on 27 February 1991, he was asked by a British journalist about the escape of the Republican Guard: "You said the gate was closed. Have you any ground forces blocking the roads to Basrah?"

Schwarzkopf answered, "No."

When the journalist pressed the issue, asking, "Is there any way they can get out that way?" Schwarzkopf again answered, "No."[14]

The damage was done. America's war with the Baathist government of Iraq would continue, at terrific human cost to the people of Iraq and enormous cost to the prestige and treasury of the American people.

Of course, the American people could not foresee the far-reaching impact of the spectacular blunder in 1991, and they did not. The generals, aided by the media, saw to that. The administration, seeking to benefit from the afterglow of victory, entered into an unhealthy alliance with the U.S. Army generals to conceal the truth of what had happened—that in fact Iraq's Republican Guard had slipped away to restore and defend Saddam Hussein's faltering regime.

Intoxicated with their easy victory, and relieved that no further test of their competence would occur, the same senior officers who asserted in the fall of 1990 that "This will be bad, we will have lots of casualties," were delighted to take credit for what the American public was told was the greatest military victory since World War II.

Throughout the spring and summer of 1991, while "victory" was celebrated in Washington, D.C., the violence beyond the demarcation line where Cougar Squadron maintained its watch on the Euphrates River grew steadily worse. Each night we watched as groups of Shiite Arab fighters crossed the line and headed in the direction of An Nasiriyah. Every morning, they would return, sometimes intact, sometimes with wounded.

The officers and noncommissioned officers of Ghost Troop developed a rapport of sorts with these fighters. The Ghost Troopers did what they could to provide the anti-Saddam fighters with water and medical supplies, but the troopers were frustrated.

Through the thermal sights on their Bradleys along the 2nd Cavalry screen line just south of the Euphrates, the soldiers could watch as Shiite Arab families were dragged out of their homes by Iraqi Republican Guard troops and shot on the spot. The soldiers naturally asked Sartiano why the 2nd Cavalry did nothing to stop it. Sartiano had no good answer. Mecca asked Sartiano the same question.

"Why not just go up there and put an end to the nightmare?" asked Mecca.

"Because we have orders not to," said Sartiano. "What the hell do you think?"

"Well, sir," said Mecca, "That's a goddamn disgrace. American soldiers should not stand around and do nothing while innocent civilians are being murdered."

"Great, what the f—k do you want me to do about it?" answered Sartiano. "Remember, I don't run the Army. I just run around in it."

Sartiano was right. None of us could do anything about it. But privately we all said the same thing: "In ten years, we'll be back."

The survival of Saddam Hussein in power meant that the war would go on. It was just a matter of time.

DESERT STORM'S LEGACY

The Napoleonic military revolution in tactics spent itself in 1815 at Waterloo, but Western military leaders worked hard for the rest of the nineteenth century to perpetuate it. Waterloo had a particularly pernicious influence over British military affairs. Even though Waterloo, as admitted by Wellington, had been a "near-run thing," it's the euphoria of its victory left the British army in an intellectual and professional state of suspended animation. As a result, the army simply fell out of touch with the forces of change in technology, society, and international affairs on the continent of Europe. It became more and more anachronistic and inwardly focused in thinking and organization.[15]

Americans confronted a similar dilemma in the aftermath of Desert Storm. The Clinton administration returned to the traditional policy of treating the U.S. Army with benign neglect, leaving critical decisions concerning the structure, content, and responsiveness of forces to the active and retired four-star generals. Far too many politicians and generals in Washington, D.C., with at most a cocktail level of familiarity with real combat, engaged in sweeping generalizations about future warfare, dismissing the Army's armored forces as strategically irrelevant in a world thought to be dominated by precision-guided munitions and information systems that would provide an increasingly perfect picture of any future enemy the United States might face, so that they could be bombarded from afar.

The upshot on the strategic level was that the Army's Cold War organization for combat, its large, ponderous divisions, and its overhead of three- and four-star headquarters, remained intact. The numbers of general officers steadily increased. Only the number of deployable Army combat troops changed, and for the worse, as the collective body of Army four-star generals arbitrarily cut the fourth company in each of the Army's combat battalions, or 25 percent of its deployable combat soldiers.

Ultimately, nothing changed. There was no impulse to establish a new institutional culture of serious, professional military study or a promotion system based on merit instead of cronyism. The Army's generals and civilian leaders deliberately missed what Andrew Grove, former chairman of the board of Intel Corporation, likes to call a "strategic inflection point"—when the balance of forces shifts from the old structure, from the old ways of doing business, the old ways of competing, to the new.[16]

Instead, the Army generals looked for and found lots of officers who aspired to be generals, proponents of preserving the status quo through a technological "makeover."[17] When poor planning, incompetent execution, and gross ignorance of the political and social conditions in Somalia resulted in the tragic loss of American Rangers in Mogadishu, accountability for the disaster was shifted from the generals who had planned and executed the mission to the civilian leadership in the Department of Defense. Hard questions were never asked. Inquiries were not made, and the wrong men were once more promoted to general-officer rank.

Despite the pointless loss of American and Somali life, the Army generals refused to acknowledge the extreme vulnerability of American light infantry. The acute need for RPG-resistant tracked armored fighting vehicles was ignored. Political leaders who could have made a difference ignored the unhealthy romanticism in the minds of the Army's generals who in Somalia had committed Army light infantry in quasi-armored Humvees and unarmored five-ton trucks rolling on flammable, air-filled rubber tires.

Before Operation Anaconda began in Afghanistan, Army generals again inaccurately read the situation. Single-service thinking and planning set the stage for potential disaster.[18] Once again, the failure of Army generals to establish an integrated joint command-and-control structure on the operational and tactical levels created a dangerous situation. However, nothing was done to hold any senior officer accountable for what could have turned into a disaster much worse than in Mogadishu. Again, nothing of substance changed inside the U.S. Army. Finally, in the spring of 2003, President George W. Bush committed American ground forces to intervene and remove the Iraqi regime from power.

Without the institutional integrity to recognize that the performance of its units in the first Gulf War, in Somalia, Haiti, the Balkans, and Afghanistan had revealed a number of substantive weaknesses in areas ranging from theater missile defense, logistics, and leadership to armor protection and tank engines, the Army's generals engaged in self-deception. Despite twelve years' experience in the Persian Gulf, the generals did nothing to prepare Army forces to cope with the complexity of operating inside the Muslim world.

The Army's chiefs of staff between 1991 and 2003 lost sight of their interwar duty: preparing for the next conflict and thinking about how differently it ought to be fought from the last war. They rested comfortably on the laurels of the hollow triumph of 1991, dispensing with all self-criticism, preferring instead to choreograph training and exercises to produce the desired outcomes. The personality types the generals promoted to general-officer rank were much like their own—those of men who thrived in the sycophantic culture of the post–Desert Storm garrison army. They were men for whom it was always easier to move up than to speak up.

After 1990, America's enemies had no navies, no air forces, weak or nonexistent air defenses, and incompetent armies that lacked either the will or the training to fight effectively.[19] America's superb combat soldiers and Marines easily overpowered their Somali, Haitian, Balkan, Arab, and Afghan enemies, whatever decisions or actions the senior U.S. military leadership took. Emergency improvisation was not needed.

Consequently, Americans forgot that to be successful, generals and officers commanding combat forces in war must be men of character and integrity, accepting risk and uncertainty as the unchanging features of war. They must demonstrate a willingness to stand up and be counted, to put country before career, and, if necessary, do their moral duty and resign. Generals must also be serious students of their profession and of their enemies. They must be able to put themselves in the position of their enemies, avoid rigid adherence to ideas and methods that are ineffective, and adopt what works in action while concentrating their minds on the essential operational and strategic tasks.

Unfortunately, in the absence of interested and competent civilian leadership in the Pentagon, the aversion of Army generals to risk, their resistance to change, and the bureaucratic culture of deceit guaranteed that billions would be wasted on the chimera of transformation. A future disaster was inevitable.

In Cougar Squadron, we already knew where it would occur—Iraq. It was only a question of when.

Postscript

Had Operation Desert Storm achieved the destruction of the Republican Guard, Saddam Hussein would have been overthrown, the United States would not have had to "contain" Saddam Hussein's regime with the use of a "no fly" zone for a decade plus, and we would not have been required to execute Operation Iraqi Freedom. More important, in 1991 the United States government was perfectly willing to stand by while the Shiite Arabs and Kurds rebelled, toppled Saddam Hussein, and formed whatever government they deemed appropriate. In 1991, no one in Washington thought a U.S. military occupation was either necessary or advisable to "oversee" the installation of a new Iraqi government. It is tragic, indeed, that the U.S. government did not reach the same conclusion in 2003.

The twelve years of containment, the 2003 combat phase of Operation Iraqi Freedom, the misguided attempt to establish a secular, Western-style democratic state in a region where it has no chance of surviving, and the Sunni Arab rebellion against the U.S. military presence cost the American people 36,000 battle casualties and a trillion dollars. The number of Muslim Arabs killed as a result of the U.S. military occupation is anyone's guess. Hundreds of thousands of Arabs have been wounded, killed, or incarcerated. At least two million Iraqi Arabs now live in refugee camps in neighboring Jordan and Syria. Two million more are refugees inside Iraq. When U.S. forces leave Iraq, more fighting is expected as the various parties inside Iraq struggle to consolidate their respective political and economic power. Only Iran benefits from these conditions.

How ironic it is that General Colin Powell and President George H. W. Bush allegedly halted combat operations at the hundred-hour mark on humanitarian grounds and from fear that the global media would castigate the United States for annihilating Iraq's remaining forces—namely, the Republican Guard Corps. And yet, the cost in blood and treasure to both the United States and Iraq would have been a fraction of what it has been thus far. Yes, 20/20 hindsight is perfect, but the case can be made that the decision to "take it easy on the defeated Iraqi enemy" was the most *inhumane* thing President Bush and his generals could have done!

Acknowledgments

For advice on writing this book, I am indebted to many of the soldiers, sergeants, lieutenants, and captains who fought by my side. Brigadier General H. R. McMaster, USA; Col. Joseph Sartiano, USA (Ret.); Dr. John Hillen, former Assistant Secretary of State for Political Military Affairs; Lt. Col. John Gifford, USA (Ret.); Lt. Col. Scott Balda, USA; Maj. Andy Kilgore, USA; Lt. Rodney Abercrombie, U.S. Army National Guard; Mr. John Mecca; Mr. Joseph Deskevich; Mr. T. J. Linzy; Mr. Charles Correll, attorney at law; Mr. Russell Holloway; Mr. T. K. Wightman; Command Sgt. Maj. William Burns, USA; MAJ John Rogler, USAF Reserve; and Sgt. 1st Class Rick Michalec, USA—all shared valuable papers and devoted time to recalling the events of those days, weeks, and months during the fall of 1990 in Germany and the winter and spring of 1991 in Saudi Arabia and Iraq.

Col. Steve Robinette, USA (Ret.), deserves special mention for helping to fill in details of events that occurred at levels above Cougar Squadron. I also owe thanks to Gina Cordero, at the National Defense University. Gina assisted me with the graphic illustrations depicting Cougar Squadron's movements and actions.

Mr. Nells Moller, the father of the Ghost Troop sergeant to whom this work is dedicated, was kind enough to share some of his son's private letters and papers, giving a poignant glimpse into the thinking and life of a heroic American soldier right up to the moment of his death in battle. Mr. Moller extended a great privilege to me, and I was humbled by the experience. I sincerely hope that the parents and loved ones of American soldiers, sailors, airmen, and Marines killed in action will find some consolation and pride in the telling of Sergeant Moller's story. Sergeant Andy Moller is a metaphor for thousands killed in action in Iraq and Afghanistan since 1991.

Bill Bode, Mike Sparks, and Lt. Mike Wood, USA (Ret.), encouraged me to pursue this project for many months before I finally started to write. They repeatedly read drafts of the work as it evolved. Their friendship, support, and encouragement were vital to this project. Also, Dr. Steve Biddle at the U.S. Army War College provided me with a long and detailed version of his published analysis of the conduct of the battle, which was very helpful.

Victor O'Reilly, the noted author, military thinker, and distinguished Anglo-Irish aristocrat, kindly read several drafts, advised on organization, did much editing, and succeeded in converting my often confusing and complex battle narratives into coherent stories. If this book succeeds in the broader goal of bringing a more accurate picture of fighting during the Gulf War and its significance to current events to the American reader, it is thanks to Victor's deep concern about the U.S. Army, unending patience, and good will.

As always, the blame for any errors of fact, or indeed of any contentious or politically incorrect opinions expressed in this book, is to be laid at my feet, not those of any of the above.

Notes

INTRODUCTION

1. Col. Michael D. Krause, PhD, *The Battle of 73 Easting, 26 February 1991: A Historical Introduction to a Simulation* (Washington, D.C.: Joint Center of Military History and Defense Advanced Research Projects Agency Project, 1991), 32, 57. Also see Stephen A. Bourque, *Jayhawk: The VII Corps in the Persian Gulf* (Washington, D.C.: Department of the Army, 2002), 328. Half of Cougar Squadron's combat force, no more than five hundred soldiers, equipped with nineteen M1A1 Abrams tanks, twenty-seven Bradley fighting vehicles, four 4.2-inch mortars, scores of M113s, and twelve M109 155-mm self-propelled howitzers, engaged the Iraqi enemy and reduced more than seventy tanks, seventy armored fighting vehicles, forty-four trucks, and thirty-two bunkers of the Republican Guard to smoldering wreckage. The numbers of enemy tanks and fighting vehicles destroyed became the subject of a dispute after the battle, when some of the Iraqi tanks and troops attacked and destroyed by Eagle Troop during the advance to the 73 Easting were subsequently credited to Iron Troop. Iron Troop, part of Wolf Pack Squadron (3rd Squadron, 2nd Armored Cavalry Regiment), had moved forward in darkness forty minutes after Cougar Squadron was already established along the 73 Easting. Iron Troop had then fallen back behind the 70 Easting. Physical inspection of the destroyed Iraqi armor by the Eagle Troop commander after the cease-fire showed that the Iraqi tanks had been shot twice, from different angles. According to Captain Miller's own account, "Iraqi resistance was sporadic." Iron Troop's actions, like Iron Troop's prewar training, had nothing to do

with the action fought by Cougar Squadron. For this reason, Iron Troop's activities on 26 February 1991 are not discussed in this book.

2. John Keegan, "Saddam's Utter Collapse Shows This Has Not Been a Real War," *Daily Telegraph*, 8 April 2003, 2; Michael R. Gordon and Bernard E. Trainor, USMC (Ret.), *The Generals' War: The Inside Story of the Conflict in the Gulf* (New York: Little, Brown, 1995), 149. Confirmation of Iraqi weakness can be found in Kevin Woods, *The Mother of All Battles: Saddam Hussein's Strategic Plan for the Persian Gulf War* (Annapolis, Md.: Naval Institute Press, 2008).

3. On 27 November 2008 the Iraqi parliament voted by a large majority in favor of a security agreement with the United States under which its 150,000 troops would withdraw from Iraqi cities, towns and villages by 30 June 2009 and from all of Iraq by 31 December 2011. Patrick Cockburn, "America Concedes," *London Review of Books*, 18 December 2008.

4. Rick Atkinson, Peter Baker, and Thomas E. Ricks, "Confused Start, Decisive End: Invasion Shaped by Miscues, Bold Risks and Unexpected Successes," *Washington Post*, 13 April 2003, A01.

5. Wayne, Leslie, "US: Former Pentagon Officials Find Wealth with Contractors," *New York Times*, 19 June 2005, 3. Also see David Barstow, "One Man's Military-Industrial-Media Complex," *New York Times*, 30 November 2008, 1.

CHAPTER 1: UNFINISHED WAR

1. In his ghostwritten account, General Franks reveals the contempt he felt for officers Rumsfeld asked him to meet with. Gen. Tommy Franks with Malcolm McConnell, *American Soldier* (New York: HarperCollins, 2004), 373.

2. Ibid., 370. McConnell cites Franks as anticipating "up to 90 days of decisive combat operations."

CHAPTER 2: GETTING READY FOR THE FIGHT

1. Gen. H. Norman Schwarzkopf with Peter Petre, *The Autobiography: It Doesn't Take a Hero* (New York: Bantam Books, 1992), 445.

2. John Levins, *Days of Fear: The Inside Story of the Iraqi Invasion and Occupation of Kuwait* (Dubai, UAE: Emirates, 1997), 289, 293, and 369.

3. Tom Clancy with Gen. Fred Franks Jr. (Ret.), *Into the Storm: On the Ground in Iraq* (New York: Berkley Books, 1997), 195.

4. Schwarzkopf, *Autobiography*, 446–47.

5. Schwarzkopf acknowledged he had serious misgivings about Franks before the ground offensive began. Schwarzkopf, *Autobiography*, 502.

6. For coalition and Iraqi dispositions, see U.S. Department of Defense, *Conduct of the Persian Gulf War*, Final Report to Congress Pursuant to Title V of Public Law 102-25 (Washington, D.C.: Government Printing Office, April 1992) [hereafter Title V], 251–58.

7. David Eisenhower, *Eisenhower at War, 1943–1945* (New York: Random House, 1986), 716.

8. Sartiano wanted the mortars to stay under the control of 1st Lt. Joe Deskevich, the troop fire-support team leader. In Ghost Troop the mortars were the responsibility of the assigned artillery officer. McMaster adopted a different tactic, one that was equally effective.

9. Heinz Guderian, *Achtung Panzer* (London: Arms and Armour, 1995), 163.

CHAPTER 3: THIS IS GOING TO BE BAD

1. Norman Friedman, *Desert Victory: The War for Kuwait* (Annapolis, Md.: Naval Institute Press, 1991), 217.

2. Gordon and Trainor, *Generals' War*, 179.

3. Schwarzkopf, *Autobiography*, 502–3.

4. British War Office, *Destruction of an Army: The First Campaign in Libya September 1940–February 1941* (London: His Majesty's Stationery Office, 1942), 55. Also see Stephen W. Sears, *Desert War in North Africa* (New York: Harper and Row, 1967), 17.

5. General der Flieger Paul Deichmann, ed. Dr. Alfred Price, *Spearhead for Blitzkrieg: Luftwaffe Operations in Support of the Army, 1939–1945* (London: Greenhill Books, 1996), 15.

6. Rick Atkinson, *Crusade: The Untold Story of the Persian Gulf War* (New York: Houghton Mifflin, 1993), 306.

CHAPTER 4: BUT WE'VE ALREADY SEIZED THE OBJECTIVE!

1. Steven Weingartner, ed., *In the Wake of the Storm* (Wheaton, Ill.: Cantigny First Division Foundation, 2000), 11. Lt. Gen. Bernard "Mick" Trainor (Ret.) enumerates General Franks' numerous decisions to halt when there was no enemy pressure to do so. What is described here is merely the first of several halts with disastrous consequences.

2. Bourque, *Jayhawk*, 235.

3. Richard M. Swain, *Lucky War: Third Army in Desert Storm* (Fort Leavenworth, Kans.: Command and General Staff College Press, 1994), 236–37.

CHAPTER 5: WHY ARE WE STOPPING?

1. Schwarzkopf, *Autobiography*, 537.
2. Atkinson, *Crusade*, 402–403.
3. Ibid., 402. Also, see Swain, *Lucky War*, 229–36.
4. Reported to the author a few days after the meeting by an officer who had been present when the remarks were made. Although now retired, the officer still wishes to remain anonymous.
5. Martin Blumenson, *The Battle of the Generals: The Untold Story of the Falaise Pocket—The Campaign That Should Have Won World War II* (New York: William Morrow, 1993), 223.
6. Schwarzkopf, *Autobiography*, 536.
7. Atkinson, *Crusade*, 422.
8. G. F. R. Henderson, *Stonewall Jackson and the American Civil War* (New York: Da Capo, 1988), 675–76.
9. For an in-depth treatment of the battle, see James N. McPherson, *Battle Cry of Freedom: The Civil War Era*, Oxford History of the United States (Oxford, U.K.: Oxford University Press, 1988).
10. Clancy, *Into the Storm*, 557.

CHAPTER 6: CLOSING WITH THE ENEMY

1. Michael Petschek, former 1st Platoon leader, Eagle Troop, statement taken in March 1991, after the battle.
2. Vince Crawley, "Ghost Troop's Battle of the 73 Easting," *Armor Magazine* (May–June 1991), 8.
3. Reported to the author by Maj. Tim Gauthier, the scout platoon leader on the right flank at the time.
4. Between 0900 and 1200 hours on 26 February 1991, the regiment halted Cougar Squadron along the 52 Easting, the 55 Easting, and the 57 Easting.
5. Statement taken from SSgt. David Lawrence's "Battle Write-Up," May 1991.
6. Atkinson, *Crusade*, 442.
7. Gen. George S. Patton, Jr., *War as I Knew It* (New York: Bantam Books, 1979), 382.

8. According to Colonel Robinette (Ret.), the instructions he passed from Franks to Holder were, "We are to continue the attack to the 60 Easting Gridline; penetrate the Republican Guard security zone and, then, report to Corps."

9. From an interview with Gen. Frederick M. Franks, Jr., in Tom Clancy's *Armored Cav: A Guided Tour of an Armored Cavalry Regiment* (New York: Berkley Books, 1994), 43.

10. Gordon and Trainor, *Generals' War*, 396–97.

11. Mission Operating Protective Posture level 4 (MOPP IV).

12. Probably in the vicinity of grid reference point PT 670005.

13. The target was probably near PT 682000.

14. Target was likely near PU 675020.

15. Targets were probably in the vicinity of PT 702025 and PT 701019.

CHAPTER 7: ACTION FRONT!

1. Estimated to be from roughly PT 684019 to PT 699061.

2. Somewhere between PT 6975 0065 to PT 7029 0034.

3. The action occurred near PT 698006.

4. Taken from Lt. Michael Hamilton's statement after the battle.

5. Minefields were scattered across the desert from PT 698021 to PT 685000. In fact, mixes of antipersonnel and antiarmor mines were present in much of the area where Cougar Squadron fought on the way to the 73 Easting.

6. Reported to the author by then Maj. John Klemenzic, regimental fire support officer, who was present in the M113 with Lute and Holder.

CHAPTER 8: DANGER CLOSE!

1. Kilgore's fight seems to have occurred from PT 690030 to PT 695001. The center of mass for the company-sized strongpoint of three tanks and thirteen BMPs, plus a hundred or more infantry, was PU 7380800.

2. Vince Crawley, "Death by Death, Minute by Minute, Ghost Troop's Fight in the Battle of 73 Easting," *Stars and Stripes*, 9 March 1991.

3. Kick is quoted by Krause, *Battle of 73 Easting, 26 February 1991*, 16.

4. Sergeant Garcia was probably located in the vicinity of PU 730095.

5. Bledsoe quoted by Krause, *Battle of 73 Easting, 26 February 1991*, 16.

CHAPTER 9: MY GOD, IT LOOKS LIKE ARMAGEDDON!

1. Quoted by 1st Lt. Danny Davis in "Artillerymen in Action: The 2nd ACR at the Battle of 73 Easting," *Artillery Journal* (February 1992).

2. Davis indicated that the enemy's center of mass was grid reference point PU 7443 0285.

3. Told to the author by then Lt. Col. (later Maj. Gen.) Larry Adair, 4-61 Artillery Battalion commander on 26 February 1991.

CHAPTER 10: SQUANDERING VICTORY

1. In his memoirs, Gen. Ulysses S. Grant recounts his experience during the U.S. Army's preparation for war with Mexico: "Too many of the older officers, when they came to command posts, made it a study to think what orders they could publish to annoy their subordinates and render them uncomfortable. I noticed, however, a few years later, when the Mexican War broke out, that most of this class of officers discovered they were possessed of disabilities, which entirely incapacitated them from active field service." Ulysses S. Grant, *The Personal Memoirs of Ulysses S. Grant* (New York: Konecky and Konecky, repr. 1982), 32. Also see the excellent research essay by Col. John Patrick Leake, "Operational Leadership in the Gulf War: Lessons from the Schwarzkopf-Franks Controversy" (AMSC 1/Canadian Forces College, 24 November 1998).

2. Gordon and Trainor, *Generals' War*, 149. General Schwarzkopf actually made his case for not attacking Iraq in the *Atlanta Journal and Constitution*: "Now we are starting to see evidence that the sanctions are pinching," Schwarzkopf told the newspaper. "So why should we say, 'Okay, gave 'em 2 months, didn't work. Let's get on with it and kill a whole bunch of people?' That's crazy."

3. Peter Turnley, "Special Report: The Day We Stopped the War," *Newsweek*, 20 January 1992, 18. Estimated numbers of Republican Guard Corps troops that escaped vary from 30,000 to 60,000 or more. For discussion of Iraqi numerical inferiority, see Gregg Easterbrook, "Operation Desert Shill: A Sober Look at What Was Not Achieved in the War," *New Republic*, 30 September 1991.

4. Patrick Sloyan, "U.S. Faced Fewer Iraqis; Casualty Estimates Also Being Lowered," *Newsday*, 24 January 1992. For an attempt to explain Iraq's defeat primarily on the grounds that American doctrine and leadership were superior, see James Blackwell, *Thunder in the Desert: The Strategy and Tactics of the Persian Gulf War* (New York: Bantam Books, 1991), 220–23.

5. Schwarzkopf, *Autobiography*, 499–500.

6. Weingartner, ed., *In the Wake of the Storm*, 30.

7. Alan Cullison and Andrew Higgins, "A Once-Stormy Terror Alliance Was Solidified By Cruise Missiles, Al Qaeda Had Sour Days in Afghanistan, but a U.S. Attack United bin Laden, Omar," *Wall Street Journal,* 2 August 2002, 1. Also see Scott Baldauf, "Al Qaeda Massing for New Fight," *Christian Science Monitor,* 9 August 2002, 1.

8. Atkinson, *Crusade,* 442.

9. John Hillen, "Where Was Leaders' Warrior Spirit during Persian Gulf War?" letter to the editor, *Army Times,* 3 October 1991. For a historical perspective on why leadership from afar does not work, see Walther Goerlitz, *Der deutsche Generalstab: Geschichte und Gestalt, 1657–1945* (Frankfurt am Main: Verlag der Frankfurter Hefte, 1950), 100.

10. General Schwarzkopf issued a verbal directive prohibiting battalion-level commanders and above from actively engaging in any fighting. This was a serious mistake.

11. Henderson, *Stonewall Jackson and the American Civil War,* 689. Also see Lewis Sorley, *Thunderbolt: General Creighton Abrams and the Army of His Times,* 2nd ed. (Bloomington: Indiana University Press, March 2008).

12. Maj. Gen. Abner Doubleday, *Chancellorsville and Gettysburg* (Stanford, Conn.: Longmeadow, 1999), 203.

13. Ibid., 208.

14. Transcript of news briefing, U.S. Central Command, Riyadh, Saudi Arabia, 27 February 1991.

15. Saul David, *Military Blunders: The How and Why of Military Failure* (New York: Carroll & Graff, 1997), 307.

16. Andrew S. Grove, *Only the Paranoid Survive: How to Exploit the Crisis Points That Challenge Every Company* (New York: Currency Books, 1999), 33.

17. Dr. Richard Kugler, *Anaconda Lessons Learned* (Washington, D.C.: Center for Technology and National Security Policy, National Defense University, 28 November 2002).

18. Maj. Mark Davis, U.S. Army, "Operation Anaconda: Command and Confusion in Joint Warfare" (thesis presented to the faculty of the School for Advanced Aerospace Studies, Maxwell Air Force Base, June 2004).

19. Michael Howard, *The Franco-Prussian War* (London: Methuen, 1981), 15–19. The French army from 1830 to 1870 had a reputation for excellence against enemies far weaker than itself. But victory over Arab, Berber, Russian, and Mexican enemies let its generals preserve an anachronistic

military system. When war came with Prussia only five years after the French withdrew from Mexico, the same generals, exalted in the French press for their brilliant leadership in Mexico and North Africa, shocked the French nation by surrendering armies to the competent and effective Prussians in the space of only a few months. The French generals, quite capable of defeating weak enemies, were incapable of defeating a competent adversary. The same condition afflicts today's American general officers.

Index

A-10 Thunderbolt aircraft, 69, 80, 179–80
Abercrombie, Rodney "Rod": battle, probability of and readiness for, 112–13; bombing campaign, 62–63; cease fire, 187; chemical munitions, concern about, 124; contact with enemy, 135, 148–49, 151, 169; Cougar Squadron, attack on, 75; courage of, 77; instructions to Ward, 73–74; Macgregor, preoccupation with battle by, 112, 126; mine, damage from, 203–4; souvenirs, collection of, 98; treatment of wounded Iraqi soldiers, 76–77
Adair, Larry, 67–68, 163–64, 202, 232n3
Afghanistan, 4, 212, 220
Armored Cavalry Regiment, 2nd: advance orders, 128–29; ammunition for, 86–87; assignment to, 11; capabilities of, 96; cavalry, job of, xvi; combat critical status, 86–87; command-and-control exercise, 43–46; competence of, 15–16; digging in, 20; equipment of, xvii; force strength, xvii; FRAGPLAN 7, 100–101; halt orders, 96, 97, 198–99; hasty defense, 92–93, 99–100, 102–5; mission of, xvii; operations officers, 11; organization of, xvii–xviii; predeployment seminars, 46–48; pursuit of Iraqi forces, 100–101, 105; regimental coin, 1–2; relief of, 202–3; reserve status of, 101, 103, 106–7, 128; shark analogy, 24–29, 42–43; Stand

To, 21–24; TOC, 10–11, 13–17, 54–57; training of, 11, 24–29. *See also* Cougar Squadron
Armored Division, 1st, 75, 95, 206
Armored Division, 2nd, 104
Armored Division, 3rd, 105, 106, 155, 163, 169–70, 178, 181, 191, 195, 196, 199, 201–3, 204–5, 206
Armored Regiment, 66th, 2nd Battalion, 201
Artillery Brigade, 210, 196, 202
artillery fire, 123–24, 126–27, 164, 211–12

Binder, Werner, 23, 201–2
bomblets, 81, 117, 123, 171, 180–81, 186
Breaking the Phalanx (Macgregor), 2
British Armored Division, 1st, 105
British Army, 218–19
Burns, William: bump up, 89; character of, 22; cobras and rats, 58–59; competence of, 25; contact with enemy, 152, 167; dreams, 60; EPWs, 192; fall back orders, 172–74; flak jackets, sitting on by Hillen, 138, 147; Macgregor, preoccupation with battle by, 126; machine gun fire and EPWs, 205; responsibilities of, 25; Rommel photo, question about, 205–6; scouting with tanks, 132–33; shooting philosophy of, 58; Sid Vicious nickname, 22; souvenirs, collection of, 98; speed of attack, 60; Ward's driving into minefield, 147

About the Author

Douglas Macgregor, Colonel, USA (Ret.), is a decorated combat veteran, an author of four books, and a PhD. He is also the lead partner with Potomac League, LLC, based in Reston, Virginia. Macgregor's concepts from his groundbreaking books on transformation, *Breaking the Phalanx* (1997) and *Transformation under Fire* (2003), have profoundly influenced thinking and organization inside America's ground forces.